Other Times Books coauthored by Bob Andelman:

Mean Business: How I Save Bad Companies and Make Good Companies Great, by Albert J. Dunlap

The Profit Zone: How Strategic Business Design Will Lead You to Tomorrow's Profits, by Adrian J. Slywotzky and David J. Morrison

Other books by Bob Andelman:

Stadium for Rent: Tampa Bay's Quest for Major League Baseball (McFarland and Company)

Why Men Watch Football (Acadian House)

Bankers as Brokers: The Complete Guide to Selling Mutual Funds, Annuities, and Other Fee-Based Investment Products, by Merlin Gackle (McGraw-Hill)

BUILT FROM SCRATCH

BUILT FROM SCRATCH

How a Couple of Regular Guys
Grew The Home Depot
from Nothing to $30 Billion

BERNIE MARCUS and **ARTHUR BLANK**
with Bob Andelman

TIMES BUSINESS

RANDOM HOUSE

ISBN 0-8129-3058-4

Library of Congress Cataloging-in-Publication data is available.

Random House website address: www.atrandom.com
Printed in the United States of America on acid-free paper

98765432

First Edition

BOOK DESIGN BY HELENE BERINSKY

For our wives,
our children,
our parents
and
our associates

CONTENTS

CONTENTS

PART III

15

THE FUTURE   297
"Responding to Change Is One of the Reasons for
the Success of The Home Depot"

16

LEGACY   313
"We Took a Lot of Chances"

Index

Acknowledgments

We would like to thank the dozens of current and former Home Depot associates, vendors, friends, and family members who spoke openly about their experiences in the founding and development of the company.

We also are indebted to the *National Home Center News,* a valuable resource in reconstructing parts of this story.

BERNIE MARCUS
ARTHUR BLANK
Atlanta, Georgia
November 1998

■ ■ ■

There are several people whose contributions I'd also like to acknowledge, starting with The Home Depot's director of internal communication Rob Hallam, who served as my orange guide and explained everything that was otherwise inexplicable, and Nancy Beliveau, who worked closely with me to coordinate schedules and research materials, and never lacked a kind word of encouragement. There was also a coast-to-coast army of secretaries and assistants at the company who worked hard and graciously to smooth my path. I'm grateful to all of you.

A few other thank-yous: to my editor, John Mahaney, and his assistant, Luke Mitchell; to my agent, Joel Fishman of the Bedford Book Works; to my overworked and much appreciated tape transcriber, Becky James; and to Marcella Ziesmann, whose good humor and hard work are missed.

I'd like to thank my daughter, Rachel, for not growing up too fast while I was writing this book. My mother, Phyllis, and my mother-in-law, Helga Holsgen, deserve kudos for helping out in so many ways. And finally, my wife, Mimi, who showed uncommon grace and patience with my many nights on the road or chained to the keyboard. I love you all.

BOB ANDELMAN
St. Petersburg, Florida
November 1998

Introduction

"We Take Care of the Customer and Each Other"

You want a formula for success? Take two Jews who have just been fired, add an Irishman who just walked away from a bankruptcy and an Italian running a no-name investment banking firm. Add—then subtract—Ross Perot. Lease space from a shrinking discount chain, fill a space the size of a football field full of hardware (and a few hundred empty boxes), and you've got a company.

At least that's the way we did it.

■   ■   ■

The creation of The Home Depot began with two words in the spring of 1978: "You're fired!"

Twenty years ago, we were two out-of-work executives. Our situation was not a lot different than millions of others who were shown the door. We had little in the way of capital and faced some daunting personal and legal challenges as we tried to get our careers back on track.

In our early years, we lived on the edge, with no balance sheet and a lack of financing. It took great romancing to establish the vendor base necessary to open and maintain the broad product selection for which we quickly became known. We were always pushing boundaries beyond where our industry's conventional wisdom suggested we could go.

And it paid off: In just twenty years, our company, The Home Depot, has multiplied exponentially from four stores in Atlanta to 775 stores, 160,000 associates, and $30 billion in sales. Almost all of our growth has come from internal expansion and very little through acquisition. How did we and our associates do it?

Building The Home Depot was a tough, uphill battle from the day we started in a Los Angeles coffee shop shortly after we were fired. No one believed we could do it, and very few people trusted our judgment. Or they trusted our judgment, but just didn't think the whole concept of a home improvement warehouse with the lowest prices, best selection, and best service was going to work. They certainly didn't realize that what we were planning would turn out to be a revolution in the retail business.

While we want to tell the story of The Home Depot because it's a great entrepreneurial tale, our larger goal is to convey what we learned along the way about customers, associates, competitors, growing a business, building a brand, and many other topics everyone in business needs to know.

We're two regular guys from similar modest personal backgrounds and religious orientation who were given a strong drive to succeed by our respective parents. The values that form the core of The Home Depot's business philosophy are bigger than one person. They developed from our families as well as from key business experiences in the early days of our careers.

This book is the story of that virtually unparalleled growth and the values and culture that nourished it.

But we're not a company that's just about numbers. The numbers are important as a measure of our success. But we've attained them because of a culture that is agile and flexible enough to change direction as quickly as events demand it. When something isn't working in our stores, we don't keep doing it the wrong way simply because the rules say to do it that way. Instead, we do it the right way and change the rules. We do things because they're the right things to do for our customer.

A set of eight values has been our bedrock for the past twenty years. Although they were not put in writing until 1995, these values—the basis for the way we run the company—enabled us to explode across the North American landscape and will be the vehicle for reaching our ambitious goals in the international marketplace.

We're only as good as our people—especially the men and women working in our stores every day. If the front line isn't absolutely committed to the cause, we can't win. That's why we believe a sure way of growing this company is to clearly state our values and instill them in our associates. Values are beliefs that do not change over time; they guide our decisions and actions. They are the principles, beliefs, and standards of our company. We call this process of enculturation "breeding orange."

In summary, we care about the customer and we care about each other. As you'll see throughout this book, our values are not platitudes that are dead on arrival on a lobby wall plaque, but are the spine that shapes the way we do business. These are The Home Depot's core values, although they are so universal that they should apply to every company:

- **Excellent customer service.** Doing whatever it takes to build customer loyalty.
- **Taking care of our people.** The most important reason for The Home Depot's success.
- **Developing entrepreneurial spirit.** We think of our organizational structure as an inverted pyramid: Stores and customers are at the top and senior management is on the bottom.
- **Respect for all people.** Talent and good people are everywhere, and we can't afford to overlook any source of good people.
- **Building strong relationships with associates, customers, vendors, and communities.**
- **Doing the right thing, not just doing things right.**
- **Giving back to our communities as an integral part of doing business.**
- **Shareholder return.** Investors in The Home Depot will benefit from the money they've given us to grow our business.

Our values empower people to be their best. If we can implant a value system that lets them apply their basic goodness and ingenuity to The Home Depot and its customers, that's all we need to succeed. That will allow them to do all the right things without us having to constantly tell them.

Nobody loves a company. A company is just a sign. Nobody loves brick and mortar.

These values are our company. They are our belief system, and we believe in them as much today as we did when the first Home Depot stores opened in June 1979. Without them, we're no different than our competition. Our competitors could copy them just as they've copied our stores, products, and merchandising ideas. But they would have to believe in the ideas underlying these values to make them effective, and that's a tough step to take.

The Home Depot—and other companies, such as Wal-Mart— have helped create a consumer revolution through low prices and wider availability of products that was unimaginable twenty years ago. Many of the products now offered by The Home Depot were either too expensive or available only through contractors. Contractors could only get them from distributors or wholesalers and, after all of the markups, many home improvement projects were beyond the means of many middle-class people. Who would have thought that today an average person could walk into a store and buy a complete designer kitchen for $3,000 and get the knowledge to install it at no extra cost? We helped create a market of male and female "weekend warriors" who confidently glide from project to project—and call on us for assistance whenever they hit a rough spot.

In 1981, before we went public, Bernie made speeches locally in the Atlanta area, where we are based. Standing before 400 members of a local Rotary Club, he asked, "How many people consider themselves real do-it-yourselfers?" He described a DIYer as someone who owned power saws, electric drills, etc., or who could change a light fixture. How many, he asked, could repair a toilet themselves rather than call a plumber? "A do-it-yourselfer is somebody who really can do those things," he said.

Out of 400 people, maybe 20 raised their hands.

In 1997, he made another speech to the same group and asked the same question. This time, only 15 out of 450 people did *not* raise their hands. We had changed America.

■　　■　　■

Our employees, customers, and investors all want to hear the story of The Home Depot. "Tell us how it started," they ask. Every colorful detail, every unforgettable, crazy character. When we do store visits, they ask endless questions about the early days of the company. They want to hear what happened, even the most familiar of business legends, in our own words.

Naturally, we enjoy telling these stories. But what's even more important to us is sharing what is learnable and transferable from our experience. For example, while we are still busy on a day-in, day-out basis as cofounders and senior executives, The Home Depot is not a cult of personality. One of our greatest accomplishments is hiring a cadre of people who are smarter than we are and who will one day run this business without us—even better than we did—and not miss a beat.

That's a vital issue to us. Because somewhere around the opening of the 300th Home Depot store a few years ago, we realized there would now be Home Depot stores that we would never visit in person, associates we would never shake hands with or personally welcome aboard.

For people like us who started the business and personally tagged and shelved merchandise and took care of customers in our first stores, to think that today we are opening up stores that we will never see is a scary thought. It is a sobering thought. That speaks to the growing size of the company and the importance of passing on what we know to others.

That raises another issue: It's one thing to have corporate values, but another thing to communicate them. When we had four stores, it was easy. We knew everyone by name and saw them on an almost daily basis. But with 761 stores and 160,000 associates, the challenge is much more complex. We can't control everything that goes on in that many stores. But our values are the magic of The Home Depot.

By consistently and emphatically teaching and enculturating them through the ranks of managers and on to the people working in the stores, we know that each and every one of these 160,000 folks will take care of the customer and each other. The rest takes care of itself.

So as you read, we hope you'll pick up a few ideas for building your own business along the way.

■　■　■

Finally, there may come a day twenty years from now when we will want to go back and remember the truth about The Home Depot. That's the real reason we wrote this book. So we can sit rocking on a porch swing and say to each other, "My God, is that what happened? What a story that was; is it true?"

It is; every word of it. Cross our hearts and swear to bleed orange.

BERNIE MARCUS
ARTHUR BLANK
Atlanta, Georgia
November 1998

PART I

1

Two Regular Guys
"We Can Finish Each Other's Sentences"*

My parents were Russian immigrants who came to America with no money. So courageous, these people. I think often about their lives, how in desperation, they picked up and left the only life they and generations before them had ever known. They had nothing. They came with nothing. They arrived in America looking forward to freedom and safety. They didn't speak the language. They were special people for whom courage was second nature.

I grew up in a fourth floor tenement at the corner of Belmont Avenue and Rose Street in Newark, New Jersey. It was freezing in the winter and hot as hell in the summer. I tell the joke that it was so bad that they tore it down to build a slum.

It was the only home I knew, of course, and I loved it. We were surrounded by other kids in this tenement, and I loved my life, me and my friends hanging from the fire escapes, using our imaginations to entertain ourselves. It was so much fun; just ourselves and our minds.

My mother was the matriarch and peacemaker of the family. She was such a positive human being that it was difficult to depress her spirit. She could find the bright side of any situation, even death. Mother was a great optimist. She often used the Jewish word *b'sheirt,*

* Bernie Marcus

3

which means "it is destined to be." And to her, everything that was destined to be was always very positive. In other words, even if somebody died, she would find a good reason—"they didn't suffer" or "the family didn't suffer." She could make anything into a positive.

My mom taught me most of the beliefs I possess today, especially that you have only so much physical and mental energy. Don't spend time replaying the past; it only keeps you from focusing on the future. Don't spend time on things in which you can't make a difference. She also taught me that the way you handle and deal with life's setbacks creates the basis for what you'll accomplish in the future.

I often think of Willy Loman, the central character in Arthur Miller's great play *Death of a Salesman*. Willy's glory days as a star salesman were clearly behind him. If he wanted to keep his job he needed to change. Instead, he blamed everyone but himself for his failures. My mom was just the opposite, always looking on the bright side.

A very, very bright woman, my mother had enough wisdom to qualify her to teach at our best business schools. She was bedridden in her mid-forties, crippled with rheumatoid arthritis. She couldn't walk. When my sister, Bea, was eight years old, Mother's doctor told her that the only hope she had of ever walking again would be if she had another baby. Believe it or not, I was conceived for medical reasons! Even better, after giving birth to me—on Mother's Day, no less—she *was* able to walk again. Her hands and feet were still hopelessly gnarled, but she was able to walk.

To her, I was a blessing. She loved me so because I literally saved her life. Although in unrelenting pain, she functioned for some thirty years after my birth and had an immense influence on my life.

My father was a cabinetmaker. He was strong as an ox, a great craftsman but a terrible businessman. He worked day and night, seven days a week, fifteen hours a day, and still couldn't make ends meet for his wife and four children. Without the contributions of my two grown brothers, Irving and Seymour, the family would never have survived.

As poor as we were, my mother used to take ice cream money away from my brothers and sister and me—often against our will—

and give it to charities. Her sincere belief was that "the more you give, the more you get." How right she was.

■   ■   ■

We lived in a predominantly black neighborhood, which made me a target if for no other reason than I stood out in any crowd. Black gang kids used to challenge me to fights every day after school and whip me badly, but, somewhat fearless, somewhat stupid, I always came back for more. Finally, the leader of one gang was so impressed with my ability to take what he was dishing out that he wanted me as part of the gang. At 11 years old, I not only ran with this gang of thirty black kids but I became its second in command.

Then when I was about 12½, we moved away from that neighborhood, which was getting too rough for our family.

■   ■   ■

My family was always in tough shape financially, so I started working from the age of 13. My first job was as a soda jerk after school. During summer vacations in high school, I earned money for college as a busboy in the Catskill Mountains. You could accumulate a significant (in those days) amount of money if you were frugal, because the jobs included room and board and the tips were all yours.

From an early age I had a propensity for medicine—especially psychiatry. I was particularly interested in studying the mind. I spent hours reading the works of Freud and Jung and became determined at the age of 17 that I would become a psychiatrist.

During this time, I learned the art of hypnosis. When I was a waiter at Kutsher's Country Club, I became proficient enough that I was able to perform on stage. I would put somebody into a hypnotic state, take them back in years, but I never made a fool out of anybody. I helped people with memory problems find something they lost. In fact, I did one of the original stop-smoking routines. It was a very exciting period in my life; I hypnotized as many as ten people at a time. It was here, as I got into people's minds, that I began to understand how some folks become obstacles for others.

I recognized then that my calling was in medicine, and specifically psychiatry. I registered for premed studies at Rutgers College in Newark, which allowed me to save money by living at home.

After my second year, I sought a med school scholarship. One day the dean, with whom I had become friendly, called me. He had arranged a scholarship for me to attend Harvard Medical School. I was very excited.

Then he said to me, "I will give you the address where you have to send a $10,000 check," and I just looked at him in disbelief. He explained that there was a quota on how many Jews Harvard would willingly accept into medical school. The $10,000 was some kind of kickback.

I never personally spoke to anyone from Harvard, but I was told there was an unwritten quota system regarding how many Jewish students could be accepted into various graduate schools—medical included. But if my family could come up with a $10,000 contribution, I could probably circumvent the quota. Well, my entire family—parents, aunts, uncles, and cousins—had never seen that kind of money, let alone possessed it, so my dream was quashed like a tenpenny nail being hit by a sledgehammer.

In total frustration, I quit school the next day, packed my suitcases, and hitchhiked down to Florida, where I stayed for a year. I was so despondent because I couldn't be a doctor.

After I'd had a year of real-life learning experiences and total independence, my mother prevailed on me to finish my education. All good Jewish mothers feel their children need a college degree, so I went home. I went back to Rutgers and enrolled in pharmacy school, which was far from my heart's first choice.

■　　■　　■

I was very young during World War II, but it—and the news of the Holocaust in particular—had a sobering effect on me. It dawned on me that folks like myself were massacred for no other reason than being born Jewish. If not for the courage of my parents giving up everything they knew to come to this wonderful land, I might have perished in Hitler's death camps. So at an early age, survival of the Jewish race and religion became very important to me.

We were brought up in an Orthodox religious home. Going to

synagogue—and living our lives according to the scriptures—were very important and had a special meaning to my parents and, through their eyes, to me. They had a strong belief in God, and they instilled that in me.

I was very religious myself, although I had a problem: I didn't understand Hebrew. It was difficult for me to pray to God in a language that I didn't understand. I did the chants, and I did the words. But I didn't understand it, and, as an adult, I kind of backed off on Orthodoxy. But I never backed off on being a Jew.

I understand the frustration that blacks faced in America years ago. Jews suffered the same obstacles. Large corporations, banks, and industries were devoid of Jews in positions of authority. We couldn't belong to exclusive clubs or high society. So we had to work harder and smarter to succeed. There is great jealousy of the accomplishments of Jews in America, but we fought for our share.

I believe that the value of our religion is critical. I think it has taught me values. And what I have always understood is that the human being is his own temple, that if you feel good about yourself and share your good fortune with others who are not so fortunate that you are doing the work of God. Beginning with my mother's encouragement, I have tried to conduct myself in this manner.

■　　■　　■

When I finished pharmacy school in 1954, I interned for a year. Before the year was up, the father of a friend of mine, Larry Wortzel, died, and Larry offered me a 50 percent sweat equity share of his father's Millburn, New Jersey, pharmacy business, Central Discount Drug. I accepted, but it was a mistake.

This was not a great partnership and was full of stress for both of us. A frustrated would-be doctor does not make for a good pharmacist. Lots of heated arguments ensued.

One Saturday night—we were open until nine P.M.—after I had yet another conflict with Larry that day, I was alone in the store and eating dinner at the back counter between customers. That's when fate—a little guy with a big cigar in his mouth—walked into the store and changed my life.

"Hey, kid, come here, get me a cigar," he said.

This fellow may have been two years older than I was, maybe three years at the most.

"What did you say?" I asked.

"I said, kid, get me a cigar."

So I walked up to him, and said, "Pick a window."

This big cigar dangling in his mouth, he looked at me, confused. "What do you mean, pick a window?"

"Pick a window, because you are going through one of them. I want you to have a choice in which one." And believe me, he knew I wasn't kidding.

He put up his hands in a defensive way, as if to suggest he meant no offense. But I was in a foul, foul mood, and I was prepared. Calling me "kid" was the last straw.

"Wait a second," he said. "You must have had an argument with your partner."

"How did you guess?" I asked, disarmed by his intuition.

"Hey, I've been in here before," he said. "I've seen you around your partner."

He introduced himself as Danny Kessler and said he was the chairman of a company called United Shirt Shops.

"What are you doing in this crummy store?" he asked me. "Why don't you get the hell out of here? Go into a business that is more suited to your talents."

"And what business would that be?"

"Discount stores. Concession departments. I have the men's clothing concession in a whole bunch of stores and we are making a ton of money. There are lots of great stores doing this."

"Where are they?"

"There is one not far from here in Paramus," he said, "Why don't you come visit me there tomorrow?"

So the next day, I did.

I had never been in a discount store in my life, and it was mind-boggling. I had never seen that many people in my whole life go through a store, and every department, while part of the same store in the customer's eyes, was run by a different concessionaire. Kessler took me over and introduced me to Henry Flink, who leased and ran the cosmetics department. Health and beauty aids were just flying off his shelves.

"How does a person get in this business?" I asked Kessler.

"You want to get in, I will get you in," he said.

I had no money to buy into a new venture; I was broke. Larry had no money, either; he had the store, that's all. But Kessler was true to his word and found a place for me to start, Spears Fifth Avenue, near the Empire State Building.

We hocked the drugstore to get into this new business. Wortzel didn't want to do it; I did. Another argument. But our resources were so slim, we had to do it together. I finally suggested a compromise. I said, "You stay with the drugstore, I'll run this business, and we'll be successful at it." Reluctantly, he went along.

To get me up and running, Flink agreed to sell me merchandise on credit, basically setting me up to be his own competitor. It was the beginning of a personal relationship that continues to this day.

Unfortunately, Spears was on its way to bankruptcy and nearly dragged us under with it. Plus I had other troubles. Wortzel and I owed Flink and others a ton of money.

Meanwhile, another friend of mine, Bob Silverman, told me about Two Guys. "They need you desperately," he said. "They are the best, but they are running the worst cosmetics business in the world. Maybe you can get a concession in their stores."

So I went to the Two Guys store in Totowa, New Jersey, and walked it maybe ten times over a two-week period. I was astounded. Great Eastern Mills, another well-known East Coast discount chain of that era, was good. But Two Guys was better. I asked one of the employees, "Who runs this place?"

"That guy right there," he said, pointing. "Herb Hubschman." By a twist of fate, Hubschman was in the same store that I was visiting.

"Mr. Hubschman?" I said, interrupting him.

"Yeah?"

"This is the greatest store I've ever seen," I said, exaggerating to keep his interest. "This is unbelievable."

Flattered, he personally walked me from department to department, telling me, "I buy this" and "I do this" and "I bought this for this" and "I bought this whole company out." When he finished, he turned back to me and said, "Well, what do you have to say about that?"

And I said, "For the smartest guy in the world, you are the biggest schmuck I ever met in my life."

He looked at me, stunned, a hurt expression in his eyes. "What are you talking about?"

"Look at how brilliant and innovative you are," I said. "You have food in the store, you have appliances, you have this and you have that. But your cosmetics department is the worst I have ever seen. It's disgraceful! How can you let this happen?"

"Well," he said sheepishly, "my brother runs it."

"Now I know what's wrong. Your brother runs it.

"Herb," I continued, "from now on, I will run this part of your business. What your brother is doing in sales now I will pay as rent and I'll make a profit over that."

"You can't possibly make that deal," he said.

What he said he believed and what he wanted to believe were two different things. I wanted that cosmetics department and he wanted me—enough for him to buy the concession departments I had at Spears and another store, Webster's, for all of the debt that I owed, including paying off Henry Flink and Larry Wortzel. I separated myself from Larry—we weren't talking at all at that point, anyway. I left him with the drugstore, and I went with Two Guys.

The owners of Two Guys, which was one of the foremost discounters in those days, bought our inventory and paid our debts. I took over the cosmetics department and in a short time did what I said I would do. They also gave me the sporting goods department, followed by major appliances. By the time I was 28, I was overseeing approximately $1 billion worth of business, all of the hard goods of the Two Guys companies.

I ascended the ladder of success at Two Guys by learning how important the folks are with whom you surround yourself. I loved teaching people the business. Why have I been successful my whole life? Because I've always surrounded myself with people who are better than I am. That's one of the lessons that guided Arthur Blank and me when we started The Home Depot and one every businessperson in America needs to learn.

■   ■   ■

I later became friendly with Wal-Mart's founder, Sam Walton, and remain close today with the company's current chairman of the board, David Glass. We have a lot of common experiences and interests.

One day, Glass and I were walking through one of his superstores in Georgia. I said, "You think this superstore of yours is a great invention, right?"

"Oh, yes," he said proudly, having played a part in Wal-Mart's birth.

"Well, we did this at Two Guys back in the early fifties," I said. "We had a supermarket. We had linen and major appliances. We had a little restaurant. We had all of the things that you have here now. We didn't have the systems that you have. We didn't have the help that you have. Today, we have computers to help run these businesses. Back in those days, it was run by grunts, who did a lot of real grunting. It was a tough business. Everything in your stores is a carbon copy, it's as though the world came around."

David then remembered! He had been in Two Guys stores.

"Some of it worked," I said, "some of it didn't work."

Seton Hall University in New Jersey did a study in the late 1960s and discovered that 70 percent of the appliances that were bought on the East Coast were bought in Two Guys stores. Something like 60 percent of lawn furniture was bought at Two Guys.

But in the end, they blew it.

Herb Hubschman, the founder of Two Guys, died. And when his brother subsequently exited the business, it was taken over by outsiders who destroyed it by overexpanding.

One of their last smart decisions was acquiring Vornado, which was probably the largest fan company in the world at the time. Two Guys was the major buyer of their fans. When they ran into bad times, our private company, Two Guys, bought their public company, Vornado, and created a new public company under the Vornado name. I subsequently went out selling their product to other people.

Another acquisition, Food Giant, a supermarket company in California that built emporiums and discount stores, was the arrogant move that destroyed Two Guys. We overexpanded and paid a heavy penalty for it. Guys like me were drowning in the mess of it all. The rising waves of red ink made me sick.

As a conglomerate, Two Guys was a disaster. People in the company focused on their own careers, not the customers. As a result, the customers disappeared and careers sank. The history of retailing is filled with once-great companies that disappeared off the face of the earth, Two Guys included. I carried the lesson I learned about the importance of customers throughout the rest of my career.

I left Two Guys in 1968 because I couldn't deal with it anymore.

I'd had it with cold weather, anyway. One freezing, miserable day, there was ice on the ground, snow and sleet were falling, it was disgusting. My car window iced up while I was driving. I pulled over, got out of the car, and as I scraped the ice, some of it went down my sleeve. Just then, a car whizzed by and sent a wave of ice over my head and down my back. "That's it," I shouted to everybody and nobody. "I am out of here! Next chance I get, I am gone."

A week later I got a call to go to California.

■   ■   ■

In June of 1968 I joined a manufacturing company called Odell, Inc., as president and chief operating officer. Odell was a $50-million-a-year manufacturer of consumer products such as Esquire shoe polish, Tintex, and Tidy Bowl.

I stayed at Odell for two years, enduring a hostile-takeover battle with Papercraft. In June 1970, I read the handwriting on the wall and left Odell for Daylin Corporation as a vice president in its North Bergen, New Jersey, offices. My initial responsibilities included supervising the 34-store Millers/Gulf Mart Discount Stores operation, working with Dave Finkle, chairman of the executive committee, to coordinate the corporate-wide merchandising of our hard-goods lines, and supervising drug and toiletries merchandising in the chain of Great Eastern Discount Stores—a direct competitor of Two Guys.

I never had any real money to speak of in those days, despite holding lofty titles in some of America's best retail companies. And by 1972, I had an ex-wife, Ruth, two kids in college, Fred and Suzanne, and a new wife, Billi, and another child, Michael Morris. No matter what I was paid, it wasn't enough. Real money is in equity, and that I didn't have.

But when I was handed the reigns to another Daylin chain, Handy Dan Home Improvement Centers, it forever changed the course of my life.

■　　■　　■

I* grew up in the borough of Queens in New York City. We lived in Sunnyside until I was 11, then the family moved to Flushing.

People assume that because we cofounded the world's largest home improvement chain, we must be real whizzes around the house. But I never had the opportunity to be handy because I was raised in an apartment. I was always out in the street, playing ball and running around with my friends. There was nothing made of wood around our house—everything was cement, bricks, and block. I didn't live in a single-family home until I was 31 years old.

My dad was a very kind person. You couldn't help but notice how everybody liked being with Max Blank. He was just an easy person to be around. And while he worked hard, he was always available to play ball or do whatever I asked.

One of the things I have always remembered about Father was his natural affinity for speaking Spanish. When I took Spanish in high school, he would help me with my homework after dinner. He would sit on the corner of my bed, shake his head, and say, "How come you don't get this?" It came so easily to him and so hard to me. I was a good student when it came to science and math, but I couldn't get Spanish. "Why is this hard for you?" he would ask. "What is the matter here?" (In 1998, when we opened our first store in Chile, I was reminded again of how useful it would have been to learn Spanish.)

I have such fond memories of my father. As a pharmacist, he was always helping people. Back then, a pharmacist was kind of a sec-

* Arthur Blank

13

ondary doctor. Medical doctors weren't as accessible or as abundant as they are now, so my father spent a lot of time talking to people about their health, giving them advice. It's somewhat ironic that my partner, Bernie, has a grounding and experience as a pharmacist.

When my father worked for his brother, it was only a couple of blocks from where we lived. Mother would make his lunch or dinner and I would take it to him at the drugstore. I would sit there and watch while he mixed prescriptions—the way pharmacists really used to do it—and he talked to me between customers and sneaking a bite of food.

I remember how hard he worked when he started his own business, Sherry Pharmaceutical, a mail-order pharmaceutical company selling direct to hospitals, doctors, and nursing homes across the country. At night he would come home and be on the phone for hours doing deals.

One of the great losses in my life happened when my father died in 1957 of a heart attack. He was just 44 and I was 15. My uncle also died of a heart attack sometime later. My brother, Michael, who is two and a half years older than I am, was always convinced that he would never live past 44. Really. He just "knew" that he was going to die because Dad died so young. Today, Michael is 60 and still in good health.

I never had that fear. I have always pushed myself hard, but it was never because I thought I wouldn't live a long life. I do, however, think one of the reasons I have had an extreme emphasis on health and exercise in my life is my father's death. In the mid-1970s, a doctor at the Scripps Clinic in San Diego warned me against smoking. "You have one big strike against you," he said. "Your father's heart condition."

That had a big effect on me. On the plane ride home, I read Kenneth Cooper's first book, *Aerobics,* all about running and staying in shape. When I got home, I ran a mile. Cooper had a test in which your physical fitness starting point was running as far as you could in twelve minutes. I was able to run a mile in twelve minutes, which today is ridiculously slow. Then, it was a major accomplishment. The next day, I did it again. Pretty soon I was running a mile or two every morning. People would see me out running—this was before it became a national obsession—and they would say, "What were you doing? What is that about?" It was such a strange thing to do then.

So I think my father's death affected me in a lot of ways. Maybe at some level, deep down inside, I have always had a sense of urgency about getting things done and accomplishing things and moving on with things, and maybe some of that has come from him. But I never consciously had a fear of dying at an unusually young age. In fact, I am probably in better condition and fitter than most men half my age.

One of the great losses that I feel I have is that I never really knew my father as an adult. There have been times when I had been under stress and I took great comfort in recalling childhood conversations with my father and imagining how we would discuss the current issues in my life.

When you see a person through your eyes at age 15, and that is the end of the relationship, you don't really know him as an adult would know him. And as I have gone through the growth in life, my first marriage to Diana, our three children, Kenny, Dena, and Danielle, all the business situations, building The Home Depot in the last twenty years, my second marriage to Stephanie, and our son, Joshua, I wish my father could have been there through it all.

■　　■　　■

My mother, Molly, was 37, a young woman, when my father died. How much his death affected her, nobody will ever really know for sure, but I think it was probably greater than any of us ever suspected. Not only because she had to go into his business and run it with no experience, but because it was really a small business then that she built from the ground up. If she had tried to sell it right after my father died, it wouldn't have been worth very much.

She was concerned because she had to put two sons through college, both in expensive private schools. The issue of being able to support us was paramount for her.

My father did not have a lot of life insurance. The life insurance that he had was in dispute because he had taken it out only a year or so prior to his heart attack. There were questions of whether or not he had made a full disclosure about his health.

So Mother became the breadwinner, trying to, as she put it, "be a mother and a father to two sons." Of course there is no way that a mother can be a father to boys, anyway.

The pressure our situation exerted upon her was enormous, and it took a lot out of her over the years. My father's death affected her, not only because she lost her husband, but because it put much more stress on her and made her life a lot more difficult in many, many ways. It changed my relationship with my mother, who is a very remarkable woman. She is a very bright lady, a principled person, a perfectionist, with strong social-liberal leanings.

My mother, who really had no business experience, went into the business and ran it as best she could. And she did a very good job.

■　■　■

I have always been athletically inclined. Today I run marathons; back in high school I was a baseball and football player, as well as running track.

Being competitive has always been at the core of my nature, although it didn't kick in with regard to academics until I got to college.

In high school, sports were my consuming passion. I did okay in school in terms of academics, but mention sports and my attention was truly riveted. In baseball, I started off as a centerfielder, but I eventually threw my arm out and couldn't make any long throws. So I became a catcher, a position that suited me because I was in the middle of almost every play.

I apparently got my athleticism from my father. He went to Columbia University, where he set then–New York City records for both the mile and the 100-yard dash, an unlikely feat today because athletes tend to specialize in distance or sprint races.

When I started at Babson College, a small business school just outside of Boston, I took school seriously for the first time. And there's nothing like applying yourself: I was elected vice-president of my junior class, president of the senior class—I did everything in school that you could possibly do, plus, I was a straight-A student and made the dean's list.

One of the ways I paid for my college education was running my own landscaping business. Freed from the confines of city life, I discovered a love of being outside. I ran my own laundry business as well, picking up laundry on campus several nights a week.

My brother, Michael, earned a degree in pharmacy from the University of Michigan. On paper, our skills sounded like the perfect combination for taking over the family business and finally relieving our mother of the pressure caused by Dad's premature death. Michael would be more on the technical side, I would handle the business side.

But after graduating with a bachelor of science degree in accounting in 1963, I postponed joining the family business a while longer and took a job with the Big Eight accounting firm of Arthur Young & Company. I was the youngest staff person they ever recruited in New York City and I stayed for almost five years.

Some of the work I did at Arthur Young was in management consulting. I was 20 years old when I started, so I was never the senior person on major assignments, but I did do some consulting, as well as staff accounting. I enjoyed that, and I was very good at what I did. It was important for me to get some outside experience in the business world so I could eventually bring a greater expertise to our own company.

I was on the verge of becoming an audit manager in 1968, when I chose to join the family business instead. The company had been growing and doing well, and my mother and brother were anxious to have me finally take my place beside them. One of my father's brothers was involved with it, as was a cousin. It truly was a family business.

It was very different than what I had expected after all those years. I was prepared to roll up my sleeves and do what it took for the business to be successful, and I understood the responsibilities that I would have then would be very different than what I had at Arthur Young, and they certainly were. The environment, certainly, was very different. But that was okay with me. And I enjoyed my work when I was there. I worked very hard, very long hours. But it was not a growth situation from a professional standpoint.

It was hard for me to work with my brother and my mother. I loved them both very much, but it was impossible. I spent a couple of years working there, and then my mother sold the business to the Daylin Corporation on June 1, 1968. When my father died in 1957, it was a very small business. By the time she sold it, my mother had built the company up to several million dollars in volume. Daylin was a conglomerate centered in the retail business, with an emphasis in pharmacy and health goods.

If you have a family where family members can work together, that is wonderful. But it doesn't often happen, and it didn't happen in our situation. I love my mother, I love my brother, but we were not meant to work together every day. And I think Mother finally saw that, too.

I think selling the company was the right decision for her. As a widow and mother, her primary interest was not building a huge business but conserving its equity and resources. She was too concerned about her own future at that time to think in terms of risk and expansion.

When Daylin took over, we all stayed with the business for a while longer, but I really didn't feel that staying in that business was what I wanted to do long-term. It was still hard for me to work with my mother.

Fortunately, Daylin was a company of infinite opportunity.

■   ■   ■

In 1970, Daylin named me chief financial officer of Elliott's Drug Stores/Stripe Discount Stores. Two years later, I became president of Elliott's/Stripe and relocated the company and my wife and our three children to Griffin, Georgia. They actually call it "The First City South of Atlanta."

Between 1972 and 1974, my responsibilities at Elliott's/Stripe included being named assistant treasurer of the parent company. Max Candiotty, the president of Daylin, and Leon Beck, the corporation's senior vice president and lead financial officer, adopted and mentored me. They saw potential in me and were very supportive during my career there.

When I became president of the division, it was kind of a shock to the rest of the Daylin organization because I was a very young man in my late twenties. I hadn't run a business of that magnitude. I had only been involved in business at Arthur Young from the work I had done there, and, of course, my family business. So it was a major move, but it turned out well. I did a good job for them, and I grew the business and gave them the kind of earnings they were looking for.

I remember having many good personal relationships at Daylin in those days. It was a less structured, less hierarchical corporate environment, a family culture where people supported each other and cared for each other.

Becoming president of that division at an early age fed my entrepreneurial spirit. It encouraged my capacity for starting and running a business, for wanting to make decisions, for wanting to be a part of everything.

In July 1974, Daylin was going through some very difficult times. That's when it decided to sell off some divisions, one of which was mine, the freestanding drug stores. I said, that's fine. I'm 32 years old—I'll do something else.

That's when Bernie called me from Handy Dan. We had met a few years earlier at Daylin corporate events and established a solid rapport. He named me corporate controller of Handy Dan; later, my title changed to vice president of finance.

In baseball, the pitcher is often the center of attention. That was Bernie. But the catcher is in the middle of the action, helping set the pace of the game. During our time at Handy Dan and subsequently at The Home Depot, Bernie and I have been effective as team players in roles in which we both feel comfortable.

Origins

"You've Just Been Kicked in the Ass by a Golden Horseshoe"*

He called himself "Ming the Merciless."

It wasn't a nickname used behind the boss's back. The sign on the CEO's office door at the Daylin Corporation impressed upon all who entered how proud Sanford C. "Sandy" Sigoloff was to be known as "Ming." Ming, of course, was the villain in the old Flash Gordon movie serials of the 1930s.

Sigoloff, a former nuclear engineer who once worked for the Atomic Energy Commission, is today best remembered for his later stint atop Wickes Cos.—which he bought in bankruptcy with the help of junk bonds wizard Michael Milken. Wickes had a reported $400 million in losses and 250,000 creditors when Sigoloff took it over in 1982, but within three years, the company emerged from bankruptcy. He also ran L. J. Hooker Corp., whose divisions included the already-bankrupt B. Altman & Company and Bonwit Teller retail chains.

He was a nice looking, sharp-dressed man, very smooth, slick, and articulate, a chief executive who couldn't just fire an underling and get on with business. When people leave Sigoloff, he once told me in a coffee shop, it was very important that he affect them economically,

---

* Bernie Marcus

20

emotionally, and physically, so that people think twice before they ever turn on him.

I was shocked at such tactics. "When you treat people like that, it comes back to haunt you," I said. "People are fearful of you."

But Sigoloff *wanted* people to be fearful of him. He didn't want to let a person out with dignity. He wanted to see them destroyed. That was his style. He didn't call himself Ming the Merciless for nothing.

■   ■   ■

Gary Erlbaum once ran a small chain of Philadelphia-based home improvement stores called Panelrama. In 1976, Erlbaum and his Park Avenue investment banker, Ken Langone, president of Invemed Associates, talked about the future of Erlbaum's industry.

"Let's start with a benchmark of who is the best in this business," Langone said. "Who do you think are the best operators?"

"The best is a company out of California called Handy Dan," Erlbaum said.

That worried Langone.

"Gee, Gary," he said, "if my memory serves me right, those guys are in bankruptcy." If that was the fate of the best, little old Panelrama didn't have a prayer.

"I think that while the majority of Handy Dan is owned by a company named Daylin Corporation, 19 percent is owned by the public," Erlbaum said. "Daylin went into bankruptcy; Handy Dan didn't."

Later that same day, back in New York, Langone got out his Moody's Investors Service and Standard & Poor's manuals, books packed with data on publicly held companies. Not only was Handy Dan not bankrupt, it was a solid company doing very well—despite the woes of its parent company.

Handy Dan Home Improvement Centers, headquartered near Los Angeles in the City of Commerce, began in 1955 as a small hardware store in El Monte, California. Two decades later, it was under *our* management and had become one of the nation's most respected and successful home improvement chains. Handy Dan stores were 30,000 to 35,000 square feet and generated the highest volumes in the industry. Our best store did $5 million a year in sales, unheard of in those days in the home improvement business. The average store was closer to $3 million.

Langone was further intrigued that it was selling for $3 a share and it appeared likely to earn $1.50 a share. Even in 1976 terms, that was awfully cheap.

Erlbaum had mentioned that he and I were good friends, a relationship begun when I had considered acquiring Panelrama. And while I ultimately passed up the deal, a close personal relationship blossomed between us. Langone asked Erlbaum to call me and make an introduction.

"Bernie," Erlbaum said, "this guy, Ken Langone, wants to meet you. He is a very tough guy. *Really* tough. This is one of the most aggressive people I have ever met. He is a tough businessman. And he can be overbearing. But I swear, this is the most honest, ethical man I have ever met in my entire life. And when he tells you something, you can believe it. I have more trust in Langone than I do anybody in the entire world."

Coming out of Erlbaum, that was a pretty strong statement.

Intrigued, I said I'd certainly take Langone's call. Half an hour later, the phone rang and I heard the following statement: "I think you have the greatest company I have ever seen in my whole life! You run the greatest business I have ever seen!"

That said, Langone was still suspicious of Handy Dan's numbers. "This doesn't make sense," he told me. "You're going to make $1.50 a share?"

"Yes," I said, "after taxes."

"In that case," Langone announced, "I am going to buy every share of stock I can in your company, and I would advise you to mortgage your house and buy the stock, because this stock is going to go straight up."

Langone, who later joined us as a cofounder of The Home Depot, was a man who formed instant, irrevocable opinions about people, and I, he decided, was the kind of man with whom he could do business. Not knowing Langone from the next potential shareholder, I was politely reserved and noncommittal.

"Would you mind if I came out to see you sometime?" Langone asked.

"Sure, sure," I said, "any time you want to come out, fine."

"Good," Langone said. "I'll see you *tomorrow* for lunch."

Langone seemed very excited. He took the first flight out of New York the next morning and landed in Los Angeles by 11:30 A.M., in time for lunch.

Still overwhelmed by the speed with which Langone operated, I took a more cautious approach. I immediately called my lawyer, Erwin Diller, a very conservative, straight-laced attorney, and invited him to lunch.

"Erwin, I am meeting a guy for lunch tomorrow, and I am not meeting him by myself," I said. "I want you there."

I was nervous about what I could and couldn't say and what I should and shouldn't say. Langone was like a fire hydrant let loose, boasting his intention of buying every single share of stock in the company. I didn't want to do anything that would land me in hot water with the Securities and Exchange Commission. And I answered to a higher authority, anyway: Ming the Merciless. I was trying to make sure I did the right thing.

Langone was the single brightest, most energetic person that I had ever met. He is intuitive, smart, and a real street fighter. Over lunch, Langone described his background and how he represented a group of investors who had every intention of buying up Handy Dan stock. He asked pertinent questions. The more he learned about the business, the more he realized how undervalued our company was—in part due to the Daylin bankruptcy—and his enthusiasm only grew.

Diller also took kindly to Langone's visit. After he had gone, Diller told me that he felt as if I could trust Langone. Certainly Langone went away happy: As soon as he returned to New York, he and his investors started buying every share of Handy Dan stock that came on the market, more than 400,000 shares in all, at prices ranging from $3 to $12 per share.

■   ■   ■

Diller was right. I could trust Langone. But I knew that for myself. The minute we met, the chemistry was right. We took an instant liking to each other and trusted each other implicitly. Of the 2.5 million outstanding shares of Handy Dan stock, about 475,000 were in the hands of the public. Langone effectively got all the stock with the exception of one block of 50,000 shares. It was owned by the Brooklyn-based Congregation of the Most Holy Redeemer, or as they're commonly called, the Redemptorists. Never shy, Langone called the priests and spoke with their financial officer, Father Ray McCarthy.

"Would you like to sell?" Langone asked.

McCarthy paused a moment. "Langone," he said. "Is that an Italian name?"

"Yes," Langone said, encouraged. "Yes, it is."

"And are you a Catholic?"

"Yes, I am."

"Then in the name of hell," McCarthy said, "tell me what I should do."

"On those terms," Langone said, laughing, "keep it. Don't sell."

■ ■ ■

Langone started buying Handy Dan stock at $3 a share. By the time he controlled most of the public issues, it was around $9 with nowhere to go because so little changed hands anymore. Still, it was a valuable stock to hold because Handy Dan was making money and had a very exciting future.

Now that he possessed so much Handy Dan stock, Langone personally visited every one of the company's stores (some of which were known as Angel's Do-It-Yourself Centers), from Southern California to Denver and Kansas City. We became fast friends, our relationship growing far beyond a common desire to see Handy Dan grow. We genuinely enjoyed each other's company and socialized whenever possible.

Sigoloff, of course, was more than a little curious about who was buying up all the Handy Dan stock, so I arranged a meeting. It was all handshakes and politeness on the surface, but that was as good as it ever got between Langone and Sigoloff. Neither liked the other and they never would. Sigoloff viewed Langone with suspicion; Langone didn't care for Sigoloff's attitude toward me.

"This is a real bad guy," Langone said after his first encounter with Sigoloff. "This is a guy that you can't trust and that would kill you in a second."

■　　■　　■

Arthur was Handy Dan's chief financial officer and my closest friend and confidant at the company. He had come to the home improvement chain in 1974 after two years as president of another Daylin division, Elliott's Drug Stores, which was based in Savannah, Georgia.

The two of us had met several years earlier at corporate meetings and discovered an instant camaraderie: I loved to tell jokes and stories, and Arthur, who enjoys laughing, is a great listener, a terrific audience. He joined me at Handy Dan as CFO after his predecessor had a stroke. With Arthur in the role, the position became much broader, with responsibilities that exceeded the realm of financial matters.

Arthur and I ate lunch together almost every day. It was very much a symbiotic relationship, despite my being nearly twelve years Arthur's senior. In the best of marriages, you marry somebody, hopefully, who has your value system but who is still different from you in lots of ways, and that is how you grow. We were two different people who fit together symbiotically.

■　　■　　■

Handy Dan wasn't the only U.S. corporation in the 1970s that was held by an 81 percent private, 19 percent public partnership. A number of holding companies like Daylin sold 19 percent of their wholly owned subsidiaries (such as Handy Dan) to the public. The holding companies kept 81 percent on the belief that the public would unlock values in the asset, creating a higher value so that the 81 percent would be worth much more than if it were completely private. (For tax purposes, the companies had to own more than 80 percent.)

But a fascinating thing happened at at least three of these companies. Brunswick Corporation owned 81 percent of Sherwood Medical and abruptly bought back the 19 percent of outstanding public shares and took it private again. TransUnion did the same with Ecodyne; National Distillers of America followed suit, buying back all the stock in Almaden Wines.

At the time, Langone was on the board of Sealy Corporation. By luck, another board member was a lawyer for two of the three companies that had repurchased their shares.

"Is there any common theme in why this is being done?" Langone asked. "Why is this stock being reacquired?"

The economics didn't work, the lawyer said, and the holding companies didn't realize as much value as they anticipated. In many cases, instead of asset values rising, the exact opposite occurred: the publicly held shares plummeted in value. Handy Dan, for example, went public at $12 and dropped as low as $3 at one point.

"Well, that and one other thing," the lawyer said.

"What is that?"

"This structure is a time bomb," the lawyer said. "We believe, theoretically at least, that if somebody were to get control of the 19 percent minority, the only way the person who held the 81 percent could really exercise their fiduciary responsibility to the minority would be to vote it in direct proportion to the way the minority votes on any issue."

Langone was thunderstruck. Not speechless, of course, just thunderstruck.

"You mean," Langone asked, "that if 60 percent or 90 percent of the 19 percent said they wanted to do something, the only way that the 81 percent owner could sanitize their vote would be to vote directly proportionate to the minority? Does this mean that the motion would carry, which means that the minority controls the company?"

"Yes," the lawyer said. "It seems convoluted, but considering fiduciary duties, that is the only way the majority owner can say, 'Hey, I didn't shout, I didn't force my will on anybody.' I think that was a stretch, okay? But it will probably work."

Langone, who controlled virtually all of the 19 percent of Handy Dan public shares, wasted little time in calling Sigoloff and asking for a meeting. Daylin was out of bankruptcy protection by then and back to business as usual.

A few days later in California, the two men shook hands and Sigoloff, completely in the dark, asked, "What's up?"

"Well, Sandy," Langone said, "I just wanted to see how you and I are going to run this company going forward."

The gauntlet was thrown down, the line drawn in the sand. Insert your own adversarial cliché; any will do.

"What do you mean, *we?*" Sigoloff erupted.

"Sandy, there is a body of thought . . ." and Langone filled Sigoloff in on what the attorney told him. "This is why these other companies are all buying their shares back, because there is a potential time bomb here. I don't want to have any trouble with you. I think what you and I ought to do is to stay in constant contact and communicate with one another the things we want to do with the company, to the best interest of everybody."

A major control freak who had no intention of ceding a whit of influence to Langone, me, or anyone else, Sigoloff was furious.

"I don't believe that, it's crazy! This is stupid," Sigoloff said. "I never heard of anything so dumb in my whole life."

"Okay," Langone said, using his most conciliatory tone and keeping as straight a face as possible. "I just hope it doesn't get to the point where one day we have to test it."

■   ■   ■

That day came sooner rather than later. A month after their first "partners" meeting, Langone received a call from Sigoloff. One of Sigoloff's lieutenants, Daylin senior vice president Jeffrey Chanin, was going to be in New York and wanted to say hello.

Langone alerted me because he expected the attorney's visit would be anything but innocent. He also put a call in to notorious corporate takeover attorney Joseph Flom, a partner at the New York firm of Skadden, Arps, Slate, Meagher & Flom, L.L.P., and a personal friend of Langone's. Flom's office was a five-minute walk from Langone's.

"Joe, I don't know if I need a lawyer," Langone said, describing the situation, "but if I do, I want you to have the meanest, toughest S.O.B. you have standing by."

"I have just the guy—Bob Pirie," Flom said.

So on the appointed day, Jeff Chanin arrived at Langone's office, took off his jacket, and sat down. He lost no time with idle pleasantries, saying that Sigoloff was taking Handy Dan private again and that Langone and his investors must sell out. If necessary, Chanin swore, Daylin would squeeze Langone out in what's called a "cramdown" merger. But that required that Sigoloff control 90 percent, something that wouldn't happen unless nearly half of Langone's investors defected.

"Jeff, cut the crap," Langone said calmly. "I control enough stock that you can't do any such thing. If that is why you are here, to threaten me, you have the wrong guy. Excuse me."

Just then, Langone picked up the phone and called Bob Pirie. "Bob," he said, "I need you."

Pirie arrived in minutes.

"Who is this guy?" Chanin demanded.

"This is my lawyer," Langone said. "Now, what do you want to talk about?"

"Look, we really don't want any trouble," Chanin said, backpedaling. "The stock is selling for about $8 a share. We know you are boxed; you can't sell any stock. You have no liquidity. How about if we pay you $10 a share?"

"No way," Langone said. "The price is $12."

Chanin was shocked. "Forget it!"

Wanting to leave Chanin swimming alone with his personal barracuda, Langone left for the men's room. Barely two minutes later, Chanin followed him in.

"Okay," he said, "$12."

"Jeff, you don't understand," Langone told him. "You offered to buy it for $10. I said no. I offered to sell it to you for $12 and *you* said no. Now you are back, wanting to buy it at $12. That offer is off the table. That's gone. We had an offer and a denial. No deal."

"What?!"

"I suggested a price of $12 in my office, right?" Chanin nodded, acknowledging Langone. "And you declined. Well, that's it. I don't want to sell it now."

"You must have some price," Chanin said.

"Okay," Langone said, "$14."

Chanin left in such a blind rage he almost banged his head on the door.

About a week later, Sigoloff called Langone.

"Let's not mess around," he said. "We will pay you $14."

"Sandy, you guys don't get it," Langone said. "I offered it to you for $14. Chanin said no. That offer is off the table."

"I don't understand," Sigoloff said.

"It is this simple. You had a chance. You turned it down. I have reconsidered my position. I don't want to sell."

Sigoloff hung up the phone, madder than hell.

■　　■　　■

Sigoloff wanted to change the Handy Dan board so that he controlled it, but I wouldn't allow that.

Sigoloff didn't like me, and the feeling was mutual; I rejected everything about Sigoloff, the way he dealt with people, how he talked down to people.

The difference between us was that I didn't need Sigoloff; Sigoloff needed me. He couldn't get rid of me even though he wanted it more than anything, because every time he moved against me, he got a call from Ken Langone. Langone would call him and threaten to sic Joe Flom on him with a shareholder lawsuit. And in that way, Langone kept Sigoloff in line.

■　　■　　■

Once Sigoloff realized that Langone was correct about the explosive nature of Handy Dan's stock arrangement, he wanted Langone out of his business. He made several more miserly attempts to buy back the publicly held stock, all rebuffed by Langone. And the more Langone resisted, the more pressure Sigoloff placed on me.

Billi and I invited the Langones to visit our home in Encino for dinner. After dinner, I turned to Langone.

"Do me a favor," I said. "Get Sigoloff off my back. Sell him the stock."

"Bernie, trust me," Langone said. "You don't really want me to sell him this stock, because if I do, I am signing your death warrant. You are a dead man."

"You don't know what you are talking about," I responded. "Sigoloff doesn't know this business. *I* know this business. He needs me to run it."

"Bernie, look, the only thing of any value in that mess Sigoloff has on his hands is Handy Dan. As long as you are there, he is never going to be able to take credit for its success, or for the recovery of Daylin."

"Oh, you don't know what you are talking about."

"Bernie, I have never been more certain of my position than I am right now. I am telling you, I can read this guy like a book. *He can't stand to see you succeed.* The more you succeed, the more pain he feels."

Not convinced, I sloughed off Langone's concern. I felt very cocky about myself, that I ran the company as well as it could be run and that Handy Dan made so much money that Sigoloff would be stupid to get rid of me.

"Don't worry about me," I said. "I am a big boy. I can take care of myself."

"It's your funeral."

"So, will you sell?"

"Yeah, sure," Langone said, "I'll sell. But I am not going to mess around on price."

On the spot, I called Ed Kaufman, a Daylin lawyer, at home. I told him that Langone was ready to make a deal. Then I handed Langone the phone.

"I want to make you an offer," Langone said. "You don't want it, that is the end of it, and let's leave it alone. If you want it, that is the price."

"Well, what's the price?" Kaufman asked.

"It's $25.50 a share."

"Why the odd number?"

"Because," Langone explained, "it has to look like we had some real hard bargaining here."

Kaufman said he would call Langone right back. Five minutes later, the phone rang.

"Be in my office tomorrow morning at ten to sign the papers," Kaufman said.

The next morning I picked up Langone at the Century Plaza Hotel. As we drove down the street, Langone tried again to dissuade me, offering to cancel the deal. But I could not be dissuaded. I honestly believed my position at Handy Dan would be more secure once Langone was out of the picture.

Daylin announced on January 9, 1978, that it had acquired all of the publicly held shares of its Handy Dan subsidiary for $25.50 per share. It effected a short-form merger of one of its subsidiaries with Handy Dan, making the home improvement company once more a wholly owned subsidiary of Daylin.

■　　■　　■

Arthur and I view bankers as people who put their careers on the line for us, and we protect them. Luther "Rip" Fleming, our banker at Security Pacific National Bank, knew everything that happened at Handy Dan before anybody else did, including the board of directors.

There are basically two kinds of banking relationships: transaction banking and relationship banking. Rip believed that relationship banking was the only way to go, just as we believed that we could succeed in retail only by building personal relationships with our customers. He sought banking relationships that would continue for years, encouraging close relationships between the officers of the company and the bank. In that way, the bankers expected to be first to learn the good as well as the bad news.

Sigoloff vehemently objected to the nature of our relationship with Rip. He thought we were too open with Rip, with whom we shared everything—good, bad, and ugly.

I even shared otherwise confidential information about Handy

Dan with Rip. He was a great supporter of ours. He would meet with anybody on our behalf, sometimes putting his own reputation on the line to protect the Handy Dan company.

Sigoloff couldn't believe the way we treated Rip. Our relationship with Rip drove him crazy. He hated it, especially when we would be discussing a sensitive issue and I would say, "Well, I spoke to Rip about it and . . ."

Sigoloff would interrupt and say, "What do you mean, you spoke to Rip? What are you talking about?"

And I would say, "Well, Rip already knows about this."

"Why do you do that?" Sigoloff would say, frustrated again.

Sigoloff told me how he had manipulated bankers all of his life. He said, "They don't know what the hell they are doing."

As contemptuous as he was of bankers, Sigoloff still needed their money to run his businesses. His oft-stated philosophy was "keep banks in the dark and feed them crap, like mushrooms." His MO was burying them in paper. And it wasn't just banks, it was anybody. In fact, he put people on his payroll whose primary job seemed to be generating those kinds of documents.

Sigoloff's approach was to hit the banks with so many facts, so many charts, that no human being could ever go through it all. And before that, confuse them. Then when you confuse them, he'd say, you'll end up with somebody who you can do anything you want with.

This is how Sigoloff wanted us to treat Handy Dan's bankers, but we refused. In fact, it was the beginning of our practice of doing everything the opposite of the way Sigoloff operated.

Sigoloff wanted to become the chairman of the board of Handy Dan, but Rip, based on covenants in loan agreements guaranteeing separation between Daylin and Handy Dan, told Sigoloff that it wasn't going to happen.

"Sandy, you are entitled to board representation on Handy Dan," Rip told him, "but you will not be its chairman."

■　■　■

Control of Handy Dan wasn't the issue for Sigoloff. What he really wanted was credit for turning Daylin around, saving it from the creditors, saving it for the shareholders, saving it from bankruptcy. But the only Daylin division that had a great cash flow was Handy Dan—my division.

As Langone had forecast, when public ownership disappeared, so too went the ability to shield ourselves from Sigoloff's dark shadow.

The day I knew I was finished with Sandy Sigoloff was the day the Daylin board of directors discussed succession. One Sigoloff-appointed board member said, "I don't know why there is any question about succession here, since you have your obvious successor right in this room, Bernie Marcus." By that time I had been promoted to chairman of the board and CEO of Handy Dan, in addition to carrying the title of president.

A quick glance at Sigoloff's ashen face told me that *that* was never going to happen. And the very notion that some on the board supported the idea made me a genuine threat to Sigoloff. The situation between us just went from really bad to dire.

The clock was ticking.

■　　■　　■

April 14, 1978, is a day that Arthur and I will never forget. We were scheduled to attend a Friday, one P.M. corporate planning meeting at Daylin's West Los Angeles offices. The plan was to spend a couple of hours reviewing our budget and plans for the coming year.

That's what it was *supposed* to be.

I still believed that if you did something well, if you made a lot of money, that people, even if they didn't like you, would tolerate you.

How wrong I was.

By this point, Handy Dan had 66 stores (the stores in Arizona and California were known as Angel's) and almost $155 million in sales. We won the Home Center Retailer-of-the-Year Award in 1976–77, which was given by the Brand Names Foundation. Best of all, the National Home Center News reported, "During fiscal year 1976, Handy Dan earned $7.8 million before taxes, while the comparable figure for Daylin, *as a whole,* was $7 million."

We arrived half an hour early and spoke casually with Bill Mallory, Daylin's chief financial officer and someone I shielded from being fired by Sigoloff. Mallory took me aside, separating me from Arthur, making innocuous conversation. He seemed nervous.

At one P.M. sharp, Mallory walked me into a room. Sigoloff was there waiting, accompanied by an assortment of lawyers, accountants, and stenographers. It was an odd group for a planning meeting. Even odder was that Arthur was nowhere in sight.

I was in one room, Arthur in another. It was a planned effort to divide and conquer us. There were several attorneys in both rooms, and it became clear this wasn't a planning meeting.

Sigoloff finally had us where he wanted us, and today was Ming's version of corporate show-and-tell. To make a long story short, I was fired and in rapid succession so were Arthur and Ron Brill.

Brill, whose family had owned neighborhood hardware stores in New York and New Jersey, had been an accountant with Arthur Andersen & Co. in Los Angeles when we first met him. His specialty was retail, and he was the audit manager for the Daylin Corp. during its bankruptcy. The end of the bankruptcy coincided with Ron's decision to leave Arthur Andersen in 1976, and we hired him as Handy Dan's director of internal audit.

Ron, like Arthur and me, never knew what hit him.

Sigoloff was well organized. He released a statement to the press by deadline on Friday afternoon, so that all the Los Angeles papers carried the story of our firing on Saturday morning.

But it was far worse than just the loss of a couple of well-paying, high-profile jobs, or a few embarrassing newspaper stories.

Sigoloff was primarily after me; for Arthur and Ron, it was more a matter of guilt by association.

We all had painful experiences telling our family and friends what happened. Walking out of the Daylin offices, Arthur went to a pay phone and called his wife.

"Diana," he said, "Bernie, Ron, and I were just fired."

She started laughing. At that moment, he may not have had a job, but Arthur felt good about his marriage. Diana knew Arthur's work ethic and manner so well, she figured he was making a little joke. The firing came so out of the blue that she thought he was kidding. After all, you don't usually fire someone for running your company well and making you piles of money.

"No," Arthur told her, "it really happened."

■　　■　　■

We have never discussed the actual charges Sigoloff made against us, but for the record, here is what happened:

We had been involved in a decertification battle with a Handy Dan labor union in San Jose, California—the only unionized stores in the chain, incidentally. A group of employees had come to us and said they wanted to decertify out of the union.

We hired an attorney who told us what we could and could not do during the decertification proceedings. I directed our personnel department to do whatever fell within the legal guidelines.

What we eventually learned was that actions were taken that apparently violated some National Labor Relations Board rules.

None of us knew about these supposed NLRB violations until some time after Sigoloff fired us.

Anybody who knew the facts behind it—including Ron Brill—also had to go. As director of internal audit, Ron knew the cost of the decertification proceedings. But he didn't think that what we were doing was illegal and, ultimately, neither did anybody else. But for nearly four years, Sigoloff made our lives miserable and cost us a fortune in legal defense fees.

Incredibly, neither the Justice Department nor the SEC instigated investigations; Sigoloff—through his attorneys—did. He made accusations to the Justice Department. He went to the Securities and Exchange Commission. His attorneys informed the Justice Department of their accusations and explained that that was why we were fired.

The labor decertification proceedings were used as a tool to eliminate me and those closest to me. These efforts did cause us emotional and financial harm, but the issue remained strictly personal. The material and "information" about the circumstances regarding the decertification that were turned over to the Justice Department and the Securities and Exchange Commission were carefully reviewed and considered. Despite all of the pressure brought to bear on Justice and the SEC to act against us, not one charge was ever made against Arthur, Ron, or me by any government agency. Ironically, the only official proceeding that came out of the entire decertification labor case was that a formal complaint charging unfair labor practices was issued by the NLRB against the union.

It cost us each a small fortune to hire lawyers to defend ourselves. And we were hardly well paid. Ron, for example, was only paid in the mid-$30,000 range. None of us owned stock in Handy Dan; all of our hard work and innovation seemed to have enriched everyone from Ken Langone to Sandy Sigoloff, but not us.

I had options in the company, but they were wiped out. Sigoloff also voided my contract, daring me to sue. "The only problem for you," Sigoloff taunted me, "is that I am going to fight you with the company's money, and you are going to have to fight me with your own money, which you don't have."

And he was right.

Traumatic as our experiences at Handy Dan were, they played an important part in developing Home Depot's values. For example, Sandy Sigoloff rewarded people who were his loyal followers with an inordinate amount of money. There are people who are for rent, and he bought their souls. We learned that love and compassion do a hell of a lot more than just buying people.

■　■　■

It was late Saturday when Ken Langone returned home and called me.

"Kenny, a terrible thing has happened," I said, describing Friday's events. "You told me what would happen to me. You told me that I would get fired, and it happened. And now he is trying to destroy my life."

But Langone wasn't at all sympathetic. Not one bit. And he wasn't interested in wasting time on "I told you so," either. What he actually said was more upsetting.

"Oh, man, that's great, that's unbelievable," Langone said.

"What the hell are you smoking?" I asked.

"This is the greatest news I have heard," Langone continued. "This is . . . I am so happy. I cannot tell you."

"What is the matter with you, Kenny? Did you hear what I said?"

"No, no, you don't understand!" Langone insisted. "You have just been kicked in the ass with a golden horseshoe. This is the greatest opportunity! Now we can open up that store you talked about when we were in Houston!"

Langone actually thought being fired by Sandy Sigoloff was a blessing.

I thought he was crazy.

"Kenny," I said, "I was just fired. There's nothing golden about that."

"Are you kidding?" he said. "That is the greatest news I have ever heard!"

I thought he was a raving lunatic—which he is. "What the hell is the matter with you?" I said. "I just got *fired*."

Langone just breezed right over that.

"Now we can open up the store you talked about back in Houston!" he said again, his excitement growing. "You guys have been really hamstrung and haven't been able to do a lot of the things you wanted to do, and it is pretty clear to me, as an investment banker and financier, that you have a lot more capacity than what you can do here. Don't view this as a negative.

"Bernie," he continued, "you never know where life is going to take you. This is a great opportunity for you to do your own thing— let's go into business together."

Frankly, I was surprised he remembered. We had been opening another Handy Dan store in Houston. Langone flew in from New York for the occasion. As we were walking the store, Langone stopped short and asked, "Why are you opening so many stores in Houston? It appears that you already have a store on every major street corner in the city."

"Because some day," I said, "somebody is going to open a store that is going to make all of our stores obsolete."

"What do you mean?"

"There is a store that I have created in my imagination that is going to make Handy Dan obsolete."

"What will it look like?"

"If I tell you, then you will know," I said. "Right now, only I know."

In 1976, I already envisioned the prototype of The Home Depot, a massive store unlike anything in the United States at that time.

"If Handy Dan has fifteen stores in Houston," I told Langone, "three of my new stores would make these obsolete."

Langone couldn't imagine it.

"Well, I am not going to tell you about it," I said. "And I am just praying that no one else thinks of it. I won't share it with anybody else. Not yet."

That was the daydream behind The Home Depot. But still in shock after being fired without warning, I was not in a mood for daydreaming.

"Bernie," Langone said, "you have repeatedly told me how Handy Dan and this whole industry is vulnerable. Too many small chains, no national companies, and prices are too high. Do you still believe that?"

"Yes."

"Good. Then let's you and I meet as soon as we can."

"I have no money," I protested.

"Well, how much would you need?"

I threw out a number. "Twenty-five million."

At that, Langone let the subject drop without further comment and said good-bye.

■   ■   ■

With very little cash on hand, my reputation at issue, and, at the age of 49, my future prospects shaky at best, I hired a lawyer to pursue approximately $1 million in salary, stock options, and other benefits that I believed Sandy Sigoloff had stolen from me.

This was a lawyer apart from the one who would defend my name and reputation as Sigoloff dragged me through the courts via the Justice Department and SEC.

My attorney said, "You have a great case. We can win." But every time I talked to him, it cost $200 an hour.

That's when I ran into an old acquaintance, Sol Price, founder of the Price Club discount membership warehouse chain. About the same time that Sigoloff fired me, Price was conducting his own legal maneuvers against a German company that had bought one of his companies. The Germans violated their contract with Price, and he sued them.

Over dinner, I told Price how Sigoloff turned me out. There was a lot of self-pity on my part: Why did this happen to me? I was drowning in my own sorrow, going several nights at a time without sleeping. For the first time in my adult life, instead of building, I was more concerned with surviving.

Price invited me to spend more time with him in San Diego. When I arrived a few days later, Price immediately walked me into a room that was piled from floor to eye level with documents.

"What is this?" I asked.

"These are depositions," Price explained. "This is what I have spent the last three years of my life going through."

I shook my head in awe—and fear. I saw my own future looming before my eyes.

Price said the lawsuit consumed every day of his life. Wherever he was, whatever he was doing, all he thought about was the lawsuit. "The attorneys are sucking me dry," he said. "In the final analysis, even if I win, I lose." Which ultimately is what happened. Price won, but he lost. All the energy and time he had to put into it wasn't worth it. He drained his body, his energy, his thoughts, and his money.

"Do you have money to pursue this?" Price asked.

"No, I really don't."

"Are your attorneys at least representing you on a contingency basis?"

"No."

"Bernie," Price said, sympathetically putting his hand on my shoulder, "when I sold my company, I went right out and started the Price Club. I had the money, so we were able to do that *and* sue these bastards. You don't have money to waste."

He paused while I considered that.

"Bernie, do you think you are talented?" Price asked.

"Yes, I think I am."

"Do you think you have the ability to build something, to create something, do you feel good about yourself?"

"Yeah, I do," I said quickly. "I feel all those things. I think I can be very successful."

"Then why don't you just tell Sigoloff to go —— himself? And get on with your life. Pay your lawyers what you owe them and walk away from it."

I drove back to Los Angeles that night, rolling over and over in my mind the things I saw and heard. By the time I got home, I realized that Price was 100 percent right.

It was time to get on with my life.

■　　■　　■

Arthur was not happy being out of work, but he did enjoy the time it gave him to spend with his wife and young children while he considered his future. He also became more dedicated to his fitness, using the time to train for and run his first marathon.

His friend Leon Beck—himself late of Daylin—suggested they open a CPA practice together, but that wasn't the direction Arthur saw himself going. He also declined opportunities to run the Wickes and Handy City chains of home improvement stores, which was later somewhat ironic when Sigoloff was hired to turn that parent corporation around, too.

And there was the growing talk of a new challenge, the home improvement store of the future. I had Langone's interest in raising money and had made it clear I couldn't even think of going forward without Arthur. Arthur quickly realized that, win or lose, his destiny was deeply entwined with mine.

We met several times a week, first at the old Hyatt coffee shop in the City of Commerce, a point halfway between our homes—Arthur's in Fullerton, mine in Encino—and later in space lent to us by our attorneys, Buchalter, Nemer, Fields, Chrystie & Younger. (Stuart Buchalter later became chairman of Standard Brands, somewhat of a competitor.) Starting with a clean yellow pad of paper, we put a business plan together. I dreamed aloud of wide open warehouse stores as Arthur tried to make sense of the numbers. It was an interesting exercise, because the numbers didn't work.

Our vision was of an immense warehouse store, anywhere from 55,000 to 75,000 square feet and with high ceilings. The biggest Handy Dan store was just 35,000 square feet. Handy Dan carried a small assortment of selective merchandise, the best-sellers in every category.

Unlike Handy Dan, we would insist on buying directly from the manufacturers. Manufacturers would send merchandise directly to our stores, cutting out middlemen and warehouses, so we could give their profit back to the customer in price reductions.

Per store volumes would be $7 million to $9 million in annual sales. That was insane at a time when the best Handy Dan store averaged $3 million.

We imagined gross profit margins of 29 to 31 percent. That, too, was unheard of. Prevalent in the industry at that time were margins of 42 to 47 percent. To make payroll, traditional stores needed higher margins. But we believed that high-volume stores would do much more business than Handy Dan or any other stores in existence in those days, because of the low prices at which we would sell the merchandise. We would have immense amounts of merchandise and great assortments, stacked to the ceiling, so consumers would be overwhelmed when they walked in, and they would virtually smell a bargain.

Finally, and most important, this superstore would star highly trained people on the selling floor who could not only move product but help even the least mechanically inclined customer through most any home repair or improvement.

That was the theory behind The Home Depot.

In my mind, the concept was simple. But it was Arthur's job to make the business plan work on paper. And it didn't. It just didn't.

"The numbers don't work," Arthur said.

"Why don't they work?" I asked.

"The margins and the volume don't support the profit."

"What do we need?"

"More sales."

"Okay," I said, "that's easy. Let's write in more sales."

"Just put them in?" That went against Arthur's straightlaced financial training. "I can't do that."

"Arthur, just do it," I said. "Just raise the sales. Look, this whole thing is not a fact; it's a product of my imagination. A business plan is just a creation. Just raise the sales. What do you need, a million, two million dollars? Put it in. Because if you don't do it, I will."

Arthur didn't give in easily, but he did give in, stretching the numbers only as far as he could go without feeling guilty.

We both felt good about the concept, even if we weren't exactly sure how the numbers would unfold in the marketplace. We even formed an operating company, MB Associates, short for Marcus/Blank.

It was something to do while we waited for fate to find us.

The Financier

"My People Don't Drive Cadillacs"*

Nothing happened for a couple of weeks as we assessed all of our opportunities. One day, my phone rang. The caller was Ken Langone.

"I got $2 million," he said.

"From who?" I asked, astonished.

"Ross Perot," he said.

■　■　■

Ken Langone is a man of truly unusual qualities, about as far from the cold, bottom-line-oriented investment banker as you will ever find. And for all his bombast, he's also a man who likes being in the background but making a difference. He can effect more positive change in a day of phone calls than most people accomplish in a year.

Ken's investment banking career with the firm of R. W. Pressprich, headquartered in New York City, had been on the upswing for ten years when he met Jack Hight at a social event, a man who became a lifelong friend and golf partner. At the end of the evening, Hight mentioned that the company he worked for was ready to go public. He even offered to arrange a face-to-face meeting with the chairman of the board.

* Bernie Marcus

"Call me on Monday," Hight said, "and I will get you an appointment."

By the time Ken called on Monday morning, it was all arranged. "You have an appointment at 11:30 Wednesday morning in Dallas," Hight said. "Be here exactly at 11:30. You have thirty minutes. You will be out of there at 12:00, and whatever you do, *don't swear!*"

The company was Electronic Data Systems, EDS for short, and its founder and chairman was H. Ross Perot.

It was a scary thing, even for a well-traveled man like Ken. He arrived early, took a seat, and was looking at the second hand of his watch when, precisely at 11:30, he and two young associates were escorted into Perot's office. *This guy means business,* Ken realized.

Now, mind you, despite his decade-long experience, Ken had never conducted an initial public offering.

"Let me tell you who I have been talking to and what they are telling me," Perot said, not wasting any time on introductions. Among the thirteen firms already bidding on his IPO were Goldman Sachs, Merrill Lynch & Co., Salomon Brothers, Allen & Co., and G. H. Walker. Perot then summed up what each had told him. Ken's thirty minutes were quickly spinning by.

After twenty-nine minutes, Perot said, "Okay, what do you think about what I have been saying?"

"I think I will say good-bye, Mr. Perot," Ken said.

"What are you talking about?"

"Well, Jack Hight told me I had thirty minutes. I have about fifteen seconds left, so I think I will say good-bye, and maybe some other time you can see me, and I can tell you about us."

"Whoa!" Perot said. "Let's talk a little bit more. Tell me what you think about what I just said."

Taking a deep breath, Ken figured he had already blown the thirty-minute rule; he might as well blow the other rule as well.

"Mr. Perot," he said, exhaling quickly, "that is the biggest pile of horseshit I ever heard in my life."

"What do you mean?"

"Well, Mr. Perot, it is very simple. I am going to try to get you to sell stock, and I will find somebody to buy that stock. It's that simple.

All the stuff in the middle is bureaucracy. You want to sell, I gotta find a buyer. They want to buy, I gotta find a seller. That's it."

Perot didn't care for profanity, but he valued straight talk even more. He kept Ken talking till one A.M., during which time the two discovered they were married at the same hour on the same day of the same year. Scary, isn't it?

Ken went to Dallas that day with the intention of going home that night, but thirteen hours later, he and his associates were in Perot's car, searching for a motel with a vacancy.

Meanwhile, at Ken's urging, Perot postponed making a final decision. Over the next several months, Ken made repeated trips to Dallas, learning Perot's business and expanding their personal rapport. Two more different men you could not find, but that seemed a common denominator in most of Ken's business deals.

Early in their discussions, Perot said, "Next time you come down, bring all the prospectuses of all the deals you have done."

"Uh, sure."

At the end of their next meeting, Perot asked, "Did you bring the prospectuses with you?"

"No," Ken said.

Perot was surprised. Ken was not forgetful. "Did you forget them?"

"No."

"Why didn't you bring them?"

Ken finally fessed up. "Because there are none. You are it."

"*What?*"

"Yours is the first deal I am going to do."

Perot just stood there, slack-jawed. He couldn't believe what he was hearing.

"Bear in mind one thing, Ross," Ken continued. "You have such a great company, nobody can screw it up. An idiot can do your deal. If I blow it, I am out of business. But if I do a great job for you, my reputation is set. I have every incentive, and I promise you, I will personally handle this deal myself."

After time, Perot narrowed the field to two, Allen & Co. and R. W. Pressprich. By then, Perot had figured out a couple of things about going public. Number one, it didn't matter who brought a company public. What mattered was the person who actually led the deal to the public, because if that person exerted a lot of effort and influence, the company would enjoy a successful underwriting. If that person didn't do his job, the biggest name in the world couldn't help.

Perot asked Milledge A. "Mitch" Hart, who was then executive vice president of EDS, for his opinion. (Mitch was later an original investor in The Home Depot and a member of our board of directors.)

"The safe bet is Charlie Allen [of Allen & Co.]," Hart said, "because he has been there and done that so many times and has such a great reputation. But Langone is the guy that I would pick."

"Why?"

"For one thing, he is so excited about this he can hardly stand it. He desperately wants to make a name for himself and he sees us as his best shot."

In June 1968, Perot made his decision. He called Ken and said, "The deal is yours." But there was a catch: Ken had to agree to bring EDS out at a multiple of 100 times earnings, which was an absolutely, outrageously stretched number.

On September 11, 1968, the night before EDS went public, Ken and Elaine Langone and Ross and Margot Perot were in the back of a limousine, driving through the Holland Tunnel from New York to New Jersey. The time was midnight. In those days, you would actually sign all the papers for a stock offering in Jersey, then turn around and come right back so you didn't have to pay the New York State transfer taxes.

The Perots were in the backseat looking forward, the Langones opposite them, looking backward.

"Ross, I have something to tell you about tomorrow," Ken said. "We won't be bringing EDS out at 100 times earnings after all."

"I knew it!" Perot said, pointing his finger. "Everybody on Wall Street told me that you will say you will do the stock offering at 100 times earnings and, at the last minute, say, 'Sorry, we can't do it.' You are just like everybody else. This is exactly what they warned me was going to happen."

"Ross, wait a minute; hold it," Ken said calmly. "I don't want you upset. If that's what you want, we will do it at 100 times earnings."

"Well, a deal is a deal. You said 100 times. . . ."

"Fine, fine. We will do it at 100 times earnings."

Just then, Margot spoke up.

"Ken, what were you going to say a minute ago?"

"Just that instead of 100 times earnings, I was going to do it at $16.50 a share, 118 times earnings," Ken said, watching Perot turn from a slow burn to a big red-faced laugh. "But if he only wants 100 times, then that is okay with me."

■   ■   ■

Because he was the only person Ken Langone knew with $2 million to spare, Ross Perot nearly became the majority owner of The Home Depot. And this is probably one of the great "What if . . ." business stories of all time.

In the world of technology, EDS was to the 1960s and '70s what Microsoft has been to the 1980s and '90s. It brought a whole new dimension to the business of computer services. EDS was eating up the business world, although Perot was not yet the household name and folk hero he is today.

Ken took me to meet Perot in Dallas. My first impression was that of a gregarious and enthusiastic man who was a model of the American free enterprise system. He was a patriot for the entrepreneurial spirit who literally created something out of nothing. A former IBM salesman and look at him now! I thought. America had been good to him, and he frequently talked about giving back to his country.

Ken told Perot—who was always cordial but never cracked a smile—about how Arthur and I had built this great business, Handy Dan, and the injustice Sigoloff had committed against us. Ken told the story in a way that we could not, and Perot ate it up.

There were a few structural and compatibility issues that I felt I needed to run by Perot right from the beginning to see if we would be compatible.

"Ross," I said, "I am not interested in doing anything with you unless I know that I am going to deal directly with you. I don't want to deal through intermediaries and I will not become part of your existing organization. If I have a problem, I will call you, and you and I will agree on how we proceed. I am not going to a captain or a lieutenant. I am not interested in that nonsense. If we get caught up in corporate crap, I won't be part of it."

It was my way of throwing down a gauntlet, challenging Perot to accept me for who and what I was. I didn't change my personality for Sigoloff; I wasn't going to do it for Perot, either.

"I like straightforward people," Perot said. "No, I wouldn't put anybody in between us, you have my word."

With an understanding of our positions in place, we agreed to explore a relationship. I introduced Arthur to Perot at the next meeting.

Arthur was unsure what he was going to do with his life. While he sorted out his options, Ken arranged for Arthur to do some consulting work in Philadelphia for Gary Erlbaum's Panelrama chain.

During this time, Perot hired a consultant named Brian Smith, who had been a general director of the board of Texas Instruments. Perot gave our presentation materials to Smith for a second opinion.

At our next meeting, the new man was alongside Perot. Perot introduced Smith and I could see a barrier already developing between me and Perot.

Ken raised the issue later, and Perot waved it away. He said that because of his intense travel schedule, we would need someone who could act and make decisions in his absence. Smith was that man. Uneasy, I let it slide for the time being.

But Smith thought our retail concept was a bad idea. At that time, gross margins in the industry were about 44 percent, really big markups, but we were talking about our gross margins being as low as 29 percent. We expected to make up the difference—and more—on volume. But Smith just couldn't get Perot's wallet wrapped around the concept.

"How are you going to do it?" he asked at a subsequent meeting. "If you are selling at these margins, you will lose a pile of money."

"No, that's not right," I insisted. "The idea is that the volume of business we will do in these stores will give us a different kind of benchmark."

Levy's was a chain of four home improvement stores in Louisville, Kentucky, owned by the Levy family. At that time, they produced some of the biggest sales volume in our industry, roughly $4 million per store annually. Our model was based on at least double their volume. The profit percentage would be lower, but the gross margin dollars, the actual dollars that the margins would convert into, would be substantially higher.

Ken turned to Perot.

"I just don't agree with Brian," Ken said. "He doesn't understand the concept."

Perot wasn't one who worried much about stepping on the views of his underlings. He wanted to do what was best for business. Smith, meanwhile, remained resistant to the deal.

For his $2 million, Perot would own 70 percent of the company, as yet unnamed, Ken would get 5 percent, and we would own 25 percent. Out of our 25 percent, we would bring in a team of people such as Ron Brill and others.

We made one final trip to Dallas intended to iron out a few final details.

There were strong signals of future culture conflicts, however. We were more than a little discomfited by the military nature of EDS, including the corporate uniforms—everybody had to wear a shirt and tie, and the only acceptable shirt color was white—and the guard who met every car entering the corporation's campus.

During a discussion of what perks would go with my salary, I told Perot I had a small problem. While my salary and perks would be similar to those I enjoyed at Handy Dan, there was the matter of a company car.

The leased car I had been driving was still being paid for by Handy Dan, but the company would repossess it unless I planned to take over the lease or buy it for the depreciated value. This was a good deal for a new company.

"We ought to try to save as much money as we can," I said. "I would like to buy it outright at the depreciated value. Would you like me to buy it, and then I will just charge it to our entity, or do you want to give me a check, and I will pay for it?"

"That's fine," Perot said. "You can either do that or buy a new car, I don't really care."

But then Perot decided to test me.

"What kind of a car is it?" Perot asked in that peculiar Texas drawl of his.

"It's a Cadillac."

Perot didn't like that answer at all.

"My people don't drive Cadillacs," he said. "My guys at EDS drive Chevrolets."

"That's fine," I said. "I think it's a good policy for you, but this is a new company we're forming, not EDS. Look, this is a four-year-old car and I'm a big guy. It is cheaper to have an old Cadillac than it is to go out and get a new Chevrolet. So how do we pay for it?"

Not that the question meant anything.

"My people don't drive Cadillacs," Perot said again. And again. "My people don't drive Cadillacs."

And when he said it the third time, I realized this was never going to work. Going from "Ming the Merciless" to Ross Perot was no improvement. Perot was establishing who and what his position was and what mine was, partners or not.

My mind flashed back to the day Sigoloff and I nearly came to blows during a board of directors meeting. When we went into another room to hash out our disagreement privately, Sigoloff told me that he was the boss. He controlled my career, and I needed to understand that. Then he demanded that I literally repeat that back to him.

I said nothing of the sort.

Instead, acknowledging that he was right about one thing—he was the boss—I nonetheless told him to go —— himself. Nobody controls my life but me. He owned shares of stock, the controlling shares of stock in Handy Dan, but he would never control me or my career.

Now I was looking across a different table, staring at Ross Perot, my blood pressure rising, my face turning red. And I was hearing Sigoloff's words coming out of Perot's mouth. "I am the boss; I control your life. I will tell you what to do and what not to do."

Regaining my composure, I smiled. "Ross, I have to talk to Kenny for a minute. Would you mind if we step outside?"

Ken was perplexed.

"Look, Kenny," I whispered, "I know Perot is a very important person in your life, but you have to understand something. If this guy is going to be bothered by what kind of car I am driving, how much aggravation are we going to have when we have to make really big decisions? If we can't be free to run the business the way we know it has to be run, it isn't going to work. I am never going to have this man for a partner. I would rather starve to death. No way."

Now it was Ken's turn to wonder whose brains were scrambled. "You must be out of your mind! Are you crazy? My God, he is going to give you $2 million!"

"Kenny, I wouldn't touch it with a ten-foot pole. I am out of here," I said and headed down the hall.

Ken went back in, looked Perot in the eye, and never said a word about Cadillacs.

"Ross, look, we are all thinking about where we are," Ken said. "Brian obviously doesn't like the deal. This is a no-win situation for me, personally, and maybe we ought to just cool it for a while. Let's just let some time pass and then decide whether we want to get back together."

"Okay," Perot said. "If you want to come back, come on back."

Ken said that he would call in a few days. And that is how we walked away from Ross Perot.

The interesting thing is that if Perot hadn't been so hung up on Cadillacs, his original 70 percent share of The Home Depot stock would be worth approximately $58 billion today.

■   ■   ■

Later, Ken wondered if he had damaged his long-term relationship with Perot. I thanked God the deal hadn't been concluded. And Arthur felt the heavy weight of Sigoloff enshrouding him once more after briefly seeing daylight.

I was the first to speak. "What do we do now?"

"Now we are going to go raise the $2 million at 50 percent," Ken said defiantly.

"What are you talking about?" Arthur said.

"Let's put together a group of investors where you won't have to worry about that. I am going to get my 5 percent," Ken explained, "you guys are going to have 45, and the next investors will get 50 percent."

"That doesn't make sense," Arthur argued. "That means we will have a better deal by walking away from this deal."

"That's right," Ken said. "In the retail business, when you can't sell something, you mark it down. In my business, when we can't sell something, we mark it up."

■   ■   ■

The Home Depot got its start when Ken Langone reached out to his own investment group for seed money. We had convinced him that our new retail concept had such a good blend of low price, wide assortment, and customer service that it couldn't miss. It was destined to become the first nationwide home improvement store brand, and once Ken believed, he set out to convince the rest of the world on our behalf.

We had never met most of Ken's group, so he set up a meeting in New York. We felt like beggars, asking these successful people to invest in our company.

Not that that was necessary; they gave us a rousing reception.

Why? These were the people who bought Handy Dan stock between $3 and $9 a share and sold it at $25.50 a share. Of course they loved us!

Of course, while they had made tons of money, we were broke.

That irony wasn't lost on Ken.

"You guys made a ton of money on Bernie and Arthur," he told them. "Take a portion and roll it over into their new business. Sure it's a gamble, a real gamble. If you went to Vegas, you would drop a few thousand dollars a day, so what the hell, let's drop it here and see if these guys can roll sevens again."

We wouldn't have wanted anyone but Ken manhandling this crowd. He's the kind of guy who, if you were in a meeting with him and he was quiet for more than a minute and a half, you'd think he was asleep. In fact, if Ken has any faults, it's that he gives answers faster than you can ask a question.

Ken eventually cajoled forty or so players in his group into buying enough $25,000 units of preferred stock to get us to $2 million in seed capital. That's of course a far cry from the original $25 million I thought was necessary to capitalize The Home Depot. And in fact we were undercapitalized for a number of years. The idea was that they would put the money up, but it would be a preferred stock and they would get their money back. Not that selling those $25,000 units was a snap.

In the end, they gave us $2 million and two years to open up any business that we chose. The money was intended to cover our salaries, expenses, and benefits, equal to what we made at Handy Dan.

There were actually two pieces to the investment. Ken's investment group bought units consisting of preferred and common stock. Common stock is also what we bought, at pennies a share. This gave us the opportunity to be participants in the fruits of our own labors, an important and much valued opportunity we never had at Handy Dan.

This is the way our company started.

4

The Merchant, Act I

"Never Be Satisfied with How Things Are"*

Merchandising is the soul of our company. And much of our success through the years has resulted from a love of discovering and inspiring new products, putting a new sales spin on reliable classics, and our passion for seeing all of them move through the cash registers.

One of the original catalysts responsible for inspiring and propelling this passion was Pat Farrah.

■ ■ ■

While we were running Handy Dan, another old-line home improvement chain was growing quickly and gaining attention in California: National Lumber & Supply Company. It was a family-owned home center outlet dating back to 1942, when it was founded by Sol Jaffee. As the years went by, his children and grandchildren joined the Fountain Valley company. But the National Lumber employee everyone in our industry talked about was not a Jaffee. It was a young man named Patrick G. "Pat" Farrah.

Pat joined National Lumber in 1962, just out of high school. He started out as a lumber man but quickly demonstrated an acute understanding of both customer service and product. When Pat joined the company, it was doing about $2 million a year in sales.

* Bernie Marcus

Before long, the Jaffees promoted Pat to service desk manager. When National opened its second store, Pat was named the store manager.

He was a natural who loved being around freshly milled wood, a husky guy who enjoyed the physicality of the lumber yard, loading and unloading building materials. He was one of the few who could load three bundles of shingles on a truck at a time.

He also loved the instant gratification that came from serving customers and making a sale. On his days off, Pat worked with an old Swedish guy who taught him how to do mill work, building windows from scratch.

The Jaffee family opened its hearts to him, and Pat became the guy they turned to after Mel Jaffee, the oldest of Sol's three sons, took over the company as president in 1965. And as Pat's stock rose, the other two brothers faded. Pat is a natural, charismatic leader. He gets pushed to the forefront because people want to follow him.

Under his direction, National Lumber grew from two to seven stores, becoming a serious regional competitor to Handy Dan. Mel Jaffee invested his time in Pat, teaching him everything he knew about the industry. He tolerated Pat's mistakes and encouraged him to make more—even at Jaffee's expense—as long as there was a lesson to be learned. After opening the fourth National Lumber store, Pat was promoted to vice president and general manager.

One year National Lumber sold Christmas trees, and Pat hung one upside down from the ceiling. "Just think of doing something totally different," he'd say. "Never be satisfied with how things are." If sales were poor on a particular product, he would find a way to make that product outsell anything else.

He tried to take National Lumber to the place where he saw the company going, but he couldn't overcome the family's resistance.

About that time, Handy Dan needed a good lead merchant— someone to oversee the acquisition of goods for all our stores—and I had heard that Pat was a great one. One day I called Pat. We agreed to meet and I intended to pursue a doubleheader, buying out National Lumber, and acquiring Pat to run the merchandise side of the much larger Handy Dan operation.

I had every intention of stealing Pat away even if National Lumber was not available—until I met him. Within thirty minutes, however, I concluded that the man was an egomaniac, a raving lunatic, out of control, in orbit.

Did you ever dislike somebody instantly? That was my response to Pat. And Pat wasn't any more impressed with me.

Pat left the office, and I told Arthur, "I wouldn't hire this guy on a bet. He and I would be like fire and oil. It will be a distant day before I'd have him associated with me."

Besides, Pat, feeling rather cocky about his own company's rosy future, indicated he wasn't interested either.

■ ■ ■

Fast-forward several years.

In 1977, National Lumber was doing very well, and the family was spending less time hands-on, pretty much entrusting its operation to Pat's care. He and Mel Jaffee even started investing together outside the company. But a dispute over one of those investments turned both of their lives upside down.

The situation started innocently enough when Pat met Cliff Branch. Branch owned California Cooperage, which manufactured a popular line of hot tubs. Pat thought they'd be great project starters in National Lumber stores; buy the hot tub and build a deck around it. As usual, he was right. Do-it-yourselfers bought the tubs and then dropped thousands more on deck materials.

It was going so well that Mel and Pat decided to buy the company. They both liked Branch and thought he'd be helpful in refocusing National's lumber business. They negotiated a deal for an 80 percent ownership.

But the day before the deal would close and be announced in San Francisco at the National Swimming Pool Show, Mel Jaffee—the show's keynote speaker—let all of the water out of the tub.

He returned from a trip to Israel and announced he couldn't go through with the deal. "I can't make this investment now," he abruptly told Pat.

Pat didn't have the cash to do the deal by himself, and there was no way to raise the balance of the money, so they had to back out.

Pat flew to San Francisco and gave Branch the bad news in person. He felt so bad about it that on the spot, without any planning, he told Branch he was quitting National Lumber.

Five of the seven National Lumber store managers and fifty more employees, demonstrating unbelievable loyalty, walked out with Pat despite his protestations that they not. They cooled their heels while Pat gathered financing for his dream: an enormous home improvement warehouse superstore, bigger than anything the industry had ever seen.

■ ■ ■

Jack Hoffman, a tough old merchant, owned a deserted, forgotten discount store in Lakewood, California, near the Long Beach Airport. He and his brother had previously operated Cal Stores on the site, a 130,000-square-foot predecessor to the Price Club membership warehouse concept. They had fifteen years of success before national discounters such as Kmart and Wal-Mart destroyed their business.

It was at Hoffman's door that Pat and his ragtag, underfunded bunch found themselves. Pat had formed a partnership with two of his most trusted managers from National Lumber, Dan Tsujioka and Dave Alban. With the help of a manufacturers' rep who loaned the trio an office and secretary, they developed a business plan in four days. On the fifth day, Pat made a presentation and raised $75,000 in cash and a $300,000 line of credit from a local bank.

Not long after that, he made his pitch to Hoffman.

Hoffman took an immediate liking to Pat and listened in earnest as Pat described his dream store. A prince of a guy, Hoffman gave Pat the entire building for 19 cents a foot and a handshake.

"There is one catch, though," Hoffman said.

After Cal Stores closed, Jack's brother continued operating a small liquor store in one part of the otherwise-closed, cavernous structure. "You have to keep my brother in business, keep him going." Hoffman said.

Within thirty days, Pat, Tsujioka, Alban, and the rest of their National Lumber refugees staffed up his new concept store—separated from the liquor store on the inside by a floor-to-ceiling chain-link fence—ordered merchandise, bought mostly used fixtures, painted the store, did the layout, and filled the back of the store with lumber.

When Homeco opened its doors in January 1978, there were 1,500 people lined up to get in. What they experienced inside was nothing short of revolutionary. Merchandise in the 130,000-square-foot store was stocked floor to ceiling. Homeco was the first really big building materials store in California to have lumber inside and per-haps the first to use a forklift on the inside.

Employees wore khaki shorts, tennis shoes, and brown T-shirts with HOMECO on the back. Nobody walked; they literally ran to wait on the customers. *Ran.* Then they walked the customer to wherever he or she needed to go. The employees wowed everybody who walked in the door, immediately establishing tremendous customer loyalty. It was a style and attitude we later adopted with great success at The Home Depot.

Being located next to the airport was a natural for Pat, whose father was an oil surveyor and part-time flight instructor there. Del Farrah was always on 24-hour call, flying to Bakersfield or Taft to check out a potential new well field. So Pat spoke the language of the flyboys and got to know several smoke-writers, the cowboys who wrote messages in the sky. They typically flew over the beaches on weekends, advertising products such as Coppertone or wet T-shirt contests at local bars. For $200 a month, he made a deal so that whenever they got back to the airport and had any smoke left, they would do messages for him. On the Fourth of July, for example, he tied in to the liquor store with which Homeco shared the building and promoted 99-cents-a-six-pack Budweiser. Hardware and beer, how do you beat that? In a day and a half, Pat sold three truckloads of beer. It was unbelievable. The place was packed.

■　■　■

One morning, Hoyne Greenberg, a vendor and friend who sold to us at Handy Dan, called me. "I want to take you out to see a store," he said. "It is very important that you see this store. It is run by Pat

Farrah. He left the company he was working with and set up his own business. You just have to see this store."

"No thanks," I said. "Not interested. I met Pat Farrah, and I wasn't impressed. I couldn't be less interested."

"Bernie, forget about that; you have to see this store."

"Nope, not interested."

"Bernie," Greenberg said, "I am picking you up at seven tomorrow morning, and I am taking you there whether you want to go or not. Be ready."

The next morning, Greenberg picked me up in a Rolls-Royce, and drove me to Lakewood and a place called Homeco. It had been open just six months. As we walked in, I saw my dreams in living color. I was flabbergasted.

Homeco was a monstrous store with merchandise piled up to the ceiling. It was astonishing. I felt tears welling up in my eyes. I was partly overwhelmed, partly angry. I couldn't believe that Pat Farrah, this obnoxious guy I couldn't stand, had this idea. *My* idea! Pat brought it to life first, but it was almost exactly what I had imagined!

Despite it being Pat's creation, Homeco was love at first sight for me. I loved the merchandise assortment, the way it was piled to the ceiling, the awesome commitment to customer satisfaction, and Pat's offbeat ways of promoting it all.

Greenberg brought Pat over, and for the first time I saw the real Pat Farrah. All the artifice was gone. He was the most enthusiastic, irrepressibly positive guy I'd ever met. At Greenberg's prompting, Pat showed me around the store. He'd point to something benign such as hammers and say, "We sold a thousand of those last week." Cans of paint? "Eight hundred of those." And so on. I figured the numbers were inflated, but it didn't matter. Pat had the right goods, priced the right way. Even the margins were as I envisioned them.

His staff were competent, hard-working folks who knew their products intimately. And they were carved in Pat's image, entrepreneurs all, a wild man and his wild tribe, selling products like they were pieces of gold.

"We ought to get together," Pat told me. "I always liked you and I always thought . . ."

"Uh, sure," I said. I didn't understand Pat's attitude. I knew Pat didn't like me any more than I liked him. Why was he being so friendly? He knew I no longer ran Handy Dan. What was going on?

When I got home, I called Arthur and told him to head over to Lakewood, meet Pat, and check out the store.

Arthur didn't carry any of my baggage with regard to Pat. He just saw a peculiar, eccentric guy who ran the remarkable store that I had described. As for Pat, he was delighted to meet Arthur and welcomed him like some long-lost brother. When it was over, Arthur was enchanted with Homeco and Pat.

Arthur and I went back to Homeco together and studied the store more carefully. Satisfied that this was the real thing, I invited Pat to meet me in Los Angeles at my favorite Italian restaurant, Carmine's on Santa Monica Boulevard.

Dinner began just as the first meeting at my office had: ugly. Both of us were posturing, circling the other, full of testosterone and distrust.

Fortunately, the drinks started flowing. I drank tequila; Pat drank rum and Coke. We had one or two drinks more, and soon we didn't look so bad to each other—just the way many relationships begin.

The conversation turned to merchandise. In business, I love two things: number one, dealing with people, and number two, merchandise. On this, Pat and I finally found common ground, and instead of being tuned to different stations, we were at long last on the same wavelength.

Instead of being repulsed by each other, we were attracted to each other. By the end of the evening, we hugged and kissed. It was an amazing evening in which we got past our facades, discovering kindred spirits.

This sonuvabitch has to be part of our team, I said to myself. *I need this guy, and he's going to end up as a major player on our team.*

■　■　■

When Ken Langone first laid eyes on Pat Farrah, he thought we were kidding. This man was going to be our partner?

Here's what concerned him:

Arthur went to Homeco to pick up Pat, who was an hour late getting to his own store. In those days, Pat was late for everything.

When he finally showed up, the wildman with the huge Afro haircut was wearing a powder blue velvet suit that was one size too small for him. His ass stuck out the back of his pants, his shirt was unbuttoned halfway down his chest, displaying a variety of gold chains and a big, old, gold watch. And that was exactly the way he walked into the Century Plaza Hotel restaurant to meet Ken, the guy who was going to provide us with the capital to establish a new business, a really important person in our lives whom Pat had never met before. And Ken was right out of Wall Street, shirt, tie, never canceled meetings, always dressed appropriately.

Ken shot Arthur a look that said, "Is this your idea of a joke?"

But Pat Farrah is one of the most creative people any of us had ever met. Pat is to retailing what Michelangelo was to art. At least that's what Ken said by dinner's end.

■   ■   ■

We were considering buying Homeco, so due diligence was in order; an audit was planned.

The problem, though, was that Pat had no idea whether he was making money. He couldn't spell the word *audit*. We asked him what he thought his gross margin—the difference between the cost of buying products and the price for which he could sell them—was, and he said, "Well, I think it is 23 percent and we are making all this money."

Shortly thereafter we signed a letter of intent to buy Homeco—subject to our due diligence. We hired Ron Brill to act as the store's comptroller and assigned him the challenge of getting Pat's financial records straightened out.

Pat's bookkeeper showed Ron around the office on his first day. Ron noticed she avoided a particular filing cabinet.

"What's in here?" he asked, pulling it open even as he spoke. It literally exploded at him, packed as it was with unopened invoices from Homeco's vendors and suppliers.

That makes a good anecdote, of course, but the reality is that by the time Ron started opening and recording the invoices, what was in them didn't matter. Pat didn't have the cash to pay the bills.

He was doing great sales volume, and that's how he covered his payroll. By not paying for his inventory, he gave the impression of having plenty of cash. Pat and his top guys, for example, were driving Porsches or Cadillacs.

As long as Pat had cash, it never occurred to him that he was insolvent. He had no clue what his liabilities were. Fiscal responsibility was just not his thing.

We commissioned KPMG Peat Marwick to do an in-depth audit. Between them and Ron Brill, what they discovered was that while inventory was flying out the door, Pat wasn't paying the vendors for it. He was spending more on advertising than he could afford. In fact he never paid any bills, had no systems, no controls, and he was slowly but surely sinking into the sunset.

However, in conducting a physical inventory of the store, Ron discovered one of the Great Farrah's many secrets.

Empty paint cans.

If the store had four layers of paint cans, the cans on the bottom layers were empty. They were on the showroom floor for show. They gave the illusion of greater inventory.

And since the empty cans looked just like the full cans, Ron had to bang on each and every one of them to determine what, if anything, was in them.

Late one afternoon Arthur received a call from Ron. "We finished the audit," he said, "but what we are concerned about is not so much Homeco's expenses but what the store's gross margin really is."

It wasn't the industry standard 44 percent.

It wasn't the 23 percent Pat had guessed.

It was a mere 12 percent.

At National Lumber, Pat had a financial structure in place that he rarely dealt with, let alone worried about. His whole expertise was merchandising and cultural, getting people excited, selling them on things, catering to the stuff that they wanted and making it happen.

At Homeco, business basics such as paying the bills revealed Pat's blind spot.

Bottom line, Pat was losing his ass.

Arthur was in shock. When Pat called him later that evening, Arthur said he had the results of the audit and suggested they discuss it over dinner and drinks.

"Well," Pat asked, "how did it go?"

Arthur hesitated. "Ah, the first number . . ."

"What is it, like twenty-five, twenty-four?"

"The first number is a one."

"You're kidding. The first number is a one? Oh, no."

"The second number is also a small number."

Arthur had grown fond of Pat in the short time since the buyout dance began and found delivering this news not unlike telling a child his dog had been run over by a truck. Pat was in a state of disbelief and denial.

Arthur told Pat furthermore that, based on Homeco's gross margin, and based on what Arthur knew about Pat's cash position, he had maybe six months left.

"Pat," he said, "you're getting killed. We can't possibly do this deal. This isn't going to work."

We had already committed a great deal of limited start-up capital to buying Homeco, but we realized that if we bought the company, just paying off Pat's debts would suck us dry. We would have no money left. This one store would kill us in the womb. We just couldn't do the deal.

Pat said he understood, but he was in shock. He was losing pallets of money? He was going broke? How could that be? Wasn't this the coolest home improvement store on the planet? So much of his personality, who he was, who he wanted to be, was tied up in the Homeco store.

"Why don't you just close it up," Arthur said, "and we'll all go somewhere else and start over."

"I can't do that," Pat said. "We have our own investors, and I have all these people who left National Lumber to work for me. I can't just quit on them like that. We are going to go fight it out and see if we can make it."

For Pat, our decision not to buy Homeco was far more painful than his earlier departure from National Lumber. About three months later, Homeco couldn't pay enough bills to stay afloat, and Pat filed for bankruptcy—both business and personal.

■   ■   ■

Two days after Pat closed Homeco's doors, I called him.

"Well, Pat," I said, "I still want you to join Arthur and me in this new venture."

Pat felt horrible, terribly guilty about all the money he had lost, the employees and investors he had let down. (After The Home Depot went public, he organized a get-together for the original Homeco investors and gave them all their money back—$415,000—in Home Depot stock. Nobody knew it was coming. Today that stock would be worth more than $362 million.) He was burned out on the whole business. Plus, he thought that maybe I felt obligated to offer him a job, because we didn't have a business to buy.

Despite the Homeco fiasco, I still had stars in my eyes. I could not understand why Pat didn't jump at my offer to be a part of another hardware store warehouse concept with tentative financing.

Two more days went by and I called Pat again.

"I don't think you understand what I'm saying, Pat," I said. "I can't believe you aren't taking me up on this. You are a great merchant. You have a great concept—you just don't have *us*. You need *us*. And *we* need *you*."

Pat was dumbfounded. A man of infinite energy and verbosity, he couldn't think of a single response, so I kept going.

"We are going to do the deal the same way. You will be the third partner in this thing with Arthur and me."

What was there left for him to say but yes?

5

The First Stores

"They Locked Me Up Because I Sold at Such Low Prices!"*

A key part of our plan to form what became The Home Depot was our partnership. Arthur no longer wanted to work for me—or anyone else, for that matter. We were each going to bring an equal measure of necessary ingredients to the recipe, based on our individual strengths, so we agreed to be partners.

I took the traditionally higher titles of chairman and chief executive officer because of my greater experience, and I ended up with slightly more stock for that reason, 18 percent to Arthur's 15 percent. Arthur became president. (Once Pat concluded his and Homeco's bankruptcy proceedings, he was granted an amount of stock that was almost, but not quite, equal to Arthur's holdings.) But the idea from day one was that the gap would close, both financially and in terms of the company hierarchy.

We knew that we couldn't afford to construct anything, because new stores would cost a great deal of money, so we started searching for vacant buildings that we could afford to lease. Our preference, since we all lived there, was to start in Los Angeles. But that wasn't enough justification, so we began a nationwide search. If we couldn't be in Los Angeles, where else would we want to live? We needed to be

* Bernie Marcus

near an airport with a hub that we could fly in and out of, a place from which we could grow and raise our children. We took turns visiting sites across the country, looking for real estate.

We recognized that we would be hiring talented people at every level. We needed a place where families would be happy and transportation would be easily accessible.

In our travels, we decided on several things. One, we were going to build a national chain, not a single market group of stores. Actually, we planned to open a thousand stores—seriously, we believed that was possible from the beginning, although we were careful not to put it in writing—so we needed to be in an appealing place to which we could recruit the best people.

As we looked around, the site selection process quickly narrowed to four cities: Boston, Atlanta, Dallas, and Los Angeles.

Atlanta was a place that Arthur, who had previously lived in Griffin, Georgia, knew intimately from his days as president of Elliott's Drugs, but I was not too keen on it. Newspapers all across the country had carried terrifying stories of crime in Atlanta during the mid-1970s, and it just didn't sound like the kind of place to which we wanted to move our families.

But Atlanta was where opportunity beckoned. Zayre Corporation—which operated a discount chain of the same name—had two stores in Atlanta and two in Charlotte that it wanted to unload, and we seriously considered them. Studying all the available demographics and opportunities, all roads led to Atlanta. Real estate was readily available in the Deep South, so the die was cast. Arthur and Pat were so convinced that Atlanta was the right place, even without a signed store lease, that they were living out of hotels and making plans to relocate their families.

In fact, even as we moved on the Zayre properties, Arthur met with the *Atlanta Journal-Constitution*'s advertising director, to talk about our potential ad budget.

The ad director mentioned a rumor that J.C. Penney was looking to scale back its monster 180,000-square-foot Treasure Island discount stores. He said J.C. Penney was reportedly looking to sublease 40,000 square feet in each of its four area locations. He also mentioned that Handy City was looking at the sites. (I got my job at Handy Dan when George Hanzi, the founder of Handy City and former head of Handy Dan, was starting a clone, Handy City, on the side. He had to leave, and I was given the assignment because of my personal experience with Wall Street.)

Even more ironically, Pat had already approached J.C. Penney about the Treasure Island stores. Everywhere we went while driving around Atlanta, the greatest locations were taken by Treasure Island stores. Pat already knew they were subleasing spaces on the West Coast, but they told him at the time that they weren't interested in subdividing the Atlanta space.

Arthur went straight to the nearest pay phone and called me in Los Angeles. I agreed about the desirability of the Treasure Island locations—and the opportunity to tweak Handy City—so I called Ken Langone in New York and asked if he knew anyone at J.C. Penney. "No, I don't," Ken said. "But by the end of business today, I will."

Ken got J.C. Penney's address and literally left his desk at Invemed, wandered over to J.C. Penney's real estate department, introduced himself, and opened negotiations.

Treasure Island—a latter-day knockoff of Two Guys—had failed to distinguish itself from J.C. Penney, even going so far as to carry J.C. Penney branded clothes and other products. Treasure Island stores also operated supermarkets in the back of the store, a business they had absolutely no business being in. Their whole concept just didn't work. The supermarket in the back of the store didn't generate volume in the other departments. The stores were too big and soon became a cash drain.

William E. "Bill" Harris was the executive vice president of JCP Realty, the real estate arm of J.C. Penney. He was assigned the task of subleasing space in the Treasure Island stores.

The initial program to lease those 30,000-square-foot supermarkets was a failure. They were located at the back, poorly laid out, and for the amount of rent Harris was asking, no one was interested.

Treasure Island itself wasn't performing very well, so Harris suggested another tack to J.C. Penney: consolidate the Treasure Island stores into 120,000 square feet and free up a narrow 60,000-square-foot space, including frontage space.

By the time J.C. Penney agreed, however, the retail market was extremely soft. W.T. Grant, Spartan, and Woolco were all in the process of throwing in the towel, closing stores and creating a glut of available big box space. Prices plummeted.

In December 1978, Harris received a call from a Treasure Island senior vice president who had met with Ken Langone who told him we were interested in leasing 60,000 square feet in four Atlanta-area Treasure Island stores. Harris then invited us to his office.

Arthur made that first meeting memorable. He and Pat walked into Harris's office bearing a loaf of French bread and a bottle of wine to break the ice.

The gesture—meant to suggest our sincere interest in negotiating a deal—was not lost on Harris. He understood that when we were done, we expected to break bread together as friends. It's a good thing we brought a snack, too; that first session lasted eight hours.

Harris was a deal-maker, very pragmatic. One real sticking point, however, almost quashed the deal. Harris insisted we take space in all four Atlanta-area Treasure Island stores or there was no deal. We were ambitious, but not *that* ambitious; we were uncertain we had the financial resources to open two stores, let alone four. But we gulped hard and agreed.

Arthur negotiated tremendous leases with J.C. Penney that tilted heavily in our favor.

The only reason we could ever guess why J.C. Penney did this was they thought if our concept worked, they might eventually buy us out. But that's just conjecture, because the issue was never raised by them.

Harris required a financial statement from us, as well as a business plan. It showed the $2 million that our equity partners had committed. That didn't impress Harris, but one of the names of our investors did: Colonel Frank Borman. Harris didn't recognize the names of any of the other people in the group, but everyone knew the commander of the *Apollo 8* moon mission and the then-president of Eastern Air Lines. Borman gave us much-needed credibility (although we didn't realize how much until Harris fessed up twenty years later in an interview for this book).

Our plan for a wholesale-priced home improvement operation sounded good to Harris and his associates, too. They thought it might be a more complementary draw for the Treasure Island stores than the supermarkets.

Harris made a commitment to us that he could get the lease done quickly. "Quick" in J.C. Penney parlance might mean as long as six months on a lease like this. We made it quite clear we couldn't sit on our hands that long, and he actually turned it around in a month. In fact, he ordered work started to build the walls between Treasure Island and our store-to-be-named-later even before the leases were signed.

J.C. Penney was a large company, and we were upstart entrepreneurs building our dreams. Surprisingly, they treated us with dignity and respect. Certainly Bill Harris did. Whenever we had conversations with him, he was honest and forthright. That was a great learning experience for us, that a company could be big and yet have a human face. (We liked Harris so much that, a few years later, after he had retired from J.C. Penney and returned to his native Cleveland, we hired him to guide our own real estate decisions. He was a person whose values appealed to us. Harris joined us in 1986 as senior vice president of corporate development when we had fifty stores. Over the next decade, he guided us through our five hundredth store.)

We backed out of the Zayre deal. In fact, if Arthur had not been in the newspaper's office that fateful day to hear about the Treasure Island stores, we might not be here today because those Zayre locations were terrible.

Arthur, Pat, and Ron moved to Atlanta ahead of me because I had family obligations that kept me in California. I commuted for six months. Ron crossed his fingers that the company would take off; he didn't have enough money to move back.

■   ■   ■

So now we had four stores, only we didn't have any money to purchase inventory and run them.

Try telling Ken Langone what a problem this little matter of money is. "No big deal," he'd say. "I have banks all over. [Original

Home Depot investor] Ed Cox is the vice-chairman of a bank in Dallas. We'll have plenty of money. You'll see."

One more time, Ken and I crisscrossed the country, only to be turned down by banks everywhere in the United States—including Ed Cox's. Ken, with all of his connections, wasn't having much luck.

Cox did arrange an interesting lunch with a bank in Dallas that I attended. The man next to me was Jewish, and when I asked what he did at the bank, the man explained that he met with all the bank's potential Jewish clients.

"Say that again?" I thought surely I had misunderstood.

"I am their token Jew," he explained. "I'm a businessman in Dallas; I don't work for the bank per se. But whenever a Jew comes into town, they call me. I go to the bar mitzvahs and weddings of their Jewish clients, or, if somebody like you comes into town . . ."

"In other words," I said, "they identified me as a Jew? Not a potential customer, but a Jew?"

"Yeah."

To be honest, the bank was actually very nice, despite this inauspicious start. But they turned us down, too.

■ ■ ■

One of Ken's leads was a little-known Boston-based venture capitalist who invested early in lots of good companies and made a ton of money.

His people were quite anxious to buy into our would-be business, which existed only on paper. Like Ken, they bought the vision of the first nationwide home improvement warehouse brand. For $3 million, he was buying us and our experience. And we needed that $3 million the way somebody dying of stab wounds needs blood in his veins.

This time, we agreed to terms. Afterward, with our group in a celebratory mood, I happily drove our new investor to the airport. But in the car, the man turned very serious again.

"Listen, there are things I didn't want to talk about in the office because they are very sensitive, and I want to discuss them with you," he said.

"What are they?" I asked

"First, I need two men on the board of directors."

That was easy, something I anticipated. "Okay, you got it."

"Now, when I make an investment, I like people to invest with me, and I need an investment on your part."

"What do you mean 'investment'?"

"Well, I need to have you invest."

"We started the business, we left everything in California, especially our support system," I said, puzzled. "We are sacrificing our lives here."

"No, I mean more than that," he said. "First of all, you should not have company cars."

We all had leased company cars because so much of our time was spent in cars, driving all over Georgia on company business, and none of us could afford to buy cars. Pat was broke and I was broke, attorneys having sucked us both dry. Arthur and Ron had no money either.

"That would be kind of tough for us," I said. "But if we could figure out a way to pay for auto expenses, maybe we can do that."

"Okay," the man said. "Another thing is that everybody needs to take a 10 percent cut in salary."

I stared at him in disbelief. "Everybody?"

"Yes."

"Do you know what I just went through to hire these people? I hired them from all over the United States. I brought them here. I sold them on this dream. They took less money than they ever had made before, and they left their security, all of those things, and you want me to cut their salaries by 10 percent?"

"Yes."

"Well, I guess we could do that, if that's so important to you. I don't think it's fair, but what choice do I have?"

"Now," the man said, "is the best of all. I am not paying your employees' or managers' medical insurance. I think they should get it on their own."

That was an issue reminiscent of the matter of principle that nearly caused a brawl between me and Sandy Sigoloff. The blood rose up in my eyes. I swerved and pulled the car onto the shoulder of the highway. My gut told me this was a terrible mistake, and my premonitions so far had been right.

"Get out of the car," I said. "Get out of the G-damn car!"

The man just looked at me. He thought I was crazy. We were in the middle of nowhere; cars and trucks were zipping by.

"I said, get out of the car! You are a stupid sonuvabitch! Do you think I would get in bed with an imbecile like you? Get out of the f-ing car. You can walk to the airport for all I care."

I then got out of the car and, as the man timidly got out, I tossed his luggage by the side of the road.

"Please don't leave me here!" the man pleaded. "I have to catch a plane."

After several minutes, still fuming, I relented and allowed the man back in. "Don't talk to me for the rest of the trip. I will have nothing to do with you. We are finished. This partnership is over before it has begun."

Here—*again!*—was somebody with whom I was going to have to live who had no clue about what it meant to care about people.

I am not a loose cannon. My mind was in overdrive weighing the pros and cons. I put everybody's careers in jeopardy by rejecting him that way. I didn't react to him just on emotion. I am not that crazy. I am not a crook. I am very deliberate in everything I do. I realized that I was going to get the money we needed, but I just couldn't live with this guy.

This company didn't blossom from miracles. It came from our instincts, knowing whom to do business with and whom to avoid. Remember the story I told about Two Guys founder Herb Hubschman in the first chapter? To his face, I called him "the biggest schmuck I ever met in my life." That was a calculated gamble. I read his personality. I knew what was going to get to him. Of course he wasn't a schmuck, but nothing short of calling him one would have gotten his attention riveted on me. I have often thought back over that situation, wondering what would have happened if I had said, "Mr. Hubschman, I could do a better job." Nothing would have happened. Instead, I very deliberately applied blunt trauma to his ego. Today, our board of directors knows me as someone who is very passionate, very direct, but never a loose cannon. I think things through. I am very clear in where I am going.

When I returned from the airport and relayed to Arthur, Ken, Pat, and Ron what had just occurred, they were in shock. Ron was already calculating where we would deposit the check so we could earn the most interest. Everybody thought I had screwed the deal up. But in the end, although we were still desperately short of financing to continue, they trusted my judgment.

Almost twenty years later, by the oddest of coincidences, I was unexpectedly reunited with this man on a trip to Israel. We were forced by circumstances to spend five days in each other's company. I put the group together, but somebody else invited him along. On the third day, the group was on a bus trip and each person stood up, introduced himself, and told a little story. When it was this man's turn, I challenged him. "I want you to tell everybody about your experience with The Home Depot," and he told the story, honestly and with great humility. He said, "I have made blunders in my life. This one was the beauty of them all." His $3 million investment would have been 15 percent of The Home Depot's original market value. Today 15 percent of Home Depot stock would be worth $12.33 billion.

There are some things money alone can't buy, as several would-be Home Depot investors learned.

■　■　■

Everything was moving quickly. Too quickly from a financial point of view. We had locations, merchandise ordered on credit whenever possible, and associates being hired. But if we didn't get some cash fast, our grand opening might end with a going-out-of-business sale.

Not knowing where else to turn but to the past, I called Rip Fleming at Security Pacific National Bank in Los Angeles.

"Rip," I said, "I need money. I need to have a line of credit, and I need to get it from Security Pacific."

"I am not going to give you a line," Rip said firmly.

"And *I* am not going to accept no for an answer," I responded. "I am going to come out to your office. I will have a sleeping bag, and I will camp out in your office. You will have to step over my body. I will not shower. I will not shave. I will stink. You will be embarrassed.

"My life is on the line," I said. "So is Arthur's; so is Ron Brill's. If I don't get money out of you, this whole thing is going to go down the drain."

"I just can't do it, Bernie. I'm sorry."

"Rip, it isn't a question of can't, you have to," I pleaded. "I am not asking how much can you do, but how fast can you do it."

I went to Rip's office with Arthur's financial plan under my arm. The plan impressed Rip with its promise of establishing a national home improvement brand based on the lowest prices, the widest selection, and the best customer service. I finally won him over. He already believed in us personally, but seeing it on paper helped.

What Rip liked about our plan was the one-stop home center concept, a three-legged stool that was held up in equal measure by price, selection, and customer service. Prior to this, if a homeowner or professional tradesperson was going to do a home improvement project, he had to go to a variety of places. He went to a hardware store to get tools, a lumber company for lumber, a paint store for paint. Nowhere did he get information or instruction, and all this was in our concept. One place where you can get all the materials, tools, and competent advice you need from skilled representatives. It just made sense.

Still, he wasn't sure he could convince the bank to approve a credit line.

A commercial loan of this size would normally fall beneath Rip's radar in the corporate banking department. Under different circumstances it should have been negotiated—and, no doubt, rejected—by a Security Pacific branch rather than through the corporate banking group. As we had already heard over and over, this was a very easy loan to turn down. As a matter of fact, Rip was riding up in an elevator one day when one of his fellow loan officers said, "Rip, there's no way we can make this loan." And Rip said, "Well, that's the easiest thing to say. Somehow we are going to find a way to make it."

Whether or not this company got off the ground now depended on Rip Fleming. Arthur, Ken, and I took charge of the details and negotiations went back and forth for three weeks. Despite Rip's vocal support and our own proven history with the bank as executives at Handy Dan, we kept getting turned down by the loan officers.

Finally, it boiled down to our investors putting up letters of credit as the final condition of a $3.5 million line of credit. Those letters of credit were transferable into stock in the company, so if they put up a letter of credit for $25,000, they got an equal warrant to buy shares of stock in the company at a later date. From the bank's perspective, in the event that MB Associates broke through certain protected covenants of the loan agreement, Security Pacific could call on additional capital from our investors. These covenants made us a more reasonable risk. It became the first start-up loan Security Pacific had ever written.

And it was the saving grace of the company.

Let me skip ahead five or six years. Rip Fleming was forced into retiring from Security Pacific, and he was very upset. He turned 65 and felt as if he were being thrown out of the only job he had ever known.

Meanwhile, Rip's boss, Richard J. Flamson III, called me on the phone. Flamson, who was chairman and CEO of Security Pacific, said, "We are giving a going-away party for Rip, would you come out and emcee the party?"

By this time, Security Pacific's involvement with The Home Depot had grown from providing our first line of credit to leading a consortium of banks that raised money for us. Despite the bank's initial doubts, they were now deeply in love with us. They even put us on the cover of one of their in-house magazines.

So I went to the party. Flamson stood up and spoke warmly and respectfully about what a great banker Rip was and what a terrific person he was and how everybody at the bank loved him. He reflected on how many of the people at the retirement party were customers of the bank whom Rip had invested in based on their character rather than their balance sheet, how he saw the person rather than the numbers.

I was seated next to Flamson on the dais. As other people stood up to toast Rip, I said to Flamson, "I love this guy. He is so terrific."

"Well you should love him after what he did for you," Flamson said.

"What do you mean," I said, " 'after what he did for me'?"

"He put his career on the line for you."

He then told me the story of how Rip originally presented our loan request to the bank's loan officers, who turned it down cold. The next time, he added extra points and other kickers, and still was turned down. Unwilling to give up on us, he came up with the letters of credit from our investors, and they turned him down cold a third time.

"Do you know what he did after that?" Flamson asked me.

"I guess not," I said.

"He burst into my office, literally, slamming the door open. There was someone sitting with me but Rip ordered the man, 'Get the hell out of here *now*,' and the guy ran out of the office. Rip slammed the door shut and threw an envelope on my desk. He said, 'Take this and this job and shove it up your rear end.' "

Flamson said he was shocked by how angry the normally mild-mannered, genial Rip Fleming had become.

"Rip said, 'You don't need a banker. You need a computer. Hire some young kid to come in here and do my job. I buy *people*. Bernie Marcus and Arthur Blank are good people, and you have turned them—and *me*—down three times! You obviously don't need me here anymore.'

"I looked at Rip," Flamson continued, "and I realized that when he walked out the door, that $400 million worth of accounts were walking with him."

The clients Rip had brought into the bank loved and trusted him and would go wherever he went. Turning down The Home Depot was no longer about denying a $3.5 million loan; suddenly it was a $400 million decision.

"I realized I had no choice and tore up the envelope containing Rip's letter of resignation," Flamson said. "I told Rip I would personally get the loan through the officers. Then I called the loan officers and said, 'We are making this loan whether you like it or not.' "

And that's why they loaned us the money that helped start this company.

This brought tears to my eyes. Rip Fleming had put his career on the line for me, for Arthur, for this company. And he never said a word to me about what he had done.

The story over, Flamson turned to me and said, "Is it too late for us to get warrants or options in the company?"

"You could have had whatever you wanted back then," I said, pulling myself together.

"Is it too late?" he asked.

"I wouldn't give it to *you* in the first place," I said. "And I won't give it to you now; in fact, let me tell you something. You really treated him terribly.

"You know, when we were together, if he bought a meal, I would buy the next meal. If I took him out to play golf, he would take me out the next time. We always conducted ourselves in the most businesslike manner. I am going back to Atlanta and we are going to hire Rip as a consultant for the rest of his life. He is never going to have to worry about money to support his family. We are going to make sure of that. You shafted him, but we will not."

And that's exactly what we did. To put his expertise to work for us exclusively, our board of directors hired Rip as a consultant for the rest of his life. Not only that, on his fiftieth wedding anniversary, Arthur, Ken, and I personally sent Rip and his wife on a first-class tour around the world. We love this guy. We love him to death. He was one of the breaks in our lives, not once but several times, and he did it because he bought character. He saw something in us. The Home Depot would literally not be around today if it wasn't for Rip Fleming. And he is still touring and critiquing our stores today as effectively as ever.

He taught us that when it comes to people, you must look past the numbers, past the résumés, and look at their heart and soul. And you must treat people as you would want to be treated.

■   ■   ■

Once we had financing and locations in place, we still needed a name for the stores.

Our best idea was "MB's Warehouse," which nobody liked. We retained a Toronto consultant, Don Watt & Associates, to help us. The same firm had already suggested painting our signs on bright orange circus-tent canvas, which would cost a fraction of the more common electric lighted signs.

Watt came up with a name and made a formal presentation to us in Atlanta. He was so excited!

"We have a whole marketing concept for you," Watt said. "We will call this place 'Bad Bernies Buildall.' "

Bad Bernies Buildall.

They were quite serious. But heck, it wasn't even grammatically correct.

They showed us a masked, cartoon "Bernie" behind bars, in a black-and-white striped prison uniform. "They locked me up," Cartoon Bernie said, "because I sold at such low prices!"

This was in an era when Crazy Eddie's was a hot consumer electronics discount chain in the New York metropolitan area—but before "Crazy" Eddie Antar, cofounder of the original chain, went to jail in 1992 on fraud and racketeering charges.

I didn't like it, but my wife, Billi, loved it. So I called our banker, Rip Fleming.

"Rip, we have a name for this store and I just want to pass it by you. We are going to call it Bad Bernies Buildall."

There was an eerie silence at the other end of the line.

"Mr. Marcus . . ." When Fleming called me "Mr. Marcus," there was going to be trouble. "Mr. Marcus, I don't think that the bank's loan officers are going to like that name too well. I would suggest that you look for some other name."

And that was the end of my life of crime.

We subsequently had an investors' meeting in New York and asked everyone for ideas. Driving home to Bethlehem, Pennsylvania,

Marjorie Buckley focused on the project, scribbling half a dozen names while her husband dozed in the passenger seat.

Each name included the word "Home." Her first choice was The Homeplace, because of its association with an Outward Bound school, with which she had been involved. Her next favorite, which combined "Home" with "Depot," occurred as she passed The Station Break restaurant, which was made from a former railroad car.

The next day, Marjorie mailed us her list.

The Homeplace didn't do much for us—it sounded a little soft for a place that would sell hardware, tools, and lumber by the ton—but The Home Depot wasn't bad. Not bad at all. Arthur and Pat were split. It sure beat Bad Bernies Buildall, but was it good enough?

We still had our doubts. But what's in a name? Today, when you see Macy's, you say, "Wow, what a great name." Well, it is great but only because the business created the name. Think of Saks Fifth Avenue, Bloomingdale's, or even Kmart. The name is not the most important thing; it is the entity that creates value in the name, and of course our company's name turned out to be a wonderful one.

Our signs were finished and installed with only two days to spare before the first stores opened.

■   ■   ■

On opening day we faced what at the moment was a disaster but turned out to be a publicity bonanza.

We couldn't afford a major television commercial campaign, so the primary ad announcing the grand opening of The Home Depot on June 22, 1979, was going to run the day before, June 21, in the *Atlanta Journal-Constitution*. Grand opening was scheduled for a Friday. We submitted a double-truck ad—two full pages, facing each other—to run as a tease on Thursday morning.

But guess what? The *Atlanta Journal-Constitution* did not run our full grand opening ad. It was a disaster! Because you're not really open if nobody knows about it! There would be no customers come Friday morning because there was no ad on Thursday.

I went back to our offices and called the editor of the newspaper.

My voice was choked with emotion, a ferocious mix of anger and growing panic. I was watching our lives go down the drain. No sales, no cash flow. Payroll was already eating us alive. The clock was ticking with vendors who wanted to be paid.

"You just killed us," I said. "You killed us. We are trying to get this company off the ground and you single-handedly put us out of business."

The editor was contrite. He felt truly awful about the paper's mistake.

As part of our grand opening strategy, we sent our own kids and wives into the parking lot of the stores and on the street handing out 700 one-dollar bills to try and lure customers in. But things were so bad without the newspaper ad that we literally couldn't give the dollar bills away.

On Friday, the ad finally ran, but the damage was done. Still, we got something from that incident for which we could never have negotiated. For weeks to come, the *Journal-Constitution* gave us a plum: the back page of one of its daily news sections, the prime advertising spot, which our young company never would have been able to afford. So out of something that was really bad, something really great arose. The breaks were still going our way.

■   ■   ■

Hours before the sun would rise on The Home Depot for the first time that Friday morning, Pat called me. I wasn't able to sleep anyway.

"We have another disaster on our hands," Pat said.

"What happened?" I asked.

"I cannot begin to tell you. You are going to go crazy when you see it. Meet me right away."

Pat, also unable to sleep, had come back to one of the stores early to plan an employee rally set for six A.M. What he saw shocked and dismayed him: The store was sparkling clean!

"What the hell happened?" Pat demanded. "Who screwed up the store?"

During the night, our store managers, Charlie Barnes and Ed

McGuire, thinking they were doing us a great favor, brought in crews that scrubbed the stores' concrete floors.

"We cleaned up so it would look great for the customers!" Barnes said, proud of the initiative he and McGuire took. "I had these guys come in to surprise you."

"You are out of your mind!" Pat screamed. "Get the forklifts! Get the pallet jacks!"

Pat called the other store and said, "If that floor is waxed, get your asses on the forklifts and screw it up again!"

For whatever time remained before the doors were scheduled to open for the first time, we sped around the aisles in forklifts, skidding around corners, stomping on the brakes, scuffing up the flooring so it would once more look like a warehouse.

The Home Depot isn't a supermarket, where customers need to feel they could eat off the floor. Our stores are action places! The idea for our stores was that they looked shopped. That is why we didn't originally put in a separate, rear entrance for the lumber buyers. It is why we had contractors and professionals go to the front registers, alongside the do-it-yourself customers. That creates action. We wanted the big stuff going out the front and loaded in the parking lots so that everyone saw it.

On top of that, the do-it-yourselfers saw that the contractor buying two units of sheet rock paid the same price as they did. There was no secret back door or discount for contractors. We were priced right for everyone—not just a select group.

Another important concept for us inside the store was that the merchandise not be constantly "fronted." We didn't want products pushed to the front edge of the shelves. If everything is perfectly lined up, that tells you it is not selling, there is no action. Besides, it takes too much energy to maintain the facade of fronting everything.

We front the products once, but never again. That way we can see what is selling and our customers feel like there is action in the aisles. "Facing" the product is another practice we don't believe in. Sears and True Value face their product, meaning they pay employees to go through the stores and turn labels out, facing customers. It looks good, but it's tremendously expensive. We find it gets in the way of offering product at the lowest possible price.

If Pat saw product fronted or faced, he thought it looked too tidy.

If we saw it, we thought it was too expensive!

The Home Depot was *supposed* to look like a warehouse! We *wanted* sawdust! We *wanted* skid marks on the floor! We didn't want it to look like a hospital; we wanted it to look like a warehouse.

We went crazy. *Nuts!* In a matter of hours, people would walk in and see this shiny floor. It was perhaps our worst nightmare—or so we thought at the time—because it was against everything that we wanted. The perception of the company would be changed. It didn't look like a warehouse; it looked like a retail store. We even pushed back products that had been fronted on the shelves so that it looked like we had already been open. By the time we officially opened, we dirtied up the store enough that it looked like a warehouse again.

We told everyone, if anyone ever did that again, we would kill them. We wouldn't fire them, because firing was not bad enough of a punishment; it had to be killing.

◼ ◼ ◼

Among the many merchandise skills Pat Farrah brought to the table was a magician's inclination toward smoke and mirrors.

When we opened, product boxes were stacked high on our racks and shelves. It was a truly breathtaking display. And some of the boxes actually had products in them!

A week before we opened, there just wasn't enough merchandise to fill the store floor to ceiling, so Pat called up the Delmar Cabinet Company on the west side of town and asked them to loan us 500 boxes of all different sizes. We folded them up and put them on the tops of the racks all around the first two stores, 250 boxes a store, so they looked full of merchandise. (We marked them with an X so we didn't count them as inventory.)

It looked fabulously legitimate. We even have video of ourselves assembling empty boxes, laughing and having a good time doing it.

Pat pulled a similar trick with our paint stacks. He had 2,000 empty paint cans sent over for each store. We put labels on them and stacked them ten feet high.

■ ■ ■

We initially had real difficulty succeeding in Atlanta, despite putting together a great store with a great merchandise mix and the lowest prices ever. This was a market where people had been doing business with traditional lumberyard stores such as Handy City and West Building Materials for years and years. Relationships were in place and the idea of shopping at our stores was as anathema to most consumers as cheating on their spouse. Our home improvement "mall" concept was antithetical to old hardware and lumber shopping habits: a paint store for paint, the plumbing store for pipes and fixtures, a lumber yard for 2×4s. One-stop shopping didn't exist in Atlanta in those days, so it was really hard to break those habits.

The first months were *slooooow*. Customers—the few we had—received great service. We could literally wait on every customer because they came in one at a time.

And the people who did walk into the stores were astounded by the sheer volume and selection of merchandise. But they didn't understand. They were a little intimidated by it all.

Low prices, double and triple the usual service levels—we felt that we were on to something big and something really different, a new concept that would cause a revolutionary change in the home improvement industry. We were the folks who were going to demonstrate that the home improvement world was round instead of flat.

We bought our products directly from about half of our manufacturers; that made our prices lower than anyone else's in the city of Atlanta. Nobody could compete with us on price. The only thing lacking was customers.

In terms of our industry, we were visionaries, even if most people didn't immediately see the vision.

One of the great reasons for our survival in 1979 was that this was a private company, because everybody in the industry predicted we would self-destruct. "Their stores are too big, there is too much inventory, prices are ridiculously low," etc. And, initially, we didn't produce the volume. Average weekly sales in 1979 were $81,700.

Between 1980 and '81, sales did begin moving upward, but we kept it a deep, dark secret. If we didn't, we might have encouraged competitors.

■ ■ ■

Those first stores really had the look of a warehouse. They weren't dirty, they weren't ugly, but you wouldn't take a lot of pictures and hang them on your wall. We never wanted a pretty store; what we wanted to do was pile the merchandise up, and *that* helped create the illusion and eventually the sales.

We laid them out in a racetrack design. When you walked in, you saw a massive assortment of unfinished furniture in the center of the store. You couldn't miss it; a third of the store was unfinished furniture. Customers loved the quality and prices, but it took up a tremendous amount of floor space.

Customers came in the entrance, went down one aisle, hit lumber in the back, and came back up the next aisle. The right-hand side of the store was paint and hardware, the left-hand side was electrical; at the front of the store were wood-burning stoves.

You wouldn't walk in and think these were strictly lumber and building materials stores because the lumber was located in the back. We did that following the logic of supermarkets. Lumber was our meat. When you go into a grocery store, you never see the meat up front, because you want everybody to buy all of the condiments before they get to the meat.

So we put the lumber in the back, making customers hunt for the 2×4s, passing by saws, doors, stain, varnish, paint, thresholds, weather-stripping, and locks. Walking around the whole store, they were drawn to items that they didn't even think that they were coming in for.

■ ■ ■

The Home Depot wasn't really born until Treasure Island died.

Treasure Island's death was inevitable. Foot traffic into its stores was dreadful; those big cavernous boxes were painfully empty. But when J.C. Penney finally read the writing on the wall and announced a going-out-of-business sale at Treasure Island stores, the public discovered us.

Every week, as Treasure Island cut its prices, first by 10 percent, then 20 percent, and on through 30, 50 and 75 percent, the cars poured into their parking lot. And once folks picked Treasure Island clean, many of them wandered over to our stores. Or while the wives went into Treasure Island, the husbands passed time in The Home Depot. Quite often, the husbands returned to their cars with more purchases than their wives.

When we did the leases with J.C. Penney, our biggest concern was that we needed *them* to be next to *us*. We depended upon them for foot traffic. If they went out of business, we feared we would lose our source of customers. Arthur negotiated a covenant of continuing operation in our lease in which J.C. Penney guaranteed us that Treasure Island *wouldn't* go out of business. So when it came time that they did, we renegotiated our lease with them and agreed to let them off the hook if they let us take more space, increasing each store another 20,000 square feet to 80,000 square feet, and gave us right of first refusal on their Florida locations.

■　■　■

At the same time Treasure Island was going out of business, an exasperating incident with Pat reinforced for us how critically important it is to sell products at the right price.

Business just wasn't booming. It just wasn't happening. We were barely covering our expenses, still having difficulty identifying with the market. Cash flow was not good; our financial resources were eroding.

Shortly after we opened our third store in Atlanta, a vendor named Bob Heller told Pat about a truckload of 3,000 fireplace screens that were manufactured for Montgomery Ward. Ward canceled the order, but the screens were already on a truck, en route to Atlanta.

Heller was a pretty creative guy and a good friend, a rep who always kept an eye out for factory deals. He knew we were looking for that one product, that special deal that would set our stores ablaze.

Thanks to some chilly winters, Atlanta was a strong market for wood-burning fireplaces, and the flush-mount fireplace screen was a popular accessory. Still, it was nearing the end of fireplace season. And 3,000 screens . . . not even Heller expected us to take them all.

"You can't sell all these," he told Pat.

"Don't tell me I can't sell them, just get a price," Pat said.

Heller was probably less concerned with whether we could sell them and more concerned with whether our check would bounce. But he was able to secure a phenomenal price for these screens, which retailed for up to $139 each.

Having already set the cost and arranged for delivery, Pat walked into my office with the news.

"These fireplace screens sell for up to $139 at Montgomery Ward," he said. "The guy needed to dump them right away, and I bought the entire shipment for an average of $33 a screen."

"How many screens is that, exactly?" I asked, gulping air.

"Three thousand," Pat said effortlessly.

This was a commitment of almost $100,000. Pat made a truck-load of fireplace screens into a life-or-death purchase for The Home Depot.

"Pat, what were you . . ."

"This will be a drop-dead thing!" he said with boyish glee. "We are putting it on the front page of the catalog."

Seeing that my partner was oblivious to the trembling in my voice and the fear in my eyes, I tried to see it Pat's way. "Wow. So you're saying that we could discount these screens $50, sell them for, say, $89, and make a ton of money!"

"No," Pat said. "Not that price. Besides, the ads have already been prepared."

"Okay, $79 is terrific. We are going to do really well at $79."

"Well . . . no," Pat said.

"Sixty-nine?"

"No."

"Fifty-nine? Fifty-nine dollars is a terrific buy for the customer. It'll be great."

Pat marked them up exactly two dollars.

"ARE YOU CRAZY?!" I asked. "Pat 'Homeco' Farrah! Have you lost your mind? Are you crazy? I don't know what you are doing—do you? We are now going to go broke—you, for the second time. You know what, the loose cannon has finally come unloosed, and now we are going to be dead in the water."

The minute the ad appeared, however, people began flocking into the stores, and we blew through the screens in about four days, the entire load. We had the cash before we had the invoice. It was that kind of a deal. We ended up selling out. The timing was perfect, the price irresistible. It was so incredibly cheap, people found it worth their while to drive fifty miles to see us. We filled the lots, and it was another early event that brought people into the stores in droves. That was another critical moment for The Home Depot. It took an insane ad to bring folks to our stores to discover the Home Depot secret.

■　　■　　■

We were never flush with cash. If a vendor wanted to see our financial statements in order to extend credit, we would say, "No, this is a privately owned company, and we are not going to share that information with you." Because we knew if we did, they would never give us credit.

The strategy worked. A manufacturer or distributor would give us a $25,000 line of credit, which was a big deal at the time, and after we paid it off, they would raise it to $35,000. When the inevitable "You are at your limit" call would come, Ron would cajole the credit manager to raise the limit again.

One of the individuals who truly believed in what we were doing at The Home Depot was Jerry Burnett, who was then the vice president of sales for the Johns-Manville Corporation.

Burnett knew we were having trouble qualifying for credit with a number of manufacturers, so he took a remarkable step: He printed business cards that said "Jerry Burnett, Credit Manager, Johns-Manville Corporation." Burnett gave us the entire box of these cards and said, "Next time you have trouble getting credit with a vendor, have them call me." So that's what we did. He must have spoken on our behalf to at least a hundred companies. "Those guys are good as gold," he'd tell them. "We've been giving them credit for years!" Ironically, it took years for us to get decent credit terms with his own company, Johns-Manville.

By the time we went public in 1981 and had to distribute our actual financial statements, it wasn't much of an issue anymore.

■   ■   ■

Back then, before we were a public company, most of us, top to bottom, were making nothing, peanuts. We were all living on the fumes of dreams. Our success today is almost taken for granted by outsiders, but twenty years ago, there was nothing taken for granted. We did not for one minute take the customers coming in our store for granted. We really wanted them back, and our entire service culture developed from that. It wasn't some lofty idea written by out-of-town consultants in a policy book nobody read. It was necessity.

Today, we feel a desire to carry on this way. Back then, it was out of pure necessity. If we didn't do whatever it took, we were out of business.

After four or five months in business, we finally started recognizing returning customers. They knew they had experienced something exceptional in our stores, and they couldn't wait to tell us about it. After a while, that spirit and enthusiasm just fed on itself.

Watching that develop was fun. And by the time we opened our third store in Marietta, we knew we had the formula down. When 1979 ended, we had three stores, 200 associates and $7 million in sales. (Our fourth store opened in 1980.) The numbers were destined never to stop getting bigger and bigger.

■   ■   ■

During our first year of operation, a heavy, bushy-faced guy in a pair of overalls was standing in an aisle with his wife and two kids. He had a bathtub on one cart, and a sink and other things on another. While I understood rural Georgia accents about as well as I did Croatian, I nonetheless introduced myself and asked what project the man was working on.

"What you see here, boy?" said the man, not in the mood to suffer city fools gladly.

"It looks like you are doing a bathroom," I said, inadvertently playing into the man's foul mood.

"You are real bright now, huh?"

"This your first trip here?" I asked, barreling ahead.

"Yeah, it's my first trip here."

"Well, did you see our ad in the paper?"

"No, I didn't see your ad in the paper."

"Well, do you read the *Journal-Constitution?*"

"Boy," he said impatiently, "I don't live here."

"Where *do* you live?"

"Macon."

"Macon," I asked, "is that near Marietta?" In my brief time here, my travels in Georgia were pretty limited to our stores and the airport.

"What are you, dumb, boy?"

"Macon, huh? How did you hear about this place?"

"My cousin from Athens called and told me about it."

Athens, I knew, was out of town—seventy miles northeast of Atlanta. "Well," I continued, unable to resist, "where did your cousin in Athens hear about us?"

Turns out that cousin had another cousin, this one in Marietta, who told him. Suddenly it all made sense. Through word of mouth, the best kind of advertising, people were traveling fifty miles and more to shop at the Home Depot stores. Somehow we hadn't made an impact on the people closest to the stores, but people were traveling from just about everywhere else because they recognized the variety of merchandise, twice as much as any other hardware store or home improvement center up until that point, and the prices were dramatically lower than anybody else's.

From that point on, we spent much more time at the registers, gently asking customers where they were from and how they heard about us. The answers were mind-boggling. They were traveling an hour and a half, two hours or more to shop our stores.

The day that happened, we knew that The Home Depot was going to be a great success.

■   ■   ■

Pat Farrah was an absolute wild man, bigger than life in the early days of The Home Depot.

He'd go out to dinner with merchants and/or vendors, and return to the stores energized. Then he'd raise hell about the arrangement of an end cap. He'd push the existing display aside and say, "Let's do it another way." Don't get the wrong idea, though. Pat's not a screamer—he didn't yell at people. But he was passionate, and he shared his passion easily. He really drove the business from the store side, raising hell, stacking stuff up and slapping things off the shelves. But Pat was also the one in there restocking alongside the associates late at night.

He set the tone for everybody working in the stores, inspiring the same incredible loyalty and respect that he had at National Lumber and Homeco. It was because of his devotion, knowledge, and personality that our associates overlooked his less attractive traits.

When Pat was in a store or an office, there was a buzz, an indescribable energy. He made our wildest dreams believable.

Pat wasn't the only one who could inspire our people. Rick Mayo and Cecil Wilson, both of whom joined us from management positions at Handy Dan, were also extremely popular leaders. They were in line with our values, always reinforcing the care and feeding of the customer above all else. Mayo was another one who would be in there at night, restocking. "Hey!" he'd announce. "We've got a big ad breaking this Thursday. Let's get ready for it!"

There was a rare chemistry at work between these men and the people who worked with them; you couldn't help but get wrapped up in it.

■   ■   ■

Pat was the guy who was always in the stores. He loved the stores; he loved the associates. When our size still allowed it, he went to every inventory and every grand opening. For years, he laid out every store and was often there when the concrete trucks poured the slabs. He took the tape and chalk lines and literally taped off where all the fixtures would be, wrote down what was going to be in those areas, and walked the store together with a group of merchants for two more days, talking about whether the store "felt" good.

Just as he had when he led our managers in constructing our first outdoor garden department (an early vision of Arthur's), Pat could be seen in our newest stores in boots and Levi's, leading the effort of newly hired associates to set fixtures, build and raise racks.

It was the greatest way ever imagined to give our people ownership of the store. Twenty years and nearly a thousand stores later, we still open about a quarter of our stores the same way we did in the early days. Setting the stores gives our people ownership. We don't own these stores; they do.

The people who started this company were not just involved but lived what we talked about. We weren't just preachers. We went out and practiced it. And rightfully so. If this thing didn't work, we were broke, out on the street again.

Pat never let a customer out of the store empty-handed, period. If there was something they needed that we didn't have, such as a quart size, he would give them the gallon size for the quart price. Pat believed you didn't let a customer leave The Home Depot without satisfying them in some way.

■ ■ ■

In the first few years, the day-to-day operating practices of The Home Depot were always fluid. They could change on a monthly basis, or even minute to minute. If any two of us were in the bathroom at the same time, someone inevitably started talking about how some product or sales approach wasn't working and how we had to do something different. And we would change. That is how quickly it came about. Common sense was an overriding factor in everything we did. Nothing but our values, ethics, and morality were set in concrete.

Meanwhile, the business plan that Arthur wrote—and I goosed—envisioned stores doing $9 million each in annual sales. Well, we never did $9 million. Within a year and a half of opening, the first two stores together were grossing $25 million, which was unheard of in the business, and we were developing a profitable bottom line.

In 1979, we lost money—almost a million dollars. By 1980, however, we were in the black by $856,000. The following year, we earned almost double that, so things looked real good.

But there is a limit to how far you can expand on starting capital and on borrowed money. The company was succeeding. We were planning years ahead and knew that future financing would be necessary if we were going to expand. We had wonderful support in Ken Langone and his ability to market securities. So it seemed obvious that the time was ripe for an initial public offering. This was a big step; going public meant losing the anonymity and cloak of secrecy a privately held business enjoyed. It meant listening to and considering Wall Street, which would become our ad hoc partner from the day we went public forward. But if we were going to grow, there was no other way.

The only reason we would have waited any longer to go public was so we wouldn't have to give as much of the company away. That, and the fact that as long as we were private, the industry perceived us as failing. If everyone knew how much money we were making, there would have been more clones, earlier.

When we went public in 1981, the home improvement industry woke up and choked on our sawdust.

■　　■　　■

Additional financing was necessary. We had four stores open in Atlanta, and we were planning on more stores in Florida.

In choosing a brokerage house to handle our initial public offering, we talked to Merrill Lynch, Drexel Burnham Lambert Inc., and Bear, Stearns & Company. Ken had a relationship with Bear, Stearns, but the firm was hesitant to do the deal, believing it was premature. It took some strategy, working one against the other. We finally told Bear, Stearns that Merrill Lynch was interested in doing the deal. "Oh, in that case, *we'll* do it," Bear, Stearns responded.

Bear, Stearns agreed to do an over-the-counter public offering of

Home Depot stock in September 1981. (We listed on the New York Stock Exchange in 1984.) Total size of the deal was going to be $7.2 million—750,000 shares at $12.00. Half the money would be used to redeem the preferred stock that Ken and his investment group bought for $2 million, and the rest would go into the operations of the business.

Taking a company public requires a magical, mystical combination of dazzling numbers, personality and a little sleight-of-hand. As the more flamboyant member of our partnership, I was the natural choice to be our main conduit with Wall Street.

Ron Brill and I conducted more than 60 percent of our dog-and-pony shows in New York and around the country, promoting the upcoming stock offering. I loved to sell, and this was a fabulous opportunity. Arthur and Ron were great with numbers, but the Street wanted to hear our dreams and aspirations. That's why Ron would cringe when they'd hear me speak of things such as reaching a thousand stores or having stock valued at $100 or more. I lived in the future.

But the Wall Street wizards loved to come and hear me pontificate, bombast and all—even if they viewed the company somewhat skeptically at the time.

Reflecting that skepticism, Bear, Stearns had a terrible time getting the deal done. The IPO waters were very choppy at the time, and we were unlike anything going in the home improvement industry, let alone retail in general.

Bear, Stearns put together a syndicate of brokers who guaranteed that they would sell the 600,000 shares of our stock. In theory, they would take advance orders and then tell us, "Okay, now that we have the orders, we are going to collectively buy the 600,000 shares."

Well, to our utter dismay, the Atlanta office of Bear, Stearns decided it didn't think the Home Depot offering was a good deal. It didn't want to sell any of the stock, and returned its quota to the syndicate. That caused a major problem—the syndicate had to find somebody else to take it. Atlanta's decision not to buy the deal made others question its value. If the Bear, Stearns office in The Home Depot's own backyard wouldn't buy in, how could we convince someone in New York?

Twenty years and several billion dollars later, we still haven't forgotten that incident. Of course, the stock did extraordinarily well, and the Atlanta office looked bad. Not us.

On September 21, 1981, the day before the IPO, Bear, Stearns called and said they intended to sell only half the deal—$3 million instead of $6 million. We were angry, but unfortunately we were not in control.

Ken was forced to contact the original investors.

"Fellas," he said, "it is this simple. If we don't take the money Bear, Stearns can raise for us, even though it is only half of what we want, we are either going to have to put the money up ourselves to keep the company going, or The Home Depot is going to go out of business."

There was no interest in putting up any more money, so Ken put together a deal converting the investment group's preferred stock into common stock. They ended up with approximately 27,000 shares of common stock for each $50,000 unit of preferred stock. Today, that $50,000 unit is the equivalent of at least 6,130,000 shares of stock and worth more than $366 million.

In the conversion from private to public company, we had our first opportunity to take some equity out of the company. This was our first opportunity to become liquid financially and pay off our own personal debts. I sold 73,000 shares of stock for $8.7 million; Arthur and Pat sold 54,800 each for $6.5 million. Today, the combined value of that stock we sold would be 41.6 million shares or more than $2.4 billion worth of stock. By the way, Ken didn't choose to sell any.

■　　■　　■

One of the reasons we needed the public offering was to finance our first four stores in South Florida. The first two opened in Hollywood and Fort Lauderdale on September 4, 1981, and the next two opened almost simultaneously with the stock sale two months later. This first foray outside of Atlanta, into four more former Treasure Island stores, doubled the company's store total to eight.

Having access to the four Treasure Island stores in South Florida was another stroke of luck due to our Atlanta store leases. In 1981, J.C. Penney decided to close down all thirty-four of its Treasure Island stores. They had held off the inevitable for a long time because they didn't want Wall Street cognizant of how frightful the operation truly was. For many years the company had represented Treasure Island as a vehicle capable of fueling growth at J.C. Penney. But it wasn't.

A clause in our rental agreement guaranteed us they would not go out of business, which suddenly put a loaded gun to their heads. "You can't close these stores," we said in mock horror. "We have a contract!" One of the things we wanted in order to let them off the hook was more stores. We were ready to expand and looked at their stores in Memphis, Charlotte, Dallas, and South Florida. We chose the four in South Florida; the new leases were almost carbon copies of the Atlanta deal with only the dates and places changed.

J.C. Penney's Bill Harris quickly organized a trio of big-box tenants at the former Treasure Island locations in South Florida, putting Service Merchandise (50,000 square feet) on one end, The Home Depot (70,000 square feet) at the other end, and Marshall's (40,000 square feet) in the middle.

Harris begged us to take his California stores as well, which were worth a lot of money and the locations of which were attractive to us. "We are so far stretched out already," I told him. "I want to do it, but we just can't handle it." Our resources—both financial and otherwise—were still limited.

■   ■   ■

Going to Florida represented our first attempt at exporting our culture. Many critics expected us to fail, figuring that while our brand of customer service might work in Atlanta, it was not the right fit for the rest of the country. How wrong they proved to be, although many of the same voices doubted us again seventeen years later when we exported our culture again, this time to Chile.

Certainly competitors in South Florida hoped we could not reproduce our Atlanta success there. One of the largest lumber companies in South Florida prepared customers, vendors, and employees

for our arrival by informing them that we were not a successful operator and would be quickly out of business. Those rumors seriously
affected hiring; we were forced to open with a bare minimum of associates because potential hires were skeptical of their future with us.

Still, opening those first stores was great fun, although everybody
worked around the clock. The night before we opened, the Fort
Lauderdale store was a mess, a total disaster from packing out boxes
for weeks. Late that night, Charlie Barnes organized everybody at the
back of the building, and they literally marched in a line to the front
of the store, picking up all the garbage that was lying around. As he
now knew better than anyone, we wanted a warehouse look—not a
dump.

When we finally opened our doors on September 3, 1981—
shades of Homeco!—there was already a line around the building.
Hundreds of people waiting to get in. Why? An ingenious Arthur
Blank promotion: $29.95 ceiling fans. (They cost us $27.)

Arthur was in the back of the store that day, beneath the fan
cloud, wearing his orange apron, ready to wait on customers. But he
never stood a chance as we were overwhelmed by a throng of customers used to paying $49.95 and more for the very same 36-inch
Caribbean Breeze fans. They weren't interested in talk; they just
wanted to *buy, buy, buy!* We had fans stacked everywhere, but people
were flowing in like water, running through the aisles. It was a frenzy
unlike anything we ever saw in Atlanta.

Everybody figured the fan price was a gimmick, a bait-and-switch
tactic, that we probably had limited quantities, so when we opened,
they ran through the store looking for these $29.95 imported Asian
ceiling fans. We sold out our vast stock immediately, but vendor
David Moss of Moss Manufacturing had a full warehouse and he
kept us well supplied. By the end of the first weekend, we sold 40,000
fans.

We didn't have an import department in the early days, so Moss
was kind of our importer of record, selling us ceiling fans and roll-up
mini-blinds. He was an innovator, going to the Orient for product.

Moss was interesting to watch because he was doing to us what we
were trying to do to the public around us: offer a huge, broad selec-

tion at a great price. He gave us a leg up on the cost side, where we could sell ceiling fans for $29.99 and still make $3 on each, whereas that same fan would have cost us $35 from a stateside distributor.

The next day, incidentally, we had a bona fide problem—but nothing like we ever encountered before in Atlanta. The bank wouldn't take our deposit! It was more than $10,000, and in South Florida, the bankers are very sensitive and suspicious about large cash deposits. As we have run the business, we have all learned a lot of new things, but that was something we never expected.

■   ■   ■

We have never been right on anticipating demand for fans—ever. Arthur started us in the fan business, and it kept growing and growing and growing and became an incredible business. But we reached a point at which we were either so out of stock or so overstocked that Pat got crazy. He marched into Arthur's office, took all of the pencils out of his partner's desk, and broke them in half.

"You know what?" Pat said. "I am firing you. You are no longer the fan buyer. I am going to do it myself."

So Pat took it over and proceeded to make the same mistakes.

One of the best ways to illustrate the fan problem is by telling a story about our longtime lumber buyer, Cecil Wilson. Cecil "owned" the lumber department, and he didn't brook interference there from anyone. "This is my lumberyard," he'd grumble. "This is where *my* stuff goes, nobody else's."

One season, Pat severely overordered fans. In some stores, there were trainloads of fan pallets filling the lumber aisles. You couldn't get a stick of lumber in or out of those stores.

Wilson saw Pat in a store and started chasing him, screaming and yelling. "What are you doing? You are killing me. You wiped me out. I can't get a customer down these aisles!"

We were always out of whack on fans. It was kind of the company in-joke. After Pat fired Arthur, he ultimately fired himself, because he didn't do any better. He couldn't wait to give it to the next guy.

■   ■   ■

Following our great success in South Florida, we were eager to expand further. Next up was Altamonte Springs, just outside of Orlando. This was our first store built from the ground up, whereas the first eight were former Treasure Island stores from J.C. Penney.

Larry Mercer was the manager of this store, having reluctantly relocated from running one of our Atlanta stores. But he got the hang of it quickly; the night before opening, as if demonstrating how much store no. 231 was his, Mercer drove his blue Toyota Corolla through the front doors and toured the inside. What a feeling! This store, the new flagship of The Home Depot, was all his.

And a devastating opening it was—for the competition, with three football fields worth of merchandise piled floor to ceiling. And this time, the boxes were all full. Customers came, and they came and they came and they came. It was a huge success.

In Florida, Scotty's was famous for its catalog, so we hung Scotty's catalogs at the end of every aisle in the new Altamonte Springs store. Every item of theirs that we carried was highlighted and discounted an additional 20 percent. The week before the opening we would stock up on Ortho Ant Killer, for example, and have the Scotty's book opened to the Ortho Ant Killer page and show the deeply discounted Home Depot price next to it.

By this time, the poorly attended store openings in Atlanta were but memories. In Altamonte Springs, the new Home Depot store was an *event*. We even hired the local police department to direct traffic at the opening. If only we had had more parking. And an even bigger store!

■　■　■

Later expansion in Florida was always successful, but it did bring unexpected complications. For instance, when we relocated from our original 87,000-square-foot store in St. Petersburg to a gigantic, 140,000-square-foot location a mile away, it briefly became the largest store in the chain. But for all the merchandise we could put in there and all the parking spaces we could offer, we had some terrible situations where elderly customers panicked because they would get lost.

In Fort Lauderdale, we were expanding a store but the city was dragging its heels on granting a permit. Pat got tired of the delay and took matters into his own hands. He jumped on the nearest forklift and drove it right through a wall—through the whole thing, back and forth, back and forth—tearing it down in about thirty minutes. The city building inspector came in a few days later and said, "We didn't give you permission to do that." The manager said, "I'm sorry, but this madman came in here and tore it up. I had nothing to do with it."

He didn't do that sort of thing as often as legend has it. It was just that he wanted our managers to know when to take action.

PART II

6

The Associates

"Make Mistakes, Learn from Them, and Move On"*

One Sunday, Bernie's regular golf game was rained out. Sitting around the clubhouse with his foursome, one of the guys told him that The Home Depot was doomed.

"You run some company," the man said. "You are going to go out of business one of these days, and you don't even know it."

"What are you talking about?" Bernie asked.

"I had an experience in your store. I am not going to tell you who it was with, but you want to talk about stupid!"

"Go ahead," Bernie said, "tell me how stupid we are."

"I was in one of your stores this week, prepared to spend $200 on a new faucet, and your stupid people showed me how to fix my old one for $1.50! You lost that sale, brother. And I am not going to tell you who did it, because you will probably fire him."

"I would like to know who it was," Bernie said.

"No way."

"How about if I give you a written guarantee that they will not be fired?" Bernie said. "How about if I tell you I am probably going to give that person a raise?"

The man's eyes lit up.

* Arthur Blank

"Why?"

"Because that person did exactly what we want them to do. We are there to save money for consumers, not to sell them products they don't need. And you know what? You are not the smartest guy in the world, but if you ever had something go wrong with your household plumbing again, where would you go?"

"Right to that person."

"You just proved the point," Bernie said. "You just proved how good our people are. The key is not to make the sale. The key is to cultivate the customer."

At The Home Depot, cultivating the customer is much more important than creating a bottom line. We teach our associates that if you can save a customer money, do it. We're not looking to fleece the customer. If I can save them $100, why not do it? That reflects one of our values: caring for the customer. Care for them today and they'll be back tomorrow.

■　■　■

People want to be part of something bigger than they are. At The Home Depot, they're part of something really special.

Everyone who works at The Home Depot is an associate of Bernie and me. That encompasses a very broad range of people, from senior managers to the cashiers and lot engineers who toil for hourly wages in the stores.

To us, "associate" implies an equal as opposed to a wage slave. That's important because of the company's inverted management structure: We value what the salesperson on the store floor says just as much—sometimes more—than what a district manager says, if they're right. That's because the salesperson touches the customer more.

Taking care of our people is understanding that every position in the company is critical. I think of the sales associates as the spinal cord of this company; they hold The Home Depot erect. The person the customer is going to interact with, the person who is going to build the image of this company with the customer, is always going to be a sales associate. They are the ones who will have the product knowledge and be able to show the customer how to use it. They are the heroes of the company, the ones who create a cult among our customers. We're trying to make our customers bleed orange.

Since customers in the stores are the center of our universe, we want everyone at The Home Depot to feel responsible when it comes to meeting their needs, whether they are a senior manager with an office in our Store Support Center in Atlanta or the salespeople or cashiers in one of the stores. In fact, associates on the sales floor are in many ways *more* empowered to make decisions than people at Store Support simply because they are at ground zero. We don't want anyone leaving a Home Depot store unhappy, so it's the job of people working in the stores to do whatever it takes to make customers happy. That gives them broad discretion to take action.

That kind of power also requires the kind of person who knows how to exercise it and when to do so. This is a tough place to work if you are inflexible. If you come to The Home Depot from a company where you checked the policies-and-procedures book before making a decision, you may not fit in well at The Home Depot.

The associate described in Bernie's golf story was more than just an employee. He wasn't solely focused on making the highest possible sale today but on cultivating a customer who will eventually spend much more than $200 at The Home Depot over his lifetime. If this associate didn't think he was being taken care of, he probably wouldn't have taken the trouble to do all the right things with that customer. But the single most important reason for The Home Depot's success is our effort to take care of our associates.

Treating our associates well includes providing them with the opportunities and training to progress into a meaningful and rewarding career. When we left Sandy Sigoloff and Handy Dan, we had made a ton of money for them but walked away with nothing. We vowed that if The Home Depot was successful, everyone who worked here would have a chance to share in the wealth.

We pay people what they are worth. That is a cornerstone of the culture of our company. That means that if an electrician comes into our store and can be productive and sell a lot of electrical goods, he or she will not be forever cubbyholed as a salesperson at a certain hourly rate. If they command a premium over our average wage and can justify their hourly rate, we hire them at that rate.

Traditionally, we hire the best people in the industry, so they make more money than their counterparts do at our competition. That breeds initial loyalty when they are hired; receiving company stock further deepens that loyalty; and then they fall in love with the way they are treated.

Whether it's through a 401(k) or a stock purchase plan, every associate at The Home Depot has an opportunity to be an owner of the company. Everyone has a stake in the company that goes beyond earning a day's wages. Associates have a real vested interest in cultivating customers and building lifelong relationships with them.

Through the Home Depot stock purchase plan, all associates can make a no-risk stock purchase at 15 percent off the going market price. That means, for example, if they buy stock at $20 per share and the price drops below what they paid, they can get a refund of their money at any time before the plan ends.

In addition to a standard 401(k) plan and the stock purchase plan, salaried associates—who represent about 6 percent of our workforce—receive stock options. Grants are based on performance and level of responsibilities. (Bernie and I, incidentally, do not receive options as part of our own compensation plan.)

No matter how our associates acquire company stock, it has proven a quality investment, appreciating by as much as 48 percent compounded annual growth since we went public in 1981. We put together a total compensation package that makes The Home Depot a financially attractive place for all associates, not just those in management. But for our hourly associates, stock options make a great incentive for moving up to salaried positions.

Walk into one of our stores and you'll find an inordinate number of people who have been there as long as the store has been open. Overall, our associate turnover is very low for the home improvement industry. Turnover among associates who have been with us more than one year is rare. After that, they tend to picture themselves building a career at The Home Depot.

Some people find our attitudes toward customers and associates a little hard to believe. But what makes us so different from anyone else in our industry is that we take the inverted management structure so seriously. Hourly associates really do lead The Home Depot; every day, their decision making and independence makes our stores better, and that reinforces customer loyalty.

Bernie and I believe it's all about trust. With the right value system and the right knowledge to do their job, people can be trusted to make the right decisions. If you can operate with that kind of trust, you don't have to micromanage. And people will do more good for the company than anyone could ever dictate.

A healthy, successful, growing organization provides opportunities to all kinds of people. This company would not be possible without the daily contribution and experiences of our associates. Their entrepreneurial and creative spirits embody the value system of the company, and we'd like to share a few of their stories.

■   ■   ■

Jeff Barrington, who is now a district manager in central Florida, was typical of our first hires, men and women who joined us in the working class, accumulated stock, and went on to become millionaires. He started out by loading customer purchases at our Marietta store, getting bags for cashiers, sweeping the front end, shagging carts in the parking lots, washing the johns, you name it. If it needed doing, Barrington was doing it.

After several months of that, we asked him to also drive a sixteen-foot flatbed truck on what were his days off. Our regular delivery driver worked five days a week, but business reached a point where we had deliveries seven days. Between that and his regular responsibilities, Barrington easily put in his share of seventy-hour workweeks. But that wasn't an issue for him. He was a team player; whatever it took to get the job done, Barrington did it.

Barrington was typical of hundreds and later thousands of Home Depot associates whose hunger for product knowledge and vision of opportunity in the company causes them to spend much of their mealtime and other breaks on the sales floor, reading the backs of boxes and eavesdropping on conversations between customers and sales associates. (Because of changes in the labor laws, we've become much stricter about hourly people working for The Home Depot off the clock.) They recognized this company's inherent, burgeoning need for informed, motivated staff who could step up, take responsibility, and be promoted quickly through a system that rewarded and encouraged entrepreneurial spirit and risk. This company became a bastion of opportunity for men and women like Barrington, many with no more than a high school education, to reach out and grab the brass ring of success.

Soon Barrington moved up from lot attendant to being responsible for loading the lumber racks. Today, lumber is forklifted onto racks, after which the metal containment bands are cut. Back in the 1970s and early '80s, it was stored lengthwise, so we had to drop a bundle, cut the band and, stick by stick, slide it in, so it looked like a bookcase. It took hours.

One afternoon, Barrington finished loading the lumber racks and put the metal bands and other assorted trash in a cart, which he wheeled to a Dumpster out back of the loading dock.

At the end of the walkway was a thirty-cubic-foot, open-top Dumpster, about the same height as the walkway, maybe a foot and a half taller. Barrington rolled his cart up to the edge, as always, pushed it up against the Dumpster, lifted up the cart, and dumped the trash.

Just then he heard somebody scream. Inside the Dumpster, Barrington was introduced to our comptroller and future chief financial officer for the first time.

Ron Brill was looking at the things we were throwing away. After getting over his umbrage at having building materials poured on him, Ron took Barrington on a tour of the Dumpster.

"Look at the stuff that is in here, Jeff," he said. He pointed to imperfect lumber that had been culled out of the bins, broken bags of concrete, and other items. Ron believed—rightly—that we could reduce the regular retail price on these items, put them out on the sales floor, and give customers at least an opportunity to purchase something that was damaged but might take care of their needs. And, of course, The Home Depot would make a little money.

Ron, it turned out, wasn't poking through our trash. He was down there looking at the company's assets. We didn't have a lot of working capital in those days, and Ron made it his business to make every nickel count. He understood that values are not something we merely preach; they're something we want practiced. He wasn't preaching to Barrington; he was demonstrating—in a rather unique way—how he protects the company's assets.

If a company's values are nothing more than words hanging in the lobby of corporate headquarters for visitors to see, they're a fantasy, dead on arrival. Values must be carried out day-in and day-out. The day Jeff Barrington encountered Ron Brill in that Dumpster, Ron—the first person this company ever hired and, to this day, still a key member of management—was an inspiration to Barrington. I'm sure that after that, he too thought more about what we were throwing out that could have somehow been sold or at least used.

It's about role-modeling.

■　　■　　■

One of our values is caring for our people: If we expect them to take care of our customers, we've got to take care of our associates. And very often, that means protecting them from themselves.

Linda Khano is now a Home Depot district manager in Minnesota, but twenty years ago she was a full-time college student putting in forty-hour workweeks at The Home Depot—which was then considered part-time. She loaded trucks alongside and kept pace with any man we hired. She lived on 45-minute naps. Her gym bag always had two changes of clothes in it, because she never knew what time she might be leaving the store and whether she'd be going home to sleep or back to class.

Some years later, after Khano had become an assistant manager, she was leaving a store one morning in a sweat suit just as I was coming in. I looked at her and cocked my head.

"Linda?"

"Yes?"

"Are you just leaving now?" I asked.

Somewhat sheepishly, not knowing which answer I wanted to hear, Khano opted for the truth. "Yeah."

"When did you come to work?"

"Yesterday."

"*When* yesterday?"

"Yesterday at six in the morning."

"And you are just going home *now*?"

"Yeah."

The next day, Khano worked all day and all night again, doing all the things she felt needed to be done before her store opened in the morning.

Once more, I passed her on her way out and my way in. I said "Hello," shook my head, and added, "Good-bye." Then I called the district manager, and asked, "Was Linda Khano here all night?"

"I don't know," he said. "Maybe."

That day, I wrote and circulated a memo that marked the end of the first Home Depot era. "Nobody will stay in a store past midnight anymore," I wrote. We did not want to kill our people.

The problem was that we all worked hard, but we didn't work smart. A highly motivated workforce will fly right into the sun. They get so energized about what they are doing that they don't realize they are damaging themselves physically.

We eventually put into effect a guideline that store managers and their assistants should work an average of only 55 hours a week. That is our goal. Somebody on the outside might say, "Wow, that's a lot of hours." But that's not us looking to increase their hours. That's an effort to *decrease* their hours. People need a balanced life. They need to use their time better.

Our people had so much pride and dedication to their work that they would not accept anything less than the best from themselves. They wanted their sales areas to look good. They wanted to be ready for the customer. They wanted to really do well. It was a lot of hard work, to really be number one. We're wiser now and try to do things smart, not hard.

■   ■   ■

Lynn Martineau, who is now president of our Western Division, had an early encounter with Bernie on the floor of the Doraville,

Georgia, store that became a commonplace occurrence for other associates through the years.

"You know, Lynn," Bernie said, "I didn't hire you to *do* . . . because you are going to have to *do* anyway. I hired you to *think*."

That was a powerful statement coming from a founder of the company. It was probably one of the most empowering statements that a young person could hear. "Through your eyes and through your knowledge, we learn what is going on with the customers," Bernie said. "We need to listen to you."

These people—men and women, although predominantly men at the time—literally had workdays where they came in as the sun was rising and didn't leave again until the next sunup. It was a fun, exciting place, an environment not likely to be duplicated in these politically correct times.

We never asked our managers and associates to do anything we wouldn't do. If an associate picked something up off the floor, it was because we did it first. We set the example. Few people ever felt that they were working *for* somebody. Hopefully, it was more like they were working *with* somebody. Everything was hand in hand.

So if we were in the stores selling on Saturday and Sunday, we didn't have any hesitation to expect it of anyone else. Working the weekend shift, as a matter of fact, was required of all managers, no exceptions.

If we didn't have a product the customer needed, we'd take their name and address and promise to get it that same day. It didn't matter where we had to go, it didn't matter if we had to get in our personal cars, pay a competitor the full retail price, and then drive to the customer's home late at night. Whatever it takes, serve the customer.

That's why so many of our longtime customers in the Atlanta area tell stories of Bernie or me rolling into their driveway with the Sherwin-Williams paint they needed—though our stores didn't even carry that brand. Or if a delivery truck wasn't available, we'd strap a piece of unfinished furniture to the roof of one of our cars and haul it wherever it needed to go.

Our managers always worked weekends. They always worked two or three nights at least. There wasn't a nine-to-five schedule for anybody. Even Ken Langone would come down from New York, roll up his sleeves, and go to work.

That rubbed off on associates, too.

When one of our store managers heard a police officer complain about the service he received at another Home Depot store, the manager gave him a big discount on the product he wanted.

"Why are you apologizing?" the cop asked. "It is not your store I had the problem with."

"Because," the manager explained, "it is *my* company you had a problem with. I don't want you going anyplace else."

He probably gained us a customer for life. That manager treated all the customers who walked into his store like they were his best friends.

And when Bryant Scott, hired as a lot engineer, now president of our EXPO stores division, heard us talk about treating the customers like they're your own family, he took that to heart. He came from a very close-knit family and thought that was a heck of an idea. What aren't you going to do for your best friend? What aren't you going to do for your dad? That is what you need to do for your customers.

■   ■   ■

Ken Langone attended a holiday party put on by one of our store managers a few years ago. The store's department head for lighting told him a little story that night that began thus: "I probably am going to lose my job when I tell you, but . . ."

He had forty customers, all regulars, who all wanted a new Black & Decker "snake" light. "We were all out," he said, "but I got them anyway."

"Tell me what you did," Ken said.

"First I called up all the other Home Depot stores in our district and asked if I could get some of their lights, and they all said no. They needed all they had, but at least I found out which stores had them. So I got in my car, drove to those stores, and I bought the lights I needed with my Home Depot credit card.

"Then," he continued, his tone a mixture of pride and fear of losing his job, "I brought them back to my store and I got a refund. Then

I went to the other side of the counter, picked up the forty lights, and called my forty customers. 'I got your lights.' "

On the spot, Ken called me at home.

"Arthur," Ken said, after repeating the story, "we have to send this guy a letter congratulating him for ingenuity. Then I want to talk to Pat about seeing if this guy wants to become a merchant."

■   ■   ■

We get new associates several ways. Most come to us, but sometimes we go out looking for them.

For example, when we opened our first store in Evanston, Illinois, our store manager visited the local Builders Square and Menard's, scouting the talent. She would feign ignorance of products, trying to uncover the competition's best, smartest, and friendliest people.

One day she was in a container store looking for something that she actually needed. The person who waited on her was so friendly, she said, "Here's my card. Come and see me."

If a salesperson approaches her first, that is a good first step. That means the person is friendly, outgoing, not afraid of customers. That is the most important thing, because you can teach anyone about a drill, but you can't teach people how to smile and be kind to other people.

Next she'll ask them for something specific. If they point and say, "Yeah, go down three rows, turn left, and it's probably halfway down on the right," then she knows they are not really into customer service. But if they say, "Let me show you where it is," they might be Home Depot material.

If they try to help, that's a good sign.

If they don't know an answer and say, "I really don't know, but let me get someone for you who does," that is another plus.

If they appear to know a great deal about something, then she'll pepper them with more probing questions: "How does it work? What's better, in your opinion?"

At one competitor's store, she saw somebody killing time, pushing labels and absentmindedly moving products around the shelves. She purposely stood right next to him, just to see if he would budge.

He didn't. She even rubbed her foot against his foot and said, "Excuse me."

He didn't say anything; he just moved over.

We say, "Thank God for people like that," because they work for the competition. And more power to them.

■   ■   ■

There is a cultural adjustment that must take place for anyone to be valuable to this company—at any level, whether vice president, store manager, or cashier. There is all sorts of baggage that people bring to the company from their prior working experiences that we have to lovingly strip away.

At Handy City, where one of our associates worked before joining us, everything had to be really neat. Employees there always carried a duster around like French maids, brushing things off and keeping the shelves in perfect order, like Nordstrom might.

After he joined us, this guy once spent hours organizing a very attractive display of wallpaper and glue products. He was very proud of it.

The next morning, he strolled around the corner, head held high, to inspect his work. But what he saw made him mad. Pat Farrah was standing in front of the display, and he didn't like it at all. As he was inclined to do from time to time, Pat was throwing it all to the floor.

"What the hell are you doing?" the associate screamed in dismay.

"I want this store to look like a warehouse. I want cut cases, not this 'pretty' stuff," Pat said.

But to this associate, Pat's approach wasn't in the least professional. Not his preference for displays, and certainly not his people skills.

"Don't you ever do that."

Just then, a store manager cut the associate off. "Hey, that's Pat Farrah. He is a vice president of the company. Don't talk to him like that."

"I don't care," the associate said. "I'm not letting anybody do something like that to my work."

That associate's situation illustrated our earliest challenge of getting new employees enculturated with our values. He came from a competing home improvement chain where he was encouraged and rewarded for keeping products and shelves in perfect order. If you recall how angry we were the night before our first stores opened, when the managers wanted to surprise us by cleaning and waxing the floors, you'll understand why the associate's neat and ordered approach didn't belong in a Home Depot store. Pat Farrah, the king of chaos, deliberately messed up a cherished display at The Home Depot as a matter of enculturation.

Our mothers taught us to clean up our rooms; we teach our associates to be messy. We don't have time in the stores for "a place for everything and everything in its place." There are too many customers to wait on, and product is being unpacked, shelved, and sold too fast for that. Besides, we know that home improvement is messy by definition.

At the same time, we don't allow any moss to gather under our mess.

Pam Scott, Bryant Scott's wife, ran the garden department of one of our Florida stores before they were married. After a store visit by a group of merchants, she was walking through the department, where she noticed something odd about the pumps on display. Looking closer, she could see that Pat had written his name and the date in the dust on the pumps, anticipating coming back the next time and seeing it again. He was challenging her not to dust the place but to rearrange the product to get it noticed and sold or send it back to the manufacturer. Home Depot merchandise shouldn't be in stock long enough to collect dust.

■   ■   ■

As a company that hires 800 new people every week, one of our critical beliefs is that you can't overlook anyone as a possible source of associate talent. There are good people everywhere, and age, race, gender, mobility, and even physical or other disabilities should play no role in a person's opportunity to become a Home Depot associate. We have often hired people with Down's syndrome who have some limitations but are thrilled to work in our environment. And because of their dedication, they inspire their coworkers.

We also believe in hiring senior citizens. We refer to them as "Bernie Boys and Girls" because Bernie was the original champion of this outreach. They are gray-haired people who were basically retired but who wanted to work, and we hired them. They are great teachers. We don't care about their age. In Florida, we have an associate who was hired at the age of 80. After twenty-five years in the hardware business, he felt retirement was too dull for him. Is there another company in America that would do something like that?

In 1997, Bernie visited the Home Depot store in Boynton Beach, Florida. An older man came over and started hugging him. "You changed my life," he said. "I am the happiest person in the world."

"That's terrific," Bernie said.

"You don't understand," he said. "You hired me five years ago, when I was 70. Nobody else would hire me." Then he said, "Let me introduce you to some of my coworkers." And he brought over a whole cadre of guys and one woman who were all in their 70s. In fact, one guy was in his 80s.

Bernie went to the general store manager, Lamar Mike, and complimented him on these associates and their enthusiasm.

"I just let them loose," Mike said. "These are the greatest. They train people for me."

So when we talk about hiring the best, number one is people with experience, and number two, people who don't have experience but are willing to learn and want to learn, who have that desire to learn. A manager interviewing people has to be able to separate these people out. That is a critical factor. And once you have them, you must invest the time and the energy into training them.

Few associates ever hired could inspire more loyalty and devotion—in both customers and Home Depot associates—than Gene Lewis.

Gene, a World War II veteran, joined us in the early 1980s after five decades in the paint business and two failed attempts at retirement. Retirement didn't suit him; he liked being around people too much. And working in the paint departments at Home Depots in the Atlanta area, it didn't take him long to attract a crowd.

Gene's product knowledge was truly extraordinary. We didn't

have computerized color matching back then like we do now, where our technology can analyze any color and create a match for it. Back then, we just had Gene. He could eyeball anything and color-match it. And he'd write the formula on the lid so you could match it again. He was an entrepreneur who created his own turn-of-the-century paint store in the middle of a Home Depot store.

"Everything you see's got a coat of paint on it," Gene always told us. "The potential in paint is tremendous. One of these days I'm going to get that potential."

Everybody remembers Gene for a different reason. Some remember him as a tireless trainer of our younger associates. He always had a joke or a wise word for somebody. In fact, his paint department was always covered with his humorous handwritten signs:

HUSBANDS ARE NOT PERMITTED TO PICK COLORS,
BUT THEY ARE PERMITTED TO PAY FOR THEM

WE ASK YOU TO PLEASE REFRAIN FROM GROANING
WHILE OTHERS ARE CHOOSING COLORS

IT TOOK MICHELANGELO FOUR YEARS
TO PAINT THE SISTINE CHAPEL.
IF HE CAME TO SEE GENE,
HE WOULD HAVE HAD IT DONE IN SEVEN DAYS!

IF THE PAINT ON YOUR HOUSE IS NOT BECOMING TO
YOU, YOU SHOULD BE COMING TO GENE.

DO NOT DISTURB THIS
EXTREMELY GIFTED,
TALENTED, GOOD-LOOKING
GENIUS, WHILE MIXING
COLORS—GENE

The purpose of the signs wasn't to show off how clever he was; it was to amuse customers waiting in line to see him. Because every day of the week, long lines of people queued up to get Gene's advice. He would hold court in the middle of the department and spend whatever time was necessary to answer each person's questions, match paint, or solve paint-related problems. We had plenty of other qualified associates, but if Gene was on duty, the customers preferred to wait for him. And if someone came in looking for Gene only to discover it was his day off, they'd leave and come back on a day when he was working.

"I want to wait on that customer the same way I want to be waited on when I walk into a retail store," Gene said. "I want to please that customer as much as possible. I want that customer to keep coming back to me, and to me only."

The kids always came around looking for Gene, too; his apron always had an extra lollipop in it.

Whereas our associates are expected to wait on customers and restock shelves, Gene was the exception. Recognizing his extraordinary value to their department, his coworkers covered his share of the restocking chores so he had more time to spend one-on-one with customers.

When The Home Depot gets calls or letters from customers complimenting one of our associates, the associate receives a customer service badge to sew on his or her orange apron. An excellent associate might earn three to five badges a year. Gene, who was with us for fifteen years, had so many—more than four hundred of them—they covered several aprons.

If we had to describe our idea of customer service in a picture instead of words, that picture would be of Gene Lewis.

■　　■　　■

Not everyone has been impressed with our hiring practices, however.

On September 19, 1997, The Home Depot—without admitting any wrongdoing—entered into a settlement agreement with plaintiffs in the class action lawsuit *Butler et al. v. Home Depot, Inc.*, in which the plaintiffs asserted claims of gender discrimination in hiring and promotion. We subsequently reached agreements to settle three other individual lawsuits, each of which involved claims of gender discrimination.

As a result of these agreements, we paid $65 million to the plaintiff class members and $22.5 million to the plaintiffs' attorneys in

Butler, and approximately $17 million for other related internal costs, including development, implementation, or enhancement of certain human resources programs, as well as the settlement terms of the three other lawsuits.

Were there ever any individual cases of discrimination in our company based on gender, race, religion, or something else? Probably. The issue for us as founders, however, was this: Do our company policies foster what the law defines as a pattern or policy that supports discrimination? The answer is no. Do we have mechanisms in place so that if we find discrimination, it is dealt with effectively and quickly? We always felt that we did—and still feel that we do.

From a personal standpoint, the accusations in the suit were so 180 degrees opposed to our personal philosophy that, in that sense, it was a shock.

The nature of employment class actions has changed in the last few years. In 1991, the law changed to give victims of employment discrimination additional remedies. They can now get general and punitive damages as well as back pay. They can also have a jury decide the issue as opposed to a judge, which has led to a huge increase in the number of discrimination cases and class actions.

The Oakland, California, law firm that represented the plaintiffs in our case, Saperstein, Goldstein, Demchak & Baller, had already been extremely successful with a gender discrimination class action formula that they had brought chiefly against grocery stores such as Lucky Stores, Albertson's, and Publix. The issue they made in those suits was that at grocery stores, the front end—the cash registers—is chiefly staffed by females. Meanwhile, sales and management positions are primarily filled by males.

In my mind, there's no intuitive reason why that would be the case in a grocery store, no obvious reason. But there *is* an obvious reason why that would be so in a Home Depot.

Our competitive advantage is having knowledgeable salespeople—people who know how to sell and use electrical products, power tools, building materials, and lumber. People who have experience in the construction trades and can educate and train our customers in how to use the products. We recruit in the construction trades; it is no secret that the construction trades are predominantly male. In fact, a scant 2.6 percent of the people working in these trades are female.

If you looked at our industry and the building trades twenty years ago, there were very few women in plumbing, electrical, lumber, and mill work. It was very difficult for us to recruit women who had professional experience in those areas.

Back then, we employed many male cashiers because there were not enough women who wanted to work in the dust and noise of a home improvement center. Many women felt intimidated by products they didn't understand and didn't use. The Home Depot was a great big warehouse, and a warehouse was not a magnet to large numbers of women.

Over the years, however, the addition of indoor and outdoor garden departments and window treatments brought women into the stores as customers and associates. Before long, women were working in all departments of the stores, including lumber.

But it *is* true that there is a statistical disparity between the number of men and women at The Home Depot.

And in this modern, enlightened age, that is the starting point for these lawsuits. But we contend there is a good reason that that statistical disparity exists. And that reason is *not* discrimination. It is due to the qualifications and choices of the applicants and candidates for the positions at The Home Depot—not a deliberate policy of exclusion or discrimination. We want our managers to have merchandising experience. We want them to be familiar with handling, demonstrating, and displaying home improvement products, turnover and return rates. These are skills needed to run a store that generally require sales experience, as opposed to working a cash register.

But the Saperstein firm has been incredibly successful in getting huge settlements out of the grocery industry and so, when they looked for other companies that paralleled the businesses against whom they had already won settlements, they came after us.

To us it seemed just outrageous, because we pride ourselves on having knowledgeable salespeople and it seemed self-evident why the numbers are the way they are. Our salespeople are predominately male, and we typically promote from within, so our management ranks are predominantly male, too. These are legitimate, nondiscriminatory reasons that are absolutely obvious to anybody who works at The Home Depot.

But because of our sheer size, the plaintiffs had the beginning of a class action, and they took it all the way.

In retrospect, we were especially vulnerable because we did not have a very structured, computerized, objective way of selecting candidates. At that time, we didn't computerize information on applications about previous jobs, and our managers conducted free-form interviews. So although it was obvious to us that we weren't discriminatory and that we have good reasons for the way our stores are staffed, we could not demonstrate that very clearly to a jury.

Bernie and I were just outraged by the lawsuit and expressed that outrage quite vocally in the early days, frustrated with the judicial system and the lawyers who engaged in such legal extortion.

Saperstein, Goldstein, Demchak & Baller filed the class action suit in December 1994 in San Francisco. A few months before that, in September, solicitation letters went out from the Saperstein lawyers to class members who they previously represented in the grocery cases, saying in effect: *You remember us, we're the folks who brought you $112 million in the Lucky Stores settlement. Now we're going after The Home Depot. Please call this 1-800 number if you or anyone you know works for The Home Depot.*

Not coincidentally, most of the eight named plaintiffs who were the representatives when the class action suit was filed in December filed their Equal Employment Opportunity Commission (EEOC) charges—which is a jurisdictional prerequisite to being a plaintiff—between September and December after receiving the lawyers' letter. And approximately four of those women had recovered money in previous employment class actions represented by the Saperstein firm.

We feel that individual claims made by the plaintiffs were weak. And some had a troubled employment history. Vickie Butler, for example, one of the named plaintiffs, had attempted to choke a male coworker, an offense for which she should have been fired.

On the basis of claims such as hers, we decided to fight the suit.

A class action has two phases. From December 1994 until January 1996, our case was in a precertification stage. Discovery was somewhat limited; the kind of information the plaintiffs could get out of us was contained.

During that time, Bernie had dinner with our legal team, plus outside counsel Thomas P. Brown IV of the Los Angeles firm Epstein Becker & Green. The strategy meeting was intended to educate Bernie about what a class action was and how it might unfold, both legally and in the press.

They went to an Atlanta steakhouse called Bones, where the steak knives are about the size of machetes. Brown was waxing forth about strategy and he used the S word—settlement. He didn't exactly advocate settlement but suggested that it was definitely an option we should keep in our minds because this could get very expensive and very public.

Bernie picked up his knife and pointed it at Brown's throat.

"Never say that word again," Bernie said.

Everyone laughed, but his point was clear: He was adamant that we were going to have our day in court. There would be no settlement, no inadvertent admission of wrongdoing. As founders of the company, still intimately involved in running The Home Depot, we took this battle very personally.

In January 1996, Federal District Court Judge Susan Illston certified the plaintiffs' class, including possibly as many as 200,000 female applicants, even though not one had complained. We went into an intense discovery phase. Video depositions began—200 in all—producing enough documents to fill entire rooms. It was a mammoth litigation.

Bernie and I—as well as the entire board of directors and senior management of the company—were sickened by the eventual settlement, both in terms of the dollar figure we gave out and the concession it implied. But even I must concede now that it was absolutely the right decision. Because we concluded two key things were against us: the judge and the jury.

Susan Illston was not the first judge on the case. The first judge was Federal District Court Judge Vaughn Walker. In the precertification phase, we were encouraged by the way he kept a very strict rein on the plaintiffs. However, one week before we were due to argue against the motion for class certification, he handed the case off to a new appointment to the bench, Illston, who had made her career in plaintiffs' securities class actions. She had actually been co-counsel with the other firm representing plaintiffs in this case, Lieff, Cabraser, Heiman & Bernstein, LLP, of San Francisco. On the basis of this knowledge, we moved that the judge should recuse herself—a formal request that she step down because of the possibility or appearance of bias. She denied our motion, and of course it didn't endear us to her. Illston is a very bright woman, a very ambitious woman, but pro-plaintiff in terms of class actions. However, she did give us plenty of opportunity to argue that the class action vehicle was inappropriate. And whenever our team argued issues before her, they always felt she listened to them and often seemed to be sort of nodding her assent. But then she would issue an order that was completely against us. As the process intensified, she ruled in the plaintiffs' favor on virtually all of our pretrial motions.

Then, two weeks before trial, she not only ordered the parties to mediate but she also imposed a limit of 80 hours per side to present the case to the jury.

When you consider that the potential class was maybe 250,000 females, the idea that we would be able to defend against these broad-ranging allegations involving a class that big in only 80 hours of trial time was devastating to us. The plaintiffs would be able to broad-brush their allegations by putting on a few sympathetic witnesses. What made it worse was another of Judge Illston's pretrial rulings: Sex harassment evidence would be admissible even though the case was not about sex harassment.

Naturally, 250,000 women have not been harassed at The Home Depot. But there have been, over the years, one or two cases that are pretty ugly and would shock a jury. And we had no doubt they were going to hear those stories and we would not have adequate time in 80 hours to fight the primary gender discrimination issue *and* put sex harassment allegations in the context of growing workplaces where thousands and thousands of women make successful, lucrative careers.

So the judge was one reason that we settled. The other reason was the jury pool.

Dr. Reiko Hasuike, the DecisionQuest jury consultant we used, said we had probably had a 50-50 chance of winning before a jury. Fifty-fifty is a helluva big risk.

That is why—against our steadfast personal beliefs that we had done nothing wrong—we accelerated the settlement discussions.

We knew it was bound to be a fairly lengthy trial—even given Judge Illston's time constraints—with fairly complicated statistical evidence. We were very afraid that the so-called anecdotal witnesses that the plaintiffs would put up would talk about an isolated incident of sex harassment and would sway the jury into believing there was a "pattern and practice" of sexual discrimination at The Home Depot.

Back in Atlanta, Larry Smith, senior vice president of legal, along with John Wymer of the Atlanta law firm of Powell, Goldstein, Frazer, and Murphy, attempted to mediate a settlement. When Smith and the plaintiffs' attorneys came to a preliminary agreement, they had to sell it to our board of directors. This was a real struggle for us to come to terms with emotionally. We had conference calls until one in the morning and the decision was not a slam dunk. In the end, however, the board was unanimous.

When we announced the settlement, two days before the trial date, it shocked and disappointed everyone from our trial team on the West Coast to many of our women managers who felt insulted by the suit. In the course of the litigation, Judge Illston had ordered that we could not talk to our own nonmanagement female employees about the case. So we used our women managers as scouts for good stories, witnesses, and testimony that would make our case. It was a very emotional process for our female managers. They felt as if they had been betrayed because they had been ready, under oath, to tell the jury that they had more opportunities at The Home Depot than they had ever had before.

But even a fool doesn't want to stick his head in a lion's mouth. So we were worried. Settling was very emotional for us because when you settle something, it indicates some wrongdoing, and we didn't feel that we did anything wrong.

We also settled because we could reach a settlement with injunctive relief that would lead to employment and advancement programs we actively wanted to do anyway. We might not otherwise have enacted them as fast, but the terms we agreed to in the consent decree made sense to us. So much sense that we implemented them nationwide, not just on the West Coast where the class action began. That really indicates that we think those things will enhance our culture going forward.

The programs we put into place will not only provide us a defense against a future class action, but they make us a stronger company for the future. We must maximize the potential of all our associates in order to staff the stores we're going to open in the next few years.

Today, all associates who want to get ahead take advantage of our product knowledge classes. They are encouraged to sign up for training to move along. Some of them really want to go back and run the lumber department, and they will one day, but they need to educate themselves on the products and how they are used.

Our fast growth means increased opportunities for well-trained, ambitious associates. We're in the training business: We offer our associates a progression of training at the divisional level that includes everything from the core fundamentals to mastering a department such as paint or lighting. There are "colleges" for learning flooring, kitchen, and bath, millwork, and even our computerized cash registers.

Our Atlanta Training Center teaches new and existing store managers and district managers how and why our culture, philosophy, and leadership approach works.

You are always going to run across someone who has a personal bias. You can't completely weed that out of any business. But our associates know how the company stands on these issues. It has been well communicated. Will the lawsuit-related employment reforms have a long-lasting effect? Yes. Out of every bad thing there can be something good, and what will happen here is that we will have a more inclusive Home Depot. It won't be an easier Home Depot, but it will be a fairer one. We can't afford to exclude anyone—there's no other practical option to fuel our need for people than to consider every warm body that applies for work with us. It's not just a corporate platitude; it's a practical business reality.

Naturally, we weren't happy about the money. We were very *unhappy* about the money. Nobody budgets $100 million for settling lawsuits.

Companies today need to be aggressive and proactive in creating an all-inclusive environment because discrimination does exist. It should really be done for two reasons. One, because it is the right thing to do, and that is what our best instincts in society demand, and two, a growing company needs an all-hands-on-deck environment.

We rolled out a new computerized application process that includes retention, central monitoring, and feedback. There are classes for everybody covering EEOC issues and guidelines. We also introduced new human resources systems to deal with all of this.

■   ■   ■

The Home Depot grew from start-up to public company to the Fortune 500 faster than almost any other organization ever. But in the early days, we were much wilder and more carefree than we could ever get away with today. Almost anything went back then.

There are hundreds of stories of outrageous behavior from our early days, stunts, pranks, and parties that slipped into corporate lore as The Home Depot grew into adulthood. While few, if any, of the things you are about to read would be tolerated today—thanks to wiser heads (ours) and insurance restrictions—there is no denying they are pieces of our history.

■   ■   ■

We weren't generally a party to such things, but on the weekends it wasn't unusual for our associates to throw some pretty wild beer parties once the last customer went home and the doors were closed. Music would be cranked up on the PA system, six-packs of beer and stacks of hot pizza would appear, and then—it was back to work.

While this would never be tolerated today—for one thing, we are alcohol-free at all stores, as well as at all official company functions—it was the norm then. Maybe it was a tradition handed down from Pat

Farrah's Homeco days, when he was just a chain-link fence away from beer at all times.

There was so much work to do almost around the clock that certain allowances were made. Our young associates in particular gave over so much of their free time and sacrificed so much that allowing them a little time to cut loose even as they worked didn't seem like such a big deal. Most of them couldn't tell you what songs, movies, or TV shows were popular from 1979 to '81 because they just didn't have the time to spare. If they hear an "oldie" on the radio today that they don't recognize, they usually guess it was a hit during that time period.

We were very lucky. The attitude, again, was whatever it takes.

Beer, hardware, and the opposite sex—what could a young person find in the outside world that he or she couldn't enjoy at The Home Depot?

We were a small company and a tight-knit unit. Parties were often the celebration of another week's survival and preparation for the next week at war. All night long, the music was cranked up, the energy was high, and a lot of work got done real quick. Surprisingly safely so. We didn't have a loss-prevention department then, and it is a miracle that we all survived some stunts.

They would work all night if that is what it took to get something done. They all worked all night and got it done, and the only thing on their minds when the sun came up was not going home but, when the customers come in, what will their reaction be?

When our first major sales record was set—a $100,000 week at the Marietta store—Pat Farrah and Cecil Wilson brought in a big galvanized Kelly washtub and filled it with beer and champagne to celebrate with the store's employees. They wanted everybody to feel good about going the extra mile at The Home Depot.

■　　■　　■

First under Pat, and later under Bruce Berg, the merchants of this company partied like crazy with the vendors in the first decade of this company.

One day in Jacksonville, two merchants made a $20 bet on who could get to the airport first. At the very end, the two cars were side by side, racing down the road. There wasn't anybody else on the road, thank goodness. When one took the lead, the other tried to pass him. Failing that, he went off the road and cut across a field, making a beeline for the rental car company's sign. The second merchant, not wanting to lose, followed suit and finally won.

Another day—actually at two in the morning—this same gang of high school truants could be found playing golf on the tops of their parked cars outside their hotel. They were good golfers, too, and discovered they could hit the ball much better on the roof of a convertible than on a metal roof.

On another occasion, Berg took his merchants to Mexico for a meeting. Everyone but Berg—who drank only alcohol on the trip, never water, and never ate food—got terribly sick with dysentery. One guy came back on a gurney. By the time Berg returned to Atlanta, word of the merchants' misadventures preceded them. Bernie walked into Berg's office and said, "Don't you ever have a meeting in Mexico again. Ever. You are forbidden. That entire country is off limits to you."

A realization came over Berg that day that it was time to clean up his act, and that of the merchants working with him. The size of a typical deal was a million dollars. Then it was $2 million and then $5 million. It struck him that they couldn't act like idiots anymore on company time. There was too much at stake.

They still have fun, of course. The merchants who have been with the company for a long time can finish each other's sentences. They sometimes look at each other and burst out laughing, remembering the deals they've done, the things they've seen.

They tended to blend together, too. If Berg grew a goatee, so would five or six other merchants. Ditto for his familiar blue jeans and cowboy boots.

It was a practice begun under Pat's influence. If Pat bought something, then you knew the other buyers would come in with the same thing. It was ostrich cowboy boots first, then Rolex watches. Pat got a Rolex watch, so they all had to get Rolex watches. Then it was cars—

Beamers. Then it was boats, because Pat was into boats. It was funny to watch, as the wealth accumulated, what they were doing with it.

■　■　■

One of our early company-wide management meetings was held in Orlando at the Marriott World Center. It used to be a tradition at the start of every annual meeting that we would jointly issue a warning to the troops: "Do not do anything stupid in regard to alcohol. Don't overindulge. You must be responsible adults, or it is going to cost you."

We always had all sorts of meetings and activities planned for the operations and merchandising people, but there was a small group of corporate support staff who were left to their own devices. One night they all went out to dinner and wound up at a place where about twenty-five of our West Coast store and district managers were having dinner.

Kerrie Flanagan, who is now our vice president of merchandise accounting, ordered a Heineken.

The waitress came back and said, "I'm really sorry, but we are out of Heineken." So Flanagan ordered a Rolling Rock. Later on, she ordered a second Rolling Rock.

This time, the waitress came back embarrassed. "Sorry," she said, "we are out of Rolling Rock."

"You are out of Heineken, you are out of Rolling Rock. What is going on?" Flanagan asked.

"There is this group upstairs from The Home Depot," she said, not knowing our people were from the same company, "and they are just drinking the place dry. We are running out of everything."

Upstairs, our people were really rocking, ordering a staggering amount of beer for their table, and a couple of the store managers and district managers got into a bash–Home Depot rant. One of the worst had been a merchandising executive who had recently been demoted to district manager. He became verbally abusive and several store managers later complained about his behavior.

As a result of that, several people were demoted and one or two were fired.

This was not one of our shining moments.

When you go back to the origins of our company, we were like the Rough Riders of retail. This was a tough group of corporate oddballs and the drinking was heavy. But what worked then didn't fit our game plan later on.

By the early 1990s we saw the destructive nature of alcohol. We had a couple of Christmas parties where we were especially troubled by it. We realized that the hard-drinking example set by the senior officers of the company was encouraging the same behavior in our young associates. Suddenly it didn't seem as much fun or as romantic.

We discussed the situation and, as parents ourselves, agreed we no longer wanted to encourage this behavior or be seen as champions of recklessness. Someone was going to get hurt or killed.

The last straw was when a young man shoved Bernie out of the way during a short welcoming speech at a holiday party. He grabbed the microphone out of Bernie's hand and proceeded to make a fool of himself and insulted everybody at the party, including Bernie's wife. Sadly, it was all alcohol. The outburst had little or nothing to do with the young man; he was just drunk as hell.

Internally, going dry was considered one of the worst calamities that could ever strike the company. Imagine having a holiday party with no alcohol. But after some time passed, most people understood why we did it. It changed the nature of the company's internal image, from one of gunslingers to a quilt of families. And where associates had stopped bringing their families to company parties, now everyone comes.

We had to take responsibility. We have the lives of these young people in our hands, and we feel acutely sensitive to that. It's a fact that we used alcohol in our early days in order to get started and get things done, but that was just one phase in our lives. The next phase of our lives, the more important and farther-reaching one, was running a company that was ethical and family-oriented.

We want to attract families. We want people to feel comfortable. We aggressively hired older people in our stores, but they didn't like the recklessness they encountered. If you didn't go out drinking after hours, you were out of the group. You were ostracized. That's not what we wanted this company to be about.

And quite honestly, what kind of an image did we portray to the world? There were articles being written about The Home Depot everywhere. Did we really want to be described as a bunch of drunken sailors?

These incidents led to what has been a good policy for the company. We decided to never again have alcohol at company functions. The only time we serve alcohol is when there are more outsiders involved in the function than insiders. For example, we served beer and wine—no hard liquor—to vendors attending Home Depot–sponsored events at the 1996 Olympics in Atlanta.

7

The Customers

"Let's Take a Walk and We'll Find It Together"*

Years ago, I read *The Big Store: Inside the Crisis and Revolution at Sears,* Donald R. Katz's behind-the-scenes look at Sears, Roebuck. It had a big effect on me, and for a number of years, I insisted that every executive in our company read the book.

The Big Store told the story about how one particular chief executive of Sears, Ed Telling, hated to be in the stores. And that was apparently why he took the world's most revered retail company into virtually every other business under the sun, from insurance to real estate. Sears bought all these other businesses that diluted its abilities and energy, and management neglected its core business. I wanted our people to read that book so that they understood how important our core business is. Telling hated being in the stores, and that was where the bread and butter was coming from. That was what paid his salary. He never understood that.

In this company, we do understand that. That is why we insist that every executive of this company works in the stores upon joining us. This policy even applies to our attorneys.

When we hired Larry Smith as our first in-house attorney, we said, "Before you assume your regular duties with us, you will be in the stores for two months."

* Bernie Marcus

132

He didn't believe it. "Are you crazy?" he said. "I am a lawyer."

"Well, if you are going to be handling lawsuits, you are going to have to understand the problems of people in the stores," we told him. "And to do that, you have to work in the stores. So that when you hear a problem, you can relate to it." He did, and ever since, Smith has insisted that all of his new attorneys and paralegals also work in the stores.

Everything in our business is about relating. Our lifeblood is the associates in the stores. They are the people who work by the hour for wages. The cashier that just started can destroy our company. The lot engineer who loads the cars is the last person who has contact with the customer. If that person offends the customer in any way, shape, or form, he or she can destroy our business. We are painfully aware of how integral each of these people is to our survival.

But at Sears, they sat up above it all in that ridiculous tower of theirs in Chicago and never went down the elevator except to eat lunch or go home. They never had a clue as to what was going on in the stores because they never spent time in the stores.

Arthur and I go into stores alone and walk around, talking to customers and associates on the sales floor, learning what's really important to The Home Depot. I love being there, because that's where the real action is, not in my office.

■　■　■

When we opened our first stores, we had so few customers that if I saw someone leaving a store empty-handed, I took it personally.

"What is it that we don't carry that you need? Why didn't you buy something?" I'd say, doggedly pursuing them to the parking lot.

"I didn't find what I came in for," was usually the answer.

"What is it that you need?" I asked. And whatever the answer, I would say the same thing: "Oh my gosh, I'm so sorry you didn't find it. We carry it, we just happened to be out. If you give me your name and address, I will deliver it to you."

That's how I often expanded our merchandise selection. First I would run back inside and order it so we'd have it in the future. Then I would personally go buy whatever it was at West Building Supplies, Handy City, or a wholesale house and personally deliver it to the customer's home, carefully removing the other store's price sticker and charging the customer a lower price than I paid out of pocket.

When we were struggling to survive, we would do whatever it took to satisfy customers. As we became more successful, that became our customer service philosophy: "Whatever it takes." There was nothing we wouldn't do for a customer.

The customer has a bill of rights in our company. These six items are, we believe, the only things a customer wants to pay for at The Home Depot:

1. The right assortment.
2. The right quantities.
3. The right price.
4. Associates on the sales floor who want to take care of customers.
5. Associates who have been trained properly in terms of product knowledge.
6. The expectation that our associates will be there when the customers need them.

Together, those six things represent excellent customer service. If you take care of those things together, you are taking care of all that a customer needs. We don't believe that, given a choice, home improvement customers are going to pay for wider aisles and brighter lights. That's *not* what they come to our stores for.

In many retail stores, the people who work there view customers as a pain in the rear end. Customers bother you. They stop you from doing your chores. They stop you from getting things done that you want to get done. They are in your way. That is not the case at The Home Depot.

We would say to our associates, "If your brother or sister came into your store, how would you treat them?" And then we would say to them, "Your brother and sister *have* to shop here. Other people don't. You have to treat other customers, strangers, better than you do your brother or your sister," and we instilled this into our people.

If I ever saw an associate point a customer toward what he or she needed three aisles over, I would threaten to bite that associate's finger. I would say, "Don't you ever let me see you point. You take the customer by the hand, and you bring them right where they need to be and you help them." This became another part of The Home Depot's way of cultivating the customer.

You won't even see aisle numbers in our stores. There is not a retailer on the face of the globe with 100,000-square-foot stores other than The Home Depot without some aisle numbers. Why? Well, if we had aisle numbers, when a customer asks, "Do you know where I can find this widget?" it would be very easy for our associates to point and say, "Aisle eight." If there are no aisle numbers, the employee has to say, "Let's take a walk and we'll find it together."

■   ■   ■

Our philosophy of customer service is "Whatever it takes." That means we'll do whatever it takes to satisfy a customer within all human reason. It's taking ownership of customer problem resolutions, even if it means going far out of our way to do it.

But we also believe in doing more than customer service. We call it customer cultivation.

What is the difference?

Customer service is asking "What are you looking for today?" then getting it off the shelf, explaining its use, and sending the customer home.

Customer cultivation is just like cultivating a tomato plant. Prepare the soil, maybe put some additives in it. Plant the seed. Water it. Prune it. Fertilize it. Apply insecticides. It will always grow bigger if you cultivate it. If you cultivate it, it will bear more fruit.

Customer cultivation is giving the same attention to somebody building a rabbit hutch as someone remodeling a kitchen. The rabbit-hutch builder might come in with a drawing scrawled on a piece of paper and a simple plan to buy a few 2×4s and a roll of screening. But with our expert knowledge, we might say, "Well, instead of using white pine, I would recommend pressure-treated lumber. You can use it outside. It won't rot. It will last longer."

"Oh," the customer will say, "I didn't know there was such a thing."

"Next, I would recommend using hardware cloth. It is galvanized, so rabbit feet won't go down through it. And let me show you how to put a door on that hutch, how to hang hinges."

What the customer will go home with are different products that he or she probably wasn't aware of, and how-to knowledge of how to assemble them a little bit smarter. The project will come together easier and we hope the end product will be better. When the project is done, our ten minutes of guidance probably increased the customer's self-confidence.

Along the way, we might also sell the customer a new handsaw or drill to complement the hammer, screwdriver, and pair of pliers in the kitchen drawer.

In our experience, we will typically see that same customer a month or so later with a little bit bigger project. This time, it might be a wood patio deck. The tasks will be more complicated, involving a power saw, goggles, and a new level of knowledge. Then the customer will go home, build it—calling us with questions along the way—and be proud enough to invite the neighbors over for a barbecue and some beers. "Hey, look what I built!"

One of our core values is building strong relationships. Well, when you have something that's moving as quickly as our company is, you come to think of it as a chain. In order for a chain to stay together and be cohesive—when it is under as much pressure as it is, being pulled in so many directions—you need to have linkage that is very, very tight. That's why it's important that we don't just develop an intellectual relationship with our customers and associates. There also needs to be a tight, *emotional* bond. At the end of the day, we're in the people business. And people need bonds with each other.

Customer cultivation helped us grow from two stores to four stores. Customers whose previous handiwork was limited to hanging pictures began taking on increasingly more complex projects, like redoing their own bathroom. In our How-To Clinics, begun in 1982, The Home Depot has taught entire generations of do-it-yourselfers. These free clinics, promoted in our ads and in-store, give customers the opportunity to watch projects ranging from installing ceiling fans to laying floor tiles come together step-by-step as demonstrated by our associates or a manufacturer's representative.

■   ■   ■

We serve a very diverse customer base. It ranges from professional repair and remodeling contractors to complete neophytes. Then there are the serious do-it-yourselfers we call the weekend warriors: Every weekend, they have a different project, and they are driven to complete it and start another. They are the men and women who are always buying the latest tools. It is their hobby. They build fences on weekends. They redo decks. They remodel kitchens.

Next we have part-time repair and remodeling contractors. They are firefighters and pilots who have professional businesses on the side. They might work for municipal organizations where they are on so many consecutive days and off so many days, or be in cities that encourage four-day workweeks, or they simply need outside income to support their regular jobs.

We sell to a whole host of professionals, too.

■   ■   ■

Ten or twenty years ago, when most people wanted to redo a bathroom, they would call a contractor. The client would give instructions about color, style, and perhaps name brands, then the contractor would pick up the plumbing and flooring items, sinks, tubs, medicine cabinets, and light bars at different places. Once The Home Depot opened, all this stuff was in one place, accessible to any homeowner.

But what the homeowner didn't have was the knowledge to put it all together.

Because we hired an army of trained plumbers, electricians, and other craftspeople as associates, organizing the How-To Clinics was a natural development for the stores. Our people were already instructing weekend warriors in an informal way. Putting on How-To Clinics became a way of formalizing the teaching and making it available to all of our customers and further cultivating their interest in do-it-yourself home improvement. Each store identified associates who were subject experts in their field. They wore a special apron that said "Pro" on it. We wrote flyers in Magic Marker promoting the clinics and printed 500 copies, posting them around the store or having the cashiers stuff them in bags. We also did loudspeaker announcements all day long. Clinics—typically held on the weekends—took place on the sales floor. Classes might be in flooring or ceiling fan installation or how to stain unfinished furniture.

In time, the How-To Clinics became more sophisticated. In addition to planning them months in advance and advertising them in catalogs and newspaper ads, we also built grandstand areas in many stores to accommodate all the people who attend and make sure everyone can see the demonstrations.

We saw people who were all thumbs before they came into The Home Depot go on to do room additions or build their own homes. That's a big part of how we created demand that never before existed.

Cost is another important factor, of course. We gave customers the knowledge to do it themselves at the right price. Today, you could install a Mills Pride kitchen yourself for $3,000 that would have cost you $25,000 and the services of a pro twenty years ago.

■　　■　　■

A few years ago, a woman called us, upset about the kitchen cabinets she ordered from one of our stores. Based on the department head telling her that the new cabinets would be in in two to three weeks, she had her contractor pull the old cabinets out and temporarily relocate the refrigerator and other appliances at the end of that time. Unfortunately, when the new cabinets arrived, they were not what she ordered, leaving her and her family kitchenless for weeks.

The department head was not sympathetic. "I'll have to reorder them, and it will take another few weeks for them to come in," he said.

"What am I supposed to do in the meantime?" she asked, furious.

"That's not my problem," he answered.

That's when she called us, explaining the situation and our department head's less than satisfactory response. "I have children to feed," she said. "What am I supposed to do?"

It was such an insensitivity on our part. First of all, you shouldn't make a promise that you can't deliver, and second, if you don't deliver on a promise that you made, you have to make good on it, because you will not be permitted to bring pain and suffering to our customers.

The reason we have our business is because customers trust us. They know they can depend on us, and when we disappoint them, we are disappointing everybody. We expect at least a hundred people will hear that woman's negative story, directly or indirectly, and we don't want people to think that that is the way we behave. It is not.

First of all, I called the store manager back.

"Yeah, she called me, too," he said. "Isn't she a pain in the ass?"

"Stay right there," I said. "I'm coming over to the store. Let's talk about this in person."

In truth what happened was a combination of the customer's fault and ours, but it was all our fault as far as I was concerned. The manager, because of his behavior, was fired. From that point until the kitchen cabinets were delivered and installed, we fed them. Every meal that they ate out was on us. That was our obligation.

"Let's turn the tables," I later told people in the store. "What if that had happened to you? How would you feel about it? What would you expect?"

■　　■　　■

We have a return policy that says you can bring a product back for any reason. No gimmicks, no tricks.

We want people to trust us. We encourage customers—weekend warriors and pros alike—to buy more than they need, and whatever they don't use, to bring back. We give them their money back, no questions asked, no hassles. We do it because it encourages people to do projects.

A woman went into one of our stores. We later found out that she owned a 200-unit resort. During her first visit to The Home Depot, she came in to buy a chandelier for her own home. She described for our salesperson what she wanted. He gave it to her, she took it home, and an electrician installed it.

But when she turned it on, she said, "Gee, that isn't going to put enough light in here."

"You're right," the electrician said. "It's too small."

The woman was embarrassed. The chandelier was exactly what she asked for. So she went back to The Home Depot and said to the lighting salesperson, "I need a bigger chandelier."

So he sold her a bigger one. "What did you do with the other one?" he asked conversationally.

"Oh, I have it at home. The electrician installed it, but it's too small."

"Well," said the salesperson, "bring it back."

"I don't know how to take it down without being electrocuted," she said.

"Tell me where you live," the salesperson told her. "On my way home, I will put the new one up for you, take the other one down, and we will give you an adjustment."

But that's not the end of the story.

About six months after this, she decided to remodel all 200 of her rental units. Every single thing she needed for those 200 units—toilets, sinks, bathtubs, carpeting, chandeliers, light fixtures—she bought from us. Why? Maybe it was the way we dealt with her $75 chandelier.

You know what the great thing about this story really is? That our salesperson had the sense to take action. He cultivated a relationship with this woman right from the beginning. You can't program that. That is either in people, or it is not. We encourage people to discover and exercise that part of their nature. This sales associate just wanted a happy customer, one inclined to come back again. He didn't know the end result would be an order for 200 toilets, sinks, etc. The right thing to do is instinctive; it lives in their hearts, not their heads.

■　■　■

Linda Khano, all of 18, was working our return desk when a woman brought in a product that she claimed was defective. Somehow, Khano decided the customer was lying through her teeth.

When she turned away from the woman to get approval for the return from a manager, an indignant Khano found me standing behind her.

"I can't believe this woman is doing this!" she said under her breath.

"If it were me," I said, "I would give her her money back."

Khano did just that, smiled and gave her the money. But as the woman walked away, Khano was fuming. I put an arm around her shoulders.

"I am going to teach you a lesson that you will remember for the rest of your life," I said. "Sometimes, in this business, you have to accept things that you believe are totally wrong."

"Excuse me?" Khano said.

"Sometimes, in this business, you have to do distasteful things," I repeated.

"Uh, okay."

"Just think about it, Linda," I continued. "This woman, she brought this thing back even though it is not defective. Don't worry about it. Even if we have to eat the cost of it or throw it away, it is no big deal, because from now on, she will have the confidence to come and buy here, and even if she goes home and tells everybody that we are stupid, that's okay, too, because now everybody is going to come shop here and take advantage of us."

The key to our no-holds-barred return policy is that people talk about it. It gets them hooked; they know they can never make a bad purchase at The Home Depot, because we don't ever want to give them a reason not to come back. There are probably some dishonest people that will take advantage of us. But they are a tiny minority. We are not going to punish the honest folks who need to trust us.

Khano's first reaction to this customer was based upon on how she thought things should be, based on what she learned before she joined The Home Depot. We had to unteach those things so she could apply Home Depot's core customer service values of going the extra mile, doing whatever it takes to build loyalty.

■   ■   ■

At The Home Depot, customer service isn't just a concept; it's actually a guy named Ben.

Ben Hill.

When we started out, we were far from perfect. We heard our share of complaints. We had a few associates who didn't get our concept of customer cultivation and service, and every so often one of them would create a huge headache for us. When customers didn't get the service they expected, or we didn't carry the product they would like to see us carry, it became apparent we needed a director of consumer affairs.

We came up with a name, a code name, so that when customers called our toll-free 800 telephone number, they knew that they were going to get the right person to help them. We didn't want to make it some sort of a name that would be intimidating, we wanted it to be somebody who sounded like he could be one of our customers—and "Jimmy Carter" was already taken.

There is a town near our Store Support Center called Ben Hill. It's on a sign between our offices and the airport in Atlanta. Ben Hill sounded like a good old southern guy you could talk to and get your problem solved. So we hired him.

Pat Farrah posed as Ben for a picture, from which artist Gwyn Raker drew a silhouetted profile that we put on big, freestanding sandwich boards at the front of every store. On it, Ben Hill asks, "Are you satisfied? If not, contact the store manager, _____, or call me, Ben Hill, director of consumer affairs, at 800-553-3199."

The number went into our main office switchboard in Atlanta. Whenever somebody called it and asked to speak to Ben Hill, we didn't ask, "What is it regarding?" The name "Ben Hill" was code red for "Expedite the call *right now.*" The call would be directed to Arthur, Pat, me, or whoever was the highest-ranking person in the company available at the time of the call.

It didn't matter if we were signing a million-dollar deal; we stopped and took the call. We wanted our customers to get to the right people and get their problems resolved.

Word got around very quickly that you don't let a customer leave a Home Depot store unhappy, because if that customer called Ben Hill, the next phone call would be from one of us to the store.

"I just got a call from a customer on the Ben Hill line, and we're in trouble," we'd say. "I would like you to run to one of our other stores, get the product the customer needs, drive it over to the customer's house, and apologize."

It worked incredibly well, both putting our associates on notice and giving customers an ombudsman. Today, Ben Hill is a nationwide concept, handled by a whole cadre of people on a regional basis. And it is still Pat's picture.

In our training classes, we will always ask, "Who was the original Ben Hill?" Once that is answered, we will ask why we did it, why we didn't just hire someone whose specific job was to handle customer complaints. Here's the answer:

Let's say we put out the word that the two of us are going to clear our calendars for the next thirty days—no meetings, no traveling, nothing, just sitting by the telephone, and we will take all the calls ourselves. What would happen to the Ben Hill calls?

They would go down. The stores would have zero customer complaints. Why? Because our associates and managers wouldn't want to deal with us directly over something that should and could have been settled in the stores.

So part of Ben Hill's purpose was to create a culture in which you will be personally responsible for the customers in your stores. Every time a customer calls Ben Hill, it reflects a failure in the store. But the managers and associates in that store have all the power and all the responsibility in the world to fix any problem that any customer has.

Your goal, we tell our training classes, should be zero Ben Hill calls from your store. We measure Ben Hill calls very closely. Store and district managers get reports on a monthly basis that detail how many calls came in because of their stores. There is "average," "above the line," and "below the line." A store does not want to be above the line. On the other hand, many divisions give awards to stores with the fewest Ben Hill calls as a recognition of that store's outstanding customer service.

An associate of The Home Depot really is responsible. Within reason, we will always give customers what they want under any circumstances. We will always make the customer happy. So they might as well do it in the store and take credit for it.

That reminds me of a story about our executive vice president of operations and group president, Larry Mercer, that became legendary within the company:

One day, a man came into one of our Atlanta stores with a set of automobile tires, demanding a refund. The Home Depot doesn't *sell* tires—never did, even when we sold some other automotive supplies—so the person running the service desk called Mercer for help.

"Sir," Mercer said, "if you bought them here, what did you pay for them?"

The man named a figure. Mercer reached into the cash register and handed the man the exact amount without another word.

Then Mercer hung the tires over the service desk to remind everybody: "The customer is always right."

8

Building the Brand

"Low Prices Are Just the Beginning"*

In the mid-1990s, a transformation of The Home Depot took place. We were no longer a big regional company but the first truly national powerhouse in our category. And lots of things changed.

Once we had critical mass and established a national presence, we could afford to do many things we couldn't as a regional player. Our new status made national television and magazine advertising a cost-effective idea for the first time. The efficiencies over regional ad placement were incredible.

The national branding of The Home Depot name as a ubiquitous reference point for home improvement stores is a recent and unexpected phenomenon. It was Dick Hammill, our senior vice president of marketing and communications, who was the champion of building "The Home Depot" name as a unique brand. He did it in part by helping us move into nontraditional arenas such as Olympic and NASCAR sponsorships, book publishing, TV shows, and advertising in women's magazines. We've created top-of-mind awareness for our entire category. People think of us the way they do Coke for soft drinks and Kleenex for facial tissues.

In just one thirty-day period in 1998, for example, The Home

* Arthur Blank

Depot was mentioned prominently on *The Tonight Show with Jay Leno*, ABC's *World News Tonight*, the *NBC Nightly News*, *Oprah* (everybody in her studio audience wore an orange Home Depot nail apron for one show), *Sally Jesse Raphael*, and ESPN.

After everything we've been through, silly stuff like that gives us all goose bumps. We can't get enough of it.

One of comedian David Letterman's Top Ten lists on *The Late Show* mentioned The Home Depot. The "Top Ten Handyman Pick-up Lines" started with Tim Allen, star of the long-running *Home Improvement* sitcom. "Number ten," Allen said. "Come to Home Depot often?"

An episode of the NBC sitcom *Jesse* revolved around a plot to sell lawn gnomes to The Home Depot. Our company was mentioned four times! (Okay, three times; the fourth reference was to "Gnome" Depot.) Even when companies buy placements, they don't get it that good. In fact, one of our big competitors, Sears, paid cash to advertise on the same show.

During an appearance on *The Tonight Show*, Ted Danson told Jay Leno he was engaged to be married and had bought a new home.

"I called your office and asked where you [were] registered," Leno said. "I wanted to get a nice present. They said you were at a . . ."

"Home Depot," Danson said.

"At Home Depot," Leno repeated. "Because you are redoing a house?"

"Yes. We were looking for toilets. We have a lot of bathrooms. Toilets, tubs."

"Really!" Leno said "I have a lovely gift for you. Can we bring it out? I went to Home Depot. . . ."

A stagehand rolled out a toilet.

"Sit down," Leno suggested. "See how you like it."

These are not sought-after mentions. They are naturally occurring, incidental branding opportunities because all kinds of people shop our stores and have an emotional connection to The Home Depot.

Our understanding of branding has evolved as The Home Depot matured. In the beginning all we were trying to do was get our name out there, including giving out one-dollar bills in 1979 just to get people in the front door. Back then, the first components of branding—not that we even used the term—were big stores, lots of stuff, low prices. That was the brand's catch points; back then it was novel. Over the years, we became more sophisticated about customer service and that was an attention-getter.

We may not have been consciously doing it, but we were building a brand nonetheless.

■　　■　　■

Frustrated with a California-based ad agency that had difficulty relating to Georgia folks and produced few results, we hired Mel Finkel's Atlanta-based ad agency, Finkel & Associates, in 1980 to handle our media buys and produce radio and TV commercials for us when we opened the first stores. Finkel is a good ol' southern advertising guy, and he understood the customer a lot better than we did in those days. He said, "You ought to have Ludlow Porch do some commercials."

We were already fans of Porch, a much-beloved Atlanta radio personality and homespun humorist, and we were excited by the prospect of him delivering our message.

"All right," Bernie told Finkel, "let's try him. Why don't I meet him at the store and explain what we are doing here."

"That is probably not a good idea," Pat Farrah said, interrupting.

"What do you mean?"

"For the last six weeks we have been telling everybody else we've tried out what The Home Depot is all about and they have not done a very good job with it," Pat said. "Why don't we just let Ludlow do it by himself? And if you promise you won't interfere with him, I promise I won't either."

Of course, neither one of them felt like he could trust the other one to steer clear. I found the whole standoff between my partners quite funny.

Two days later, Finkel invited us over to hear the first Ludlow Porch–Home Depot radio commercials.

"Listen to this," Finkel said, turning on a tape recorder.

"Folks, I have just been down to a new place on Highway 41, The Home Depot. I walked around there, and they had this and that. . . . I tell ya, if these stores were any bigger, we'd be paying Alabama sales tax. Better bring a sandwich, too, 'cause you're going to be walking around awhile."

We loved every second of it. It was one of the greatest commercials we had ever, ever heard. Finkel was right; nobody could sell The Home Depot like Ludlow Porch did.

"How much does he want for those commercials?" Bernie asked.

"One-fifty," Finkel said.

"A hundred and fifty thousand?!" Bernie was aghast. "No way! They aren't that good!"

"No, Bernie," Finkel said, "a hundred and fifty dollars."

To which Rick Mayo, who was also there, said, "Well then, they can't be any good."

Pat laughed.

"Hey, guys," he said, "what is the price that makes them good?"

Finkel, who had worked with Porch many times before, merely advised the talented young man to "Ludlow this up." Make it funny, make it southern, attract attention to it. Porch never talked to any store managers, and we never knew what he was going to say next; Porch had carte blanche. If we had a sale or grand opening or something, we would tell him about it in advance, but otherwise, we gave him his head. His voice became synonymous with The Home Depot.

His amusing observations and lighthearted commentaries caught the public's imagination. His descriptions were just colorful enough that if folks were driving by one of our stores, they couldn't help but stop and see what ol' Ludlow was talking about. He was known for his integrity and never said anything about us that wasn't true.

One of his most remembered lines about The Home Depot was when he said, "This place is so big that it has its own Rotary Club!"

■　■　■

WSB was then—and still is—the most widely listened to radio station in Atlanta. They were experimenting with talk radio phone-in shows and offered us air time to do a morning show on home improvement.

So for 30 minutes every Wednesday at nine A.M., Pat Farrah became Atlanta's other voice of The Home Depot, answering questions about the right and wrong way of hanging doors, painting outside walls, or pouring a foundation. It was a natural format for Pat the storyteller. And, of course, he could mention The Home Depot as often as seemed appropriate.

Later, as the show grew in popularity, Pat added a second show on Friday nights offering more of the same. When we opened the first group of stores in Florida, he called in the show for nearly two years before it just got to be too much with the other demands of his schedule.

■　　　■　　　■

In 1981, graphic artist Gwyn Raker—who was one of our creative managers—created the little cartoon character who evolved into our mascot, Homer. Homer brought life and wit to our ads as time wore on, giving us an identity apart from the competition.

In early ads, Homer wore a hat, plaid shirt, and jeans. He was Joe Customer, a do-it-yourselfer working in his backyard and hanging wallpaper. Over the years, Homer started wearing a Home Depot hat and apron, and since he's more recognized as our company spokesman than either of us, he must be on the payroll by now.

Homer adds a personality signature to The Home Depot the same way Mickey Mouse adds to Walt Disney. He is lovable and huggable, and he was all Gwyn's baby.

Every division has a full-size, big-headed Homer costume for grand openings and in-store appearances. The original costumes were designed by the same company that does outfits for characters at the Disney theme parks. We even did a hot-air balloon once where Homer was leaning on cans of Glidden paint.

One of Homer's less stellar moments was the time we used him to promote Closet Maid ventilated shelving in a newspaper ad. For some reason, Raker put his creation in a dress. It was obviously Homer: he had a dress on, but you could see his hairy legs, his black socks and sneakers. The whole page was full of ventilated shelving and accessories. No big deal, right? Except the headline on the page was "Closet Cases."

But wait. It gets worse.

In those days, Raker did all the cartooning and lettering of prices in our newspaper ads and catalogs. And even with all that work, he still found time for a little *Mad* magazine–inspired mischief, scribbling little notes in the corners of his cartoons. Well, in the same shelving ad, he drew a Rubbermaid trash can with the lid lifted, and Homer peeking out. A fellow artist of Raker's in the art department mentioned a guy he went to high school with who was nicknamed Frank the B., because his last name was so long. The other artist scribbled "Frank the B!" on the trash can and told him to look for his name in the newspaper.

Raker never thought any more about it. Six weeks later, Raker's boss called him in. "Gwyn, do you know anything about this?"

He showed him a letter from a gay activist in Tucson who was furious with The Home Depot.

"Who put 'Frank the Bi' on the trash can?" Raker's boss asked.

The ink had run, making the exclamation point on "Frank the B!" into "Frank the Bi." The headline "Closet Cases," plus "Frank the Bi," next to Homer in the dress, was just too much for the man in Tucson to accept as coincidence. But it was.

■   ■   ■

When we expanded outside of Atlanta, we looked for a spokesperson whose appeal would extend beyond the South. Oddly enough, we found that person at Handy Dan.

Al Carrell, the "Superhandyman," became spokesman for Handy Dan after we left the company. He brought a growing cachet of national recognition thanks to his nationally syndicated King Features newspaper column, as well as daily radio features on the NBC News and Information Service Network. WGST in Atlanta carried his radio commentaries, so Carrell was already a recognizable quantity to us.

Mel Finkel asked Carrell to become our spokesman. Unfortunately, he had never heard of us and turned us down. Besides, he was already representing Handy Dan from Texas to California and was working out a deal to become spokesman for our other nemesis, Handy City, on the East Coast.

A few days later, Carrell's phone rang again. This time, it was Bernie on the phone. Still Carrell resisted. The following week, Bernie called back and put Pat on the line. Again, Carrell declined.

"Look," Bernie tried again, "I know you are coming to Atlanta for a home show. Let me at least pick you up at your hotel and take you over to one of the Home Depot stores. If you don't think it is the greatest thing in the business, I will never bother you again."

Hoping to get Bernie off his back, Carrell agreed. He was going to Atlanta to do live remote broadcasts from the Handy City booth, so it wasn't out of his way.

In the car on the way to The Home Depot, Bernie poured on the charm. He painted a picture of our stores that was so unbelievable that Carrell wondered what he had gotten himself into. But the store was every bit as big and overstocked as Bernie described it. And Carrell was also struck by how all the associates not only knew Bernie and called him by his first name, he knew all of them by name. Several times he saw Bernie get distracted by an associate, inquiring about this one's kids, or the operation that one's wife was about to undergo. Carrell was blown away.

That store visit changed his life.

Carrell said he would definitely like to work with The Home Depot. Bernie told him that his work for Handy Dan was not an immediate problem because the two were in different markets, but that he couldn't work for Handy City and The Home Depot. Besides, Bernie said, "Handy City isn't going to last very long against us."

For the next eight years, on radio and TV, Al Carrell, the "Superhandyman," was the sole spokesperson for The Home Depot. He became so closely identified with us that people still think he's with us. And that's okay by Carrell; his unexpected stock options made him a wealthy man. That happened when we were extending Carrell's contract and Bernie took him to dinner to discuss the future.

"I want to put you on our payroll for a small part of your remuneration," Bernie said, "because I want you to take advantage of our stock option plan, and you have to be an employee to do that."

Several people had given Carrell stock in the past, but it had never been worth anything. Still, he didn't want to hurt Bernie's feelings.

"Gosh, Bernie, that sure sounds great."

After his stock split the first time, Carrell began seeing the future in the same terms we did. He exercised every option that he ever received. So it was quite okay that Bernie did him that favor. As the years rolled on, Al Carrell made more on his stock options than he was ever paid by us for all his years of promotional work combined.

■   ■   ■

During our first few years, Home Depot sales rose and fell with publication of our biweekly catalog. Customers would wait to see what was on sale, knowing that the catalog was due every other week, bringing with it greatly discounted prices on selected items.

We went crazy offering ridiculously low prices to get attention in catalogs and corresponding newspaper ads—our merchants used to call sales our drug of choice.

Sales produced a flurry of activity in the stores. This was in the days before Universal Product Codes and computerized bar coding, when every item had to be manually priced and stickered. When products went on sale in our catalog, it meant bleary-eyed associates red-tagged the items the night before. And when the sale was over, if anything was left, they removed the red stickers and repriced items by hand. It was a labor-intensive process.

Every Home Depot sale catalog guaranteed a 25 to 30 percent jump in store sales. As the sale wore on, however, sales dribbled downward. Instead of seeing a steady stream of customers day-in and day-out, we'd start with a grand rush and end up with a trickle.

Everyday low pricing at The Home Depot was an idea that originated with Sol Price and the Price Club but was encouraged by Sam Walton. Wherever Walton traveled, he would visit a Home Depot store.

In fact, when we opened the first Home Depot stores in Atlanta in those old Treasure Island buildings, Walton and David Glass were among the first in the industry to check us out. They frequently traveled to Atlanta, which was a market in which Wal-Mart competed head-to-head against Treasure Island, Richway, and Kmart. So they saw The Home Depot stores develop from their inception.

Over the years, despite being competitors in several departments, we became good friends with Walton and Glass. (In 1993, Glass told *Fortune* magazine that The Home Depot runs "the best retail organization in America today.") We feel very comfortable picking up the phone and talking to them about general retail conditions, and they have always been very candid with us. We often walk each other's stores together, sharing ideas and taking notes. We are tough but friendly competitors on a very high level.

So it should not be too surprising that while visiting Wal-Mart's corporate headquarters in Bentonville, Arkansas, Walton and Glass convinced Bernie to try everyday low pricing at The Home Depot.

The main purpose of his visit, incidentally, was to learn more about Wal-Mart's employee stock ownership plan, also known as an ESOP. We had been thinking about an ESOP program for some time and Wal-Mart's was considered a model in the industry. Our theory had always been that if we were going to get rich, we wanted our associates to get rich with us. If we were going to benefit, they were going to benefit as well. That has always been a part of our philosophy. There were men and women busting their rear ends, killing themselves, working day and night for The Home Depot; if we made it, we wanted them to make it as well. From the day we opened the stores, that was a philosophy of the company.

But Walton, probably the greatest retailer that ever lived, had something else on his mind.

"Why do you continue to run sales?" he asked. "Don't you run out of merchandise?"

"Yeah," Bernie said, "we run out of merchandise all the time. In fact, we have to hold back stuff in the back room, because otherwise people buy all the merchandise before our sale catalogs hit."

"Manufacturers can't keep up with you, is that right?" Walton asked.

"That's right."

"Why don't you go to everyday low prices, like we have?"

Walton and Glass then explained what everyday low prices meant to them. They did a thorough selling job—how it works with manufacturers, how it helps the stores, the positive effect on systems and customers.

"If you take everyday low prices as a marketing philosophy," Glass said, "and you list the pros and the cons, you would never do anything other than everyday low prices. There are very convincing arguments for it. People who come out of a different background, though, who haven't really worked with everyday low prices or thought it through, resist it."

Walton loved The Home Depot and said, "You have to do it."

Most retailers can't do it, don't have the intestinal fortitude or the vision to execute and make it happen. We were not the first or last company to whom Walton and Glass recommended everyday low prices, but few could properly execute it.

When he returned to Atlanta, Bernie told me, "We are going with everyday low prices."

Following a great deal of internal discussion—this was, after all, a momentous decision—I embraced the idea as well. I liked the logic and reliability of it. The Price Club was the originator of everyday low prices; it was a concept we had discussed and dismissed in the past.

Across the rest of the organization it was a much tougher sell. The merchants were not easily convinced. They loved sales, they *lived* for sales.

We argued that sales were actually a weakness and that everyday low prices meant more consistent sales overall, making it easier to stay in stock, and that we would give away margin right off the bat. In other words, at whatever price we would previously have discounted an item, that's the price we should be selling it at all the time. Customers should be able to get the same good deal Monday through Sunday.

In retailing, some people need to find ways of creating artificial excitement. But who wants to go shopping for a deal every day? That is what people were doing with all these sales.

Larry Mercer compared the change in philosophy to going to church every Sunday, then deciding from now on you will go to church every day. Day-in, day-out pricing became our new religion.

In order to switch to everyday low pricing in 1987, we had to mark our merchandise down. And under the retail accounting method, when you lower your retail price, that is a charge to your P & L. So if we did that and the sales didn't increase and our advertising spending didn't decrease, then our earnings would decrease. It was a one-time charge, but with our high PE ratio, one bad quarter might cause the stock to plummet. So Ron Brill was concerned.

At the time, we were probably spending more than 3 percent of gross sales on advertising. So if we had $100 million in sales, we were spending $3.3 million on advertising. If something sold for $100, we might put it on sale for $75, which is 25 percent off. When you advertise one item, you're trying to sell it and others and get a good overall margin. But people only bought the sale item, so we didn't get a good mix. Everyday low prices forced us to lower prices across the board, but because of that we were able to sell more of everything. As customers became confident that our prices were always good, we saved on advertising and better controlled our margins.

At the time, we understood Wal-Mart's advertising to be about 1.5 percent of gross sales. Our accountants thought we would never achieve that kind of number, but today, our advertising is well below that level.

It made such good sense, but it took us more than a year to mechanically switch over and years emotionally. Some days it seemed as if everyone fought us.

Our sales associates were more than a little apprehensive about customer response when we made the switch. Even though sales events meant backbreaking work for them, the approach of a new catalog every 14 days created an adrenaline rush across the stores. Associates feared that because select merchandise would no longer be offered at dramatically lower prices the catalog would become ineffectual.

Home Depot merchants, the people who made deals for the products sold in our stores, had a major problem with day-in, day-out low pricing. It was tough for them to buy in, philosophically, that everyday low prices meant that we would always be competitive. It was more of an emotional hurdle for the merchants, because they felt like we were taking away a huge piece of competitive ammunition from the marketplace.

We struggled at first to convince both the associates and cus-tomers that all prices were reduced to what we would normally sell on sale for, and then we dropped the term "on sale" altogether.

The sales curve flattened out with the switch to everyday low pricing. Initially, it felt to everyone like we were giving away business because we didn't have that spike anymore. In fact, it raised sales across the board.

There were many more good things that came about as a result of the switch. When they knew what items were going on sale, store managers had guessed the quantity that would be sold, usually erring on the high side and stacking them to the ceiling. One of two things always happened. We either ran out before the end of the catalog, which happened a lot, or, when the ad was over, we still had stuff stacked to the sky. It was a huge guessing game. Woe unto our man-agers if they ran out of an item before the sale ended. They could find themselves writing several hundred rain checks on a single item. For the managers and their assistants, it was a huge pain. Because a rain check wasn't the end of it. They still had the labor ahead of calling the customers back when the next shipment arrived to pick it up. We sub-sequently saved all the related administrative costs of the rain checks, tagging, and tracking merchandise.

The switch led to an ingenious marketing slogan we have used ever since: "The Home Depot: Where Low Prices Are Just the Beginning."

To this day, of course, some people still don't get it. They pick up an item that might be in our catalog and ask, "Is this on sale?" Sure it is—every day.

■   ■   ■

Building the Home Depot brand name today occurs in ways we couldn't have dreamed of twenty years ago: our own line of million-selling *Home Improvement 1-2-3* books in print and on interactive CD-ROMs and DVDs; sports sponsorships such as NASCAR; home and garden shows; a popular project-oriented site on the World Wide Web; and an active involvement in local TV news, featuring Home Depot associates who appear in weekly "how-to" segments.

When we first opened, primarily men came to the stores to shop; now, there are women everywhere. We started out encouraging them with classes, which always filled up. Almost overnight, we got more sophisticated and so did they, taking on the same projects that only men did in the past. Today, more than 50 percent of our customers are women.

To further our appeal to women, The Home Depot began a relationship with TV personality and designer Lynette Jennings, with whom we developed a show on the Discovery Channel called *House-Smart*. In 1997 she became an official design consultant and spokesperson for The Home Depot, giving us an opportunity to broaden our exposure to women.

She is not yet at the Martha Stewart level, but we will help her get there because of the exposure she receives on our commercials. She is already reaching a level of recognition comparable to Bob Vila's when he became a spokesman for Sears and had been host of *This Old House* on PBS.

Even better for us, she has a substantial following and credibility among women. Jennings does clinics in our stores that attract hundreds of people, creating and cultivating a connection between our stores and women.

In South Florida, Home Depot stores offer a "Divorcée University"; the first class is in how to change your lock.

Other stores around the country have their own ways of reaching out to women, including "Ladies' Night Out" on Wednesdays and "Football Widow Night" every Monday. We also developed a national wedding registry for couples getting married.

One of our most successful outreach programs, however, has been the Kids' Workshops. In their first full year, 1998, more than 1 million kids participated by building birdhouses, tool kits, and other projects. A father wrote us and said that his daughter was a regular at the kids' clinic at their neighborhood Home Depot. One day they were out running errands and he pulled into a competitor's parking lot, intending to pick up a few things. His daughter absolutely refused to get out of the car.

"All of my friends are at Home Depot!" she pouted.

■ ■ ■

The 1996 Summer Olympic Games in Atlanta was our true coming-out party as a national brand name. For the first time, we proactively positioned ourselves as a part of the fabric of North America.

In 1992, we went downtown to see the folks who were selling corporate sponsorships for the '96 Olympic Games in Atlanta.

Everybody knew that another little Atlanta company named Coca-Cola had been an Olympics sponsor for decades. We had become leaders in the Atlanta community both on a personal basis and in terms of our company and felt the time was right to step up.

Atlanta is our hometown, and we have more associates here than in any other market. The Home Depot has been able to impact the Atlanta community substantially, like Coca-Cola, Delta, or CNN. Our success and the kind of positive attention it has brought to the Atlanta community certainly has added to the equation. And being a sponsor of the 1996 Summer Olympics in Atlanta marked an enormous milestone for our company.

We didn't have stores all across the United States until the mid-1990s, so we couldn't afford to do national until then. We did big things in each community where we had a store but never on a national scale. So our sponsorship of the Olympics made a major statement that The Home Depot had arrived on the national scene.

It was our debutante ball. We spent millions of dollars on NBC television and brought thousands of associates, from Arizona to New Hampshire, to Atlanta to participate. When you become an Olympics sponsor, you are given the right to purchase a set number of packages including event tickets and accommodations for two. We had an option for 2,000 packages. Half went to our vendor-partners. The other half went to our associates. In fact, we were the only sponsor who devoted such a high percentage of our hospitality packages to our associates.

The associates we invited were being recognized and congratulated for outstanding customer service. In some cases, they were people who had never left home before, never been on a plane, taking the trip of a lifetime at company expense. And the vast majority of them were hourly employees, not managers or executives. Talk about a party!

Another highlight, at least for us, was when Larry Mercer and I personally participated in carrying the Olympic torch through the streets of downtown Atlanta. With my daughter Danielle running beside me, I received the torch from Mercer on Peachtree Street. Thousands of associates, decked out in orange, turned out for the two A.M. handoff.

Why did we sponsor the Olympics? Why not announce our status as a national company in some less costly manner? Number one, we want to be part of the fabric of North America as a company, and there is no greater sporting event on Earth than the Olympics in terms of emotion and viewership. It is the pinnacle; it is number one in terms of its mystique. It is a positive—who doesn't like the Olympics? If we were going to align ourselves with something, The Home Depot wanted it to be that.

And in all the research that we saw, Olympic sponsors are perceived by the general public as being leaders in their industries: Kodak . . . Coca-Cola . . . and The Home Depot. We liked that affiliation.

Number two, from just a raw advertising standpoint, the Olympic Games tend to be the most watched, highest rated TV programming in any given year, so running commercials during the Olympics is a very powerful way of reaching your customers.

Being able to say you are a sponsor is equally powerful—internally, if not externally. We drew analogies between our associates and the Olympians' coaches. We want our associates to go for the gold. We need that same dedication. They are like coaches, teaching, inspiring, training, and motivating their customers. In fact, we named ourselves "North America's Home Improvement Coach" during the 1996 Games.

Another element of our support: We are one of the largest providers of jobs to Olympic hopefuls in the world. Going into the 1996 games, we employed more than 100 Olympic contenders, of whom 28 made teams, and six medaled.

Hiring Olympic athletes became a morale issue as well, because our employees got behind these men and women, on the job and off, rooting them on and feeling a party to their progress. Along that line, it is not a bad recruiting tool to say that we are an Olympics sponsor. These men and women live by a higher standard because of their dedication and focus.

In the big scheme of things, however, the Olympics is just another spoke on the wheel. Even though we will spend tens of millions of dollars on it over the course of a decade, it only represents a fraction of our whole marketing budget.

We also underwrote *Olympic Glory,* the first-ever large-format, 70-millimeter film of an Olympic Winter Games, shot in Nagano, Japan, during the '98 Games. It was another way of bringing the Olympics back to our markets. The Olympics is some event far, far away. This film is allowing our customers and associates to feel the emotions and magnitude of the most powerful sporting event on Earth.

We signed on as an Atlanta Olympics sponsor back in 1992, but we were so pleased with the results that we re-upped as sponsors of both the U.S. and Canadian Olympic teams through 2004, as well as the Games themselves in Salt Lake City in 2002.

We also sponsor the Canadian and U.S. Paralympic teams. Going forward, we will continue those sponsorships and add the Puerto Rican Olympic team to our sponsorship efforts.

As we go to press on this book, all of the Olympic organizing committees are embroiled in the Salt Lake City bribery scandal. We are in touch almost daily with the U.S. Olympic Committee and the International Olympic Committee and share their confidence that these issues will be resolved so that the value of the Olympic brand is restored, especially here in North America. After all, the focus of the Olympics is the athletes. Their dedication to excellence is the reason we support them.

When you merely advertise, as we did for our first ten or fifteen years, you are only attracting people through one narrow channel of opportunity. You're just another store in the neighborhood with a newspaper ad, hoping people respond to it. Now that we're part of the fabric of North America, we want to plant seeds more subtly for consumers to consider taking on home improvement projects around the house. We want to be their ubiquitous source for the information they need to do these projects.

One of the reasons we sponsor the Olympic teams and games is because Olympians know that what won four years ago is not going to be enough to win again. That is in keeping with our values. We want to raise the bar for our own associates in the same way. Even though we won a gold medal in the past—last week, last quarter—we, like the Olympic athletes, need to reach within ourselves every day to raise that bar. The competition is always getting better; so should we.

The values of the Olympics and the athletes are very much in keeping with ours—faster, higher, stronger. That is what The Home Depot is all about.

■   ■   ■

Ten years ago, The Home Depot advertised stores that were bigger than two and a half football fields. That was a point of difference. Today, who isn't bigger than two and a half football fields? We also said we carried more than 30,000 items. That was a point of difference. Well, who doesn't have more than 30,000 items today? And who doesn't have a low-price guarantee?

If all those things have become a commodity, why is The Home Depot still so successful? It is the culture, it is the people.

That's why the real secret of our TV commercials is our own people.

We think that our 160,000 associates can send home a message better than any actor. And the public trusts our people. They don't necessarily respond as strongly to somebody who is being paid to deliver a message. Ace Hardware has John Madden. Our signature is our associates in orange aprons.

There are no scripts. We just ask them a question and turn the camera on. They are pretty passionate, and no one can speak about a price guarantee better than the people who work in our stores. You can't give that to an actor. They can't do it; it wouldn't be believable.

The lines that we get—we couldn't write stuff like this: "Our pricing guarantee is chiseled into the bedrock of this company."

9

The Competition
"Market Dominance Is Important"*

When we entered the central Florida market in 1982, Jim Sweet, the then-chairman of the board of Scotty's, which is headquartered in Lakeland, Florida, came by our new Altamonte Springs store for a chat with me.

Sweet, a distinguished, well-liked southern gentleman, made the comment that it was a big market and the two companies could enjoy a peaceful coexistence.

But I didn't want there to be any misunderstanding. I suggested an analogy from the movie *Jaws*, about a giant killer shark. "Have you seen the movie?" I asked.

"Uh, sure," Sweet said.

"Imagine we're in a backyard swimming pool together," I continued, smiling. "Now imagine that The Home Depot is Jaws."

"Hmm."

The difference between Sweet and the heads of many of our other competitors through the years is that I at least warned him of what was to come.

■ ■ ■

* Arthur Blank

162

Every industry witnesses spectacular battles between number one and number two:

Coke versus Pepsi.

McDonald's versus Burger King.

Hertz versus Avis.

And The Home Depot versus Lowe's, the largest of our many regional competitors.

The Home Depot is far ahead of Lowe's in every major measurement of success, including number of stores (761 vs. 484 in 1998, according to newly released figures), total sales ($30.219 billion vs. $12.24 billion). As a matter of fact, only 20 to 25 percent of Lowe's stores face The Home Depot as a competitor. But only 15 to 20 percent of Home Depot stores face a Lowe's. Our impact on them is worse than their impact on us.

At the end of the day, we produce on average about 40 percent more volume out of our big boxes than they do at a 40 percent greater rate of profitability.

Bob Tillman, chairman of the board at Lowe's, pinpointed the moment we became direct competitors in the book *No Place Like Lowe's,* a look back at their first fifty years in business, written by Deni McIntyre.

"I remember my first exposure to The Home Depot," Tillman said. "Lowe's had a store managers' meeting in Orlando in 1981, and we made time to visit Home Depot's store there. The store was 85,000 square feet. We were on a little bus, and we could not find an empty space in the parking lot. Leonard [Herring] was with us, and he said, 'I'll bet you could sell these parking spaces for $5 apiece.' At that moment, I knew they had built a better mousetrap—before we ever went into the store!"

Still, Lowe's stuck with its traditional store model for many more years, a lumberyard with a showroom that might have been 10,000 to 20,000 square feet. They were in smaller markets, carrying not only home improvement products but also appliances and electronics. It wasn't until 1990 that their first big-box store, 95,000 square feet, opened.

Meanwhile, another famous competitor of ours, Hechinger, also stayed its course, buying merchandise at higher cost through distributors. They didn't have the merchandise or service that we offered. But they did offer bright, clean, good-looking stores. They believed that the same formula would always work based on years of customer loyalty. We believe there is no perfect, ongoing formula, as long as your values remain constant. I don't think they understood that their customers' loyalty was based on a lack of options. When we arrived, customers made it very clear that the static Hechinger formula was not the one offering the best value. It wasn't responsive. And Lowe's wasn't either for many years. Today, they are.

But when you only copy somebody and don't really understand why they're doing what they're doing, you're never going to be as good as the original. That's Lowe's problem vis-à-vis The Home Depot. They copy almost everything we do, from store design to marketing. But the reason they still only achieve about 60 percent of our volume is that they don't understand the essence of what we do: Take care of the customers. It's not how beautiful the store is, or how wide the aisles are. People come to our stores for the product selection, the right prices, and the product knowledge. Our stores are not Nordstrom. The Home Depot is a warehouse store open to the public. People shopping for home improvement feel very comfortable in our environment.

You can copy a Black & Decker drill and sell it for the same price that we do, but you can't copy The Home Depot culture. We think we're very difficult to emulate without believing in the same values that we do.

■　　■　　■

Being a major player in a market is an important part of our growth plan. We opened in certain places—Atlanta, South Florida, and Dallas, for example—and focused our marketing in those places until we became number one. Only then did we move on to the next city.

We never go to a new market with plans for just a couple of stores. One of the reasons we didn't go into Los Angeles sooner was that our real estate vice president, Bill Harris, said that unless we were prepared to go in and open a whole bunch of stores at once and be the best against a broad array of competitors, it made more sense to stay in South Florida until we were number one with the customers there.

We follow that philosophy in terms of merchandise in our stores, too, always having the widest selection. If we can't be the best in a category, we don't carry it.

Before us, nobody had a truly national presence in home improvement except for Sears, which competes in the industry by virtue of its Craftsman tool and Weatherbeater paint lines. Sears had more business around the United States than anybody else; the rest of us ran small regional chains by comparison.

The industry knew we were edging closer and closer to them but they never prepared for us. They all knew that eventually we would present a direct threat, but they couldn't think in terms other than the way they had for decades.

They ran good businesses, they made lots of money, why change it? Hardware was a chummy regional business—"There is room for everybody!"—but the truth was that we were so revolutionary that they couldn't do business as usual with us in a market they once dominated. They had to lower prices to an extent that they couldn't financially survive. And they didn't have space for the assortment we offered or the broad array of customer services.

All the dynamics changed and the strongest of them started disappearing off the face of the Earth.

Fifteen years ago, Mike Grossman, the founder of Grossman's, walked around at trade shows with an entourage of 30 people following in his wake; he was the king of the hill. At those same shows, we also walked around, begging and pleading with people to sell to us. If Grossman walked by as we talked to a vendor, the vendor would walk away from us and seek an audience with Grossman. None of those people recognized how strong the Depot was, because even though we were a public company, the way we did business was hard for the old-timers to understand. They couldn't understand sales volume and velocity as opposed to gross margin. Their key was selling less at a higher price; ours was selling more at a lower price. They couldn't understand our dynamics or the numbers.

As our impact on regional players grew, people in the industry found new ways of describing us: "The Orange Plague" and "Agent Orange," not-so-nice references to the company's trademark color. Small business people would get together to keep the orange plague from coming to town.

Sixty years ago, grocery stores cut butter out of a tub. If you wanted a half a pound, they went in with a knife and cut it out, and we all paid for the butter and the labor. When supermarkets came along, butter was precut and premeasured. It sold for much less because it could be made and delivered much more efficiently. Efficiency should give you lower prices. Lower prices should be better for the consumer. Whatever is better for the consumer is better for the economy.

That is how we developed our business. Our competitors did not understand that, and they believed in the same thing that Handy Dan did: high margins and smaller sales, which meant inefficiency. As we have since proved, that is not what works best in the real world.

Today, there are those in our industry who have learned to be efficient and productive, who now understand the philosophy of selling at lower prices and of being competitive in the marketplace. Those are the survivors. As for the others . . . their day has passed.

Fortunately, while a good number of direct competitors have gone out of business trying to compete with us, we have also strengthened the lot of many small neighborhood hardware stores that provide extraordinary service and convenience. Around every Home Depot store you will find ten more specialty stores selling tile, carpeting, and kitchen cabinets; even though we carry those items, they survive in our milieu by offering product lines we don't, attracting the attention of shoppers drawn to us as their ultimate destination.

■　　■　　■

Every part of the country represents a different primary competitor for The Home Depot. On the East Coast, it would be Lowe's. In California, it would be HomeBase. In the northwest, it would be Eagle. (In November '98, Lowe's was negotiating to buy Eagle.) In Canada, it is REVY Home & Garden in the western provinces and

Canadian Tire, which is all over. In other words, we have a strong competitor in each market. We don't have one monster, other than Sears, which is in every market that we are in but doesn't feature home improvement goods and services exclusively.

Each regional competitor is very strong and well-financed in its own right. And each is a great concern to us.

We are always looking over our shoulder. The essence of keeping our company great is its nonstop reinvention, because if you are in constant motion, nobody can catch you. You must maintain that motion, whether it be in the physical layout of the store, merchandising, advertising, or a thousand other factors. It is no different than changing your clothes every day. If your spouse wore the same clothes every day, after a while, you'd stop looking at him or her. Well, our stores can't show up wearing the same clothes every day, either. The concept and values of how we operate stay constant, but what the customers see changes regularly, whether it means putting in new lights, moving departments around, new signage, or bringing in new types or brands of merchandise.

No matter what your business, you cannot stay still for any length of time, or your competitors will scratch and crawl over you. There is always somebody out there who is as bright or brighter than you who is looking for ways of taking away what is yours.

In our management training classes, Bernie and I tell our people it's not just an issue of competition; it's more personal than that. These people want to take away our livelihood. We're talking about their homes, about sending their kids to college. We're talking about their retirement nest eggs. We tell them about all the things that are meaningful in their lives that a competitor targets by opening up a new store nearby. This is not fun. "This," we warn them, "is your *life*. And every time they challenge you, it's a challenge to take away your livelihood and your career and your future."

So we tell our people that they must focus on the customer. This war is made up of skirmishes that go on every day. Every day is a skirmish, and we must be on our guard every single day. Competition moves in because it recognizes a weakness in your fabric. So we have to be very careful that we don't have any weakness.

■   ■   ■

Internally, we have many different opinions as to what approach we should take versus our competition. When you are the leader in the marketplace, should you even think about mentioning number two? How high a road do we want to take? Should we just sit back and ignore the competition just because they are not hurting us? We produce about eight commercial spots a day, 2,000 spots a year, so we can usually manage a little of everything.

Part of our marketing department's job is to make sure that all of the orange-blooded folks wearing our aprons are charged up and saying, "We are a kick-ass company." We won't just let the competitors come in and throw jabs at us. They haven't hit us hard yet, but they keep punching.

Should it be personal against the competition? Well, our associates do love that stuff. It depends on how edgy you want to get.

■   ■   ■

Builders Square was our most visible competitor of the 1980s. When it closed its last store in Atlanta, our store managers put on a vicious skit at a citywide store meeting.

The theme was how we deal with the competition. When the big rolling front door of the store went up, in drove a black funeral hearse. Inside was an actual funeral home director. He gently opened the back doors of the hearse, slid out a coffin, and lifted the lid. Everyone gasped at the sight of an assistant manager holding a stake that read:

BUILDERS SQUARE
REST IN PEACE

We shared a particular antipathy with Builders Square because it was founded by Frank Denny, our ex-associate at Handy Dan. He started the company in San Antonio, Texas, as Home Centers of America. It was the first Home Depot clone. In 1985, Denny sold the nine-store company to Kmart, which changed its name to Builders Square.

When we opened in Daytona Beach, Florida, Builders Square had been there for some time. Our new store manager hired an airplane to fly over the Builders Square parking lot with a sign advertising better prices at The Home Depot. There was probably a better way of spending money, but it was pretty funny and our Daytona Beach associates cheered her sense of the absurd.

Lowe's and The Home Depot both announced plans to enter the Savannah, Georgia, market at about the same time, locating just a few hundred yards apart. Lowe's opened while our store was still under construction, but that didn't stop us from having fun at their expense.

Our Jacksonville store manager chartered a bus, festooned it with Home Depot logos, and took dozens of his store's associates to the Lowe's in Savannah, where he conducted a store meeting in the parking lot.

When we arrived in the Washington, D.C., market, our first bouquet of black roses arrived from Hechinger. It quickly became a tradition that whenever we opened a store, we would find a bouquet of black roses on our door.

Then, of course, we would reciprocate. After a while, the two companies stopped doing it. But a few bouquets kept slipping through the cracks because Lowe's picked up the practice from Hechinger. On another occasion, Lowe's employees welcomed a new store of ours outside of Richmond, Virginia, by wrapping the front entrance in toilet paper.

Not that we're innocents. We used to fill a flatbed truck with our employees, hay wagon–style, and do Home Depot cheers in competitors' parking lots. This happened in the Northeast, Arizona, and Florida.

"Arthur Blank" was once paged over the loudspeaker in a Scotty's store I was visiting with Larry Mercer. And probably just as strange is that I took it in stride, picking up a house phone and saying, "Yes?"

Of course, that was a more pleasant experience than being thrown out of a competitor's store, something that happens more and more these days. When they spot us, a posse of employees will typically follow us through the aisles, not saying a word, but watching everything we do until the only smart move is to leave. Bernie had this experience at a competitor's store in Minneapolis: He was literally picked up and thrown out.

■ ■ ■

The nature of competition in our industry has changed in the last ten years, primarily because of The Home Depot.

A decade ago, the industry was smaller, we were smaller, and our competitors were more often than not the founders of their companies. We all knew each other on a first-name basis and there was a certain kind of camaraderie amongst us all. Robert Strickland at Lowe's, John Hechinger from Hechinger, and Payless Cashways' David Stanley were friends of ours when the industry was characterized by regional powerhouses. We would visit their stores; they would visit ours. Hechinger used to bring an entire senior management group to Atlanta, and we would spend several hours talking about what we were doing. We weren't yet thinking of barging into the Washington, D.C., market and he never thought of us as a competitor. Or we would visit Somerville Lumber in Boston, and they would proudly take us through their stores and show us what they were doing. We could still talk about industry economics and things of common interest.

Ten years ago, these people didn't view us as the threat to their survival that they do today. Ten years ago, they weren't openly ridiculed by industry trade magazines, analysts, and even customers for failing to keep up with changing times and consumer expectations. We worked on City of Hope and other charities together. But as you move past the founders of the company, the gloves come off. We no longer have the same kind of personal relationships. On the other hand, maybe that's no longer realistic.

The fact that we were able to design our company on a clean sheet of paper and weren't hampered by years of tradition and years of people being committed to a certain sort of business form played to our advantage with both customers and the industry.

Lowe's was number one in our industry until we sailed past them in 1989. To their credit, Lowe's finally saw the writing on the wall and understood that the only way they could compete with us was to copy our format. Around that time, Lowe's began converting to consumer home improvement superstores, moving up from its traditional 15,000-square-foot, contractor-oriented lumberyards.

As Lowe's CEO, Bob Tillman, told the American Hardware Association convention in 1997, "One of the best things that ever happened to our company was The Home Depot. As the saying goes, a good scare is worth more than good advice." According to newspaper reports, Tillman once had a life-size cutout of Homer, our cartoon mascot, in his office with a target on his chest.

Could a Lowe's and Menard or Lowe's and Eagle combine forces to better compete with us from coast to coast? Sure they could. But we would still be much bigger than they are, with stores grossing nearly twice what they do per square foot.

We take them all very seriously today, but their ability to compete with us would probably not be greatly enhanced if they were combined.

Both Eagle and Lowe's create an overall environment in their stores that is softer than ours. We will probably do more in the years to come to create more of a decor environment within certain areas of a Home Depot store. Of course, if we cut our selection to match Lowe's, we would have wider aisles, too.

■   ■   ■

The toughest competitor we faced over the years was Hechinger. In the Washington, D.C.–Baltimore–Virginia market, Hechinger had an enthusiastic consumer following, high-quality locations, a classy look and feel, and heavy advertising. If they were steak, we were hamburger. It was also the only game in town for a long time, so buying habits were formed and solid. That was a tough one to break down.

We seriously discussed a merger with Hechinger in 1984 at a point when they were well known and widely respected and we were starting to attract notice. Hechinger had money; we didn't. We waltzed around and around romancing each other. Hechinger president Dick England and Bernie took long walks down Fifth Avenue in New York, discussing the ins and outs of a merger.

The Home Depot's name would have been on the buildings after the merger. Bernie would be chairman of the merged company; on this we all agreed. And we agreed that neither John Hechinger nor Dick England would be president; they were up in age and didn't want to run a company anymore. Bernie said, "Arthur's gotta be president, because Arthur knows what he is doing." But Hechinger and England wanted John W. Hechinger Jr., a junior officer in their company at that time, to become president. He was a kid. A nice kid, but a kid nonetheless.

Over dinner at England's house, he said he couldn't do the deal if we wouldn't name John Jr. as president of the new company. Bernie told him that that was too bad, because one way or the other we were going to come up to the Northeast and compete head-to-head. A merger would have gotten us to D.C. earlier, and the Hechinger people would have been 30 times wealthier than they are today, and their employees would have been a hell of a lot better off. But they just didn't see it.

Ultimately, John Jr. became president of Hechinger, and it lost its luster, despite acquiring Home Quarters and Builders Square. It also spurned an opportunity to be acquired by Sears.

Hechinger had a great business, but the company never changed with the times. It had a formula that worked once, and that was good enough for them. Management didn't understand that the world changes, the environment changes, competition changes, people change, everything changes. Retailers can't ever stay the same. If you don't change, you are a dead duck. You must wake up every morning and wonder, "Who will destroy me today if I don't keep my eyes open?" You must constantly think about ways to outmaneuver the competition and be the number one horse.

■　　■　　■

Hechinger was not the only opportunity to merge with The Home Depot that one of our competitors squandered.

There was also Sears.

If our people mistakenly underestimate competitors who are not as big or as successful as The Home Depot, we remind them of two who are bigger: Sears and Wal-Mart. We don't want either of them to sell a single tool.

Our idea of a merger with Sears was that we would take over all of their hard goods business. We knew we had a winning concept, but we were still a small company, maybe 30 stores to their 700 or more. We didn't yet have category-killer brand names and products like Sears did with its Craftsman tools and Weatherbeater paint lines. They also had their credit card and they had consumer trust. When people were asked what retailer they trusted in those days, Sears was the common response.

We were looking for ways of accelerating our growth. This was prior to our Bowater acquisition. We thought Sears might be a good partner.

In theory, Sears would eventually stop selling Craftsman in their stores, making the brand only available in the Home Depot stores. And it would have been a huge advantage to us to have direct access to every Sears and Discover credit card holder. That was magic to us.

When we discussed the possibility of a merger with Sears in the early 1980s, Al Goldstein was their executive in charge of acquisitions.

Goldstein suggested a purchase price of no more than $300 million for our company. It was technically worth about $200 million at the time, based on the value of the stock.

"You can do what you want," Ken Langone told him, "but this company is going to be worth a hell of lot more than $300 million, and you aren't going to buy it cheap."

At that point, Sears was a diversified conglomerate with Allstate Insurance, Coldwell-Banker real estate and the Discover credit card. We saw hardware and home improvement as a sideline for them at a time when their core retail business was going down the drain. They were riding the wrong horse in the pre–Arthur Martinez days, being eaten up by their bureaucracy, unable to make quick, effective decisions.

When Bernie was president of Odell in 1969, he had an encounter with Sears that colored his view of that company for years.

Sears was making a choice between carrying Odell's Esquire and another shoe polish brand, but you'd think it was deciding between capital punishment and life in prison with all the committees the decision went through. It was a joke. Bernie spent so much time wrangling with Sears, waiting anxiously for a decision, that he threw up his hands and made it for them. "Take our product out of your stores," he said. "I don't want you selling our stuff anymore. It's just not worth it."

We could have done more for Craftsman tools in those days than Sears was doing, and they needed more room for clothing. So we gave them the out, but there was nobody there besides Goldstein willing to take the chance.

Negotiations didn't get very far. And as a result of the Sears deal failing and the subsequent issues Bowater created for us, we realized that we couldn't accelerate as simply as we thought we could. Growth required a very cautious, well-considered plan. In retrospect, we would not have been able to handle a merger with Sears, so it was a good thing for us that it fell apart. But it will probably go down in history as one of Sears's biggest mistakes ever.

■   ■   ■

I often tell our people that if we didn't have competitors we would have to create them.

We are at our best when we are competing against somebody, so our perpetual challenge is creating a competitive environment even when it doesn't materialize naturally. In markets where there is no Eagle Hardware & Garden, Menard's, or Lowe's, or strong local competition, we must make sure that our associates really believe in the competitive factor.

There are always independent lumberyards, electrical and plumbing supply houses, and specialty stores. It is just a question of making sure that our folks are really aware of them and that they recognize who and what are our real competitors. Who else is moving products? Who else is moving commodities? And who else is taking care of the customers in the marketplace? Sometimes it is companies that you are aware of. Sometimes it is companies whose names you don't know.

Competition is an important part of being aggressive and competitive. Our nature is to be in your face.

Our people really get turned on by competition. We understand that we are in the business not to destroy a competitor but to serve the customer. If, as a result of that, we end up hurting a competitor, that is fine, but it can't be our focus. Our focus has to be on the customer.

The truth of the matter is, we have to win the customer. We don't have to beat the competitor, we have to win the customer. But by winning the customer, we also take advantage of the competitor. Consider any serious competitor we have in any market. Any single competitor represents a very small percentage of the total amount of lumber and building materials, all of the products that we sell in any particular market. So even if we got *all* their business, it would not begin to support the kind of business that we have today. That's why we focus on the whole industry, where all the merchandise is being sold as well as by the name competitors that most people think of.

That said, there is a lot to be said for one-on-one competition.

When we first expanded outside of the Southeast in 1984, managers at HomeClub in Phoenix, Arizona, told *National Home Center News*, "We are going to stop The Home Depot. The orange tide stops here!" It was pretty funny to us, a company of barely a dozen stores, but it really rallied our troops. We blew that story up really big and posted it in the Phoenix store.

And when we went to California, we actually put up posters of HomeClub executives on our bulletin boards, actual posters of their faces—with big *X*es through them. Even better, we hired one of HomeClub's former ad agencies to work for us.

When Lowe's decided to take the fight to us in Atlanta, they bought full-page ads in the *Atlanta Journal-Constitution* feverishly attacking us. Dick Sullivan, our senior vice president of advertising, and his team rose to the occasion and responded by creating a series of hysterically simple ads, only one of which appeared in print. Each asked a question or made a statement and was accompanied by a photo that furthered our point.

Here's an example of one that didn't run:

"Been to Lowe's for plumbing advice?"
Photo: A man in his basement, his head barely above water.

And this is the one that was published:

"If you buy the manure Lowe's has been spreading lately, one of these may come in handy. Lowe's price $54.99. Home Depot $44.77."
Photo: Scott's Model No. 4991 Fertilizer Spreader.

Every time someone attacks our stores for not being as brightly lit as a competitor's, or for being too big, we shrug our shoulders and laugh. But if they talk about the quality of customer service in our stores not being as good as Lowe's or somebody else's, that is something that our people just don't tolerate.

Periodically we run newspaper ads that may appear targeted at consumers but are really intended to rally our own troops. The way we win the hearts and minds of customers is with merchandise, price comparisons, and sufficient stock. But that is the *mechanical* part of the business. We win their hearts and their minds with our *people*.

Growth

"It Was Like Basic Training;
You Learned How to Do a Lot of Things,
Then You Went to War and Improvised"*

One of the companies that we have admired over the years has been Wal-Mart, because, despite their success, the founders always retained a degree of humility about themselves. David Glass says one of the reasons they haven't moved from Bentonville, Arkansas, is because they always want to remember who they are and where they came from.

Sam Walton often told us that the way Wal-Mart reached $10 billion in sales was by concentrating on its stores, not on the numbers. That became the basis of our success, as well. We both opened a ton of stores because we had so much control of merchandise, distribution, finances, and infrastructure:

■ **MERCHANDISE:** We negotiate the lowest possible prices, based on enormous buying power and our willingness to pay invoices immediately. Instead of paying for merchandise on net 30 days or even 15, we pay in five days or less. Sometimes we send checks overnight. That policy is usually good for an additional discount from vendors.

And if you asked me, "What is the value of having a decentralized merchandising staff like The Home Depot's?" I'd say that *our* sales

* Arthur Blank

volume is 15 to 20 percent higher because we're making decisions locally rather than on a centralized basis.

■ **DISTRIBUTION**: Most of our vendors ship directly to our stores, cutting out middleman distributors. That saves everybody time and
money.

It's not that we're opposed to distributors. But if we buy merchandise direct from the manufacturer, we can get it at a lower price.
Then if we price it lower, we'll create higher sales volume.

We do have some warehouse operations, either for handling lumber or where it makes sense to source merchandise globally.

In a related issue, we currently spend more money on freight than
any other retailer in the country because of the size and weight of our
merchandise. So we've rechallenged ourselves to take the air and
wasted space out of delivery trucks and thereby reduce our freight
costs significantly. That enhances our gross margin not by changing
our pricing but by changing our cost.

■ **FINANCES**: This goes back to the roots of our company. We didn't
originally want to start with four stores in Atlanta; we wanted to do
two. That wasn't because we didn't have the capital to do four; we did.
What we lacked was the safety net. We needed a strong balance sheet
to grant ourselves the courage to make the tough decisions we needed
to make, even if it initially drained our resources. We didn't want to be
whipsawed by the marketplace before our concept had a fair chance.

I always tell people starting new companies to secure *twice* the
capital they think they need. Not because they need the money, but
because it gives you the confidence and the strength to do what you
think is right instead of being pushed by external financial forces.

We wanted a strong financial statement so we could ignore the immediate financial consequences and do what we knew was right, taking the long-term position. We didn't want to imply we could only
offer the best prices, selection, or service for thirty days. So we've always overcapitalized the company.

For many years, we had the weakest balance sheet in the industry.
If we had been a public company in 1979, we would not be in busi-

ness today, because the people who came to our stores had already convinced themselves we would not be in business in nine months. And we *did* lose half of our capital reserves in the first year. But having the other half gave us the courage to keep doing the right things.

Today, our excellent credit and cash reserves make financing expansion easy.

■ **INFRASTRUCTURE:** Because we plan our growth years in advance, we have invested in the human resources we will need to ramp up expansion before, not after, the fact.

An excellent example of this is our philosophy of hiring people who are overqualified for the positions to which they are initially assigned.

Charlie Barnes was a district manager at Handy City when we hired him in 1979 to run one of our first stores. We knew he'd do a bang-up job with that first store and could oversee many more after that. At Handy Dan, Rick Mayo was one of the most senior merchants in our industry. But he started with us as a buyer. Bruce Berg left Wickes (a $1-billion-per-year business at the time) and joined Home Depot as a merchandising VP when we were only a $400-million-per-year business. Lots of people took these kinds of chances on us.

Over the years, we have overinvested in people for two reasons. First, if people have that extra capacity and experience they can probably do whatever job we ask of them. Second, it gave us the opportunity to grow the company more quickly. Because these people had untapped capacity, they were not running in fifth gear. They were probably in first or second gear, and we always got a "10" in terms of performance from them.

More recently, we opened our first store in Chile with a full merchandising staff. That's an unheard-of commitment for a single store. But ours is a people-based philosophy: Hire the best people. Payroll is not an expense to us; it's an investment. And like any other investment, as long as you are getting a return on that investment, you invest in the best quality you can get.

■ ■ ■

Every young company screws up. We were no exception.

With our Atlanta and South Florida stores going great guns, we looked for ways of dramatically increasing the size and scope of the Home Depot brand. In March 1984, we bought land in Los Angeles for multiple future stores and also considered sites in Houston, San Diego, and San Francisco. Later in the year, on October 30, we also bought a fledgling, Plano, Texas–based chain by the name of Bowater Home Centers.

Bowater was a $38.4 million acquisition of a chain with nine big-box hardware stores somewhat like ours but in markets we were not in—Dallas, Shreveport, Baton Rouge, and Mobile. And when we say "somewhat" like ours, we can say on good authority that they were based on our earliest stores. That's because the American division of the London, England–based Bowater Corp. newsprint and chemical manufacturing conglomerate tried to buy The Home Depot while it was still in the conceptual stages. Bowater was another company to which we tried to sell a 15 percent equity stake in our company for $2 million.

Their American CEO, Ralph Dillon, was very affable and understood what we were trying to do and was very interested in our business concept. He sent his accounting staff in, although there wasn't much to see. This was all prior to the first store openings, so everything you could know about us was contained on twelve sheets of paper. There was no balance sheet. The money was all outbound. All investors were really buying was talent.

He saw that, liked what we were doing, and we made a deal. And then he went back to London, and the holding company turned him down flat.

But while they wouldn't approve his investment in our company, they didn't say he couldn't start his own copycat chain, so that's what he did. He literally took our blueprint and started from scratch, opening Bowater Home Centers in Texas and Louisiana. He had all our numbers and our business plan. The only thing he didn't have was the experience of how to run it.

We weren't going to get to Texas for many, many years, so copying us so blatantly probably seemed safe.

Back East in Atlanta and Florida, The Home Depot had opened up great stores boasting a wondrous esprit de corps and confidence in our retail philosophy—lowest prices, widest selection, and the best customer service anywhere. So we went down to look at the Bowater stores. Even with our blueprint, they just didn't know how to run the business. The locations were not bad, but they had old inventory, the stores were beaten-up looking, and they were only selling half the dollar volume of our stores.

Still, we believed that their locations, under good management, could leapfrog our expansion plans several years ahead, and Dallas–Fort Worth was a key market we wanted to be in.

We never anticipated the ancillary losses caused by sucking all of the great people out of our existing stores and sending them to fix the black hole that was Bowater. When you do that, you weaken yourself, which is exactly what happened in our existing stores.

The burden of recasting Bowater fell to Pat Farrah. He assumed the responsibility for changing the stores' merchandise, which was the critical area. It was a major undertaking, and a heavy burden for him.

One of the reasons Bowater taxed us so greatly was the indirect drain it put on our existing systems. The Bowater stores were in such disarray that we immediately sent some of our best talent from Atlanta and South Florida to fix them. That left gaping holes back in our own stores. So we didn't get anticipated revenues in the Bowater stores, and existing Home Depot store sales went flat in the fourth quarter of 1984.

For experienced Home Depot managers who fanned out across Texas and Louisiana, the Bowater experience was a return to the early Depot days. They worked seven days a week, twelve or more hours a day. Every third week we flew them home or flew their spouses and children to them, but it was a difficult, taxing existence. They bore the pressure of not only converting these runaway stores but also saving our rear ends back in Atlanta.

The conversion of the merchandise was difficult because Bowater only carried about half of the products that Home Depot carried. We had the task of introducing all of the Home Depot stock-keeping units (SKUs)—individual variations of product lines—phasing out the ones that we didn't carry, and then meshing them all together. Product by product, aisle by aisle, we put familiar Home Depot merchandise on Bowater shelves and dumped Bowater products onto the floor, marking them down to fire-sale prices. We couldn't wait to get them out the door.

Culturally, we were as different as night and day. Home Depot store managers spend their days on the floor, wandering their stores, solving problems for customers and associates alike. Most Bowater store managers were pencil pushers. They hid in offices, as did their assistant managers. They weren't prepared to do the side-by-side, go-go work that we expected. (One of the few exceptions was Vern Joslyn, who not only stuck with us but went on to become president of our northeast division.)

Our people sometimes took unusual steps to get across the differences in the two retail cultures. Ron McCaslin, who is now our director of store systems support, arrived at a Bowater store in Louisiana one day, pointed to the manager's offices and, with great fanfare, announced, "That is not part of The Home Depot!" Then he climbed aboard a forklift and literally plowed through the walls of the offices until they were dust.

We terminated all of the Bowater corporate executives. Almost all of them, anyway. When everyone else was gone, one older gentleman kept showing up for work each day. He'd go to his little office toward the back, shuffle papers, make phone calls, and generally give the impression of being busy. None of us knew who he was; somehow, this particular vice president slipped through the cracks. So every day he came into the office. He never talked to anybody, never said anything. Finally, somebody saw through his ruse and he, too, was fired.

We eventually interviewed all the employees and explained, one-on-one, what The Home Depot was all about. Simultaneously, we kept the stores open and yet tore them apart, remodeling and remerchandising them into Home Depots, all the while using employees who resented us.

In the end, we terminated almost 95 percent of the original Bowater crew.

Every one of us could feel the resentment. When we came in and demanded that they work the hours that we expected everybody to work, it didn't go over real well. Ironically, if the Bowater employees had channeled as much pride into Bowater while it was a going concern, it would have melded much more easily with The Home Depot.

Bowater put an unanticipated and unwelcome demand on our vendors as well. We pressured them to take back Bowater merchandise. Where they refused, we marked goods down and sold them at a loss. But some of the merchandise in these stores was so bad, we couldn't even give it away.

■   ■   ■

The Home Depot has always been a high-multiple stock. Part of the explanation for it is that the financial community *trusts us.* They know that we are aboveboard with them. They know that if something is out there on the horizon that we are concerned about, we will tell them up front.

For a time, the Bowater debacle severely tested our goodwill on Wall Street. Until we ultimately turned the situation around, it temporarily dampened the euphoria for The Home Depot.

It's not easy being a public company. You have to answer to a ton of people, you have to answer a lot of questions, and Wall Street's memory is only as good as your last quarter. Long-term for the Street is between breakfast and lunch. You always have to run your business worrying about how much somebody else says you will make—somebody who may not have enough knowledge to understand what your potential is.

But against all of those negatives, without public money this company would still be a chain of four stores in Atlanta, Georgia.

The reason we are who we are today is the public money. The fact that people bought our stock, believed in us, thought that what we were doing was right, saw in our stores exactly what we preached, that the customer service was better than anywhere else, that the product knowledge was better than anywhere else, that our pricing was better than anywhere else—they bought us based on the truth of what we told them about ourselves, and they could go see it for themselves.

Such trust is invaluable to us, and we didn't want to do anything that would puncture or endanger it.

We arranged a series of meetings in New York in which Bernie and Ron Brill, every hour on the hour for a full day, came clean with the fund managers and analysts who covered our company. Standing before each group, Bernie stood up and bluntly announced, "I am the CEO of this company, and I am a schmuck," in precisely those words. "We screwed it up; we should have closed the Bowater stores."

After that, Bernie told them about the corrective measures that we put in place to prevent a repeat in the future. He assured them that the growth and profitability would continue. And they believed Bernie.

Many CEOs would blame a Bowater-type fiasco on the economy, blame it on this or blame it on that. We didn't blame it on anybody. We blamed it on ourselves.

The seriousness of our miscalculation in Dallas rocked our fourth-quarter earnings in 1984.

In an April 17, 1985, report, Montgomery Securities analyst Bo Cheadle wrote, "Bowater held down The Home Depot's performance in the fourth quarter and we expect it will continue to impact the first quarter. However, excluding Bowater, Home Depot's fourth-quarter earnings would have been up approximately 35 percent." In a subsequent report released on November 20, 1985, Cheadle noted that "the Bowater units cost Home Depot nearly $0.04 in last year's fourth quarter, $0.06 in the first quarter of this year, and $0.01 per share in the second quarter."

We disappointed the Street for the first time and damaged our credibility to expand our concept beyond the Southeast. Suddenly, analysts said we didn't know what we were talking about. It was the nadir of the business.

This happened soon after we negotiated a $200 million line of credit with the banking syndicate led by Security Pacific's Faye Wilson. And thank God that deal was done and secure; we couldn't have made the same deal a month later. It would have been years before we would ever be able to go back to the financial community and get this kind of money.

While all the pessimists wagged fingers at us, it gave us enormous resolve to prove that we weren't an accident. We said, "We'll show these people just how good we are," and we did.

In retrospect, Bowater wasn't even a good real estate deal, because we eventually closed all the stores we acquired and built bigger, better Home Depot stores close by. If we had just passed on Bowater altogether, it probably would have gone out of business anyhow.

Bowater taught us we're never as smart as we think we are. You have to look at yourself, your talents and abilities, realistically. We thought we were better, we thought we could handle anything. Success was breeding a little arrogance, and we learned that sometimes you believe you can do more than you really can do.

On the other hand, maybe it *was* a good deal. Even though it only gave us six stores in Dallas–Fort Worth (the other stores were in Louisiana), even though the transition took longer and was more raucous than we dreamed, and even though it produced an ugly quarter for us on Wall Street, it did secure our position in Dallas–Fort Worth and the other markets. That was amazing, considering that at the time, Handy Dan had seventeen units there, Payless Cashways had thirteen, and Boise Cascade had eight. And once we started making money on those stores in 1986, we never stopped. Those stores became cash cows for this company, and the deal gave us Vern Joslyn, an assistant manager at Bowater who has gone on to become president of the northeast division.

So Bowater was a great—and hard—lesson learned.

■　■　■

After Bowater, Bernie, Ken, and I sat down for a serious heart-to-heart. We had no choice but to change the philosophy of the company. The decisions that came out of that meeting were, first, we would ask the board to pass a resolution that we could not grow at a pace exceeding 25 percent new stores a year.

The board agreed to cap our annual growth so we would never again be tempted to do more than that. We wanted the board to protect us from ourselves, and it has.

Second, we would be more cautious about buying a company and keeping its management in place, because you can't match the Home Depot culture anywhere. We have competitors that copy every single thing that we do. We just have to be so careful that no matter how they copy us, they cannot copy the essence of what The Home Depot is all about.

At the time the Bowater acquisition came crashing down on our heads, we were ready to close on some great real estate in Detroit. So our third major decision was to sell all four properties in Detroit. We simply could not go to Detroit. We no longer had the surplus of qualified people that we had before Bowater. We were stretched more from a personnel standpoint than a financial standpoint; we just couldn't afford to do it. Fortunately, the real estate in Detroit was so good that Ron Brill sold it in very fast order—and at a profit—to Pace Membership Warehouse.

We were in despair when our longtime banker at Security Pacific National Bank, Rip Fleming, retired in 1983. It was even more troubling when The Home Depot account was turned over to a new loan officer.

Neither Fleming nor we felt that this new banker had the correct vision of our future. We were a small company with 19 stores and revenues of $250 million, and he couldn't envision us as a big one. And instead of the hands-on, intimate relationship we had with Fleming, we were being handled in a traditional manner by the bank's small-business group. We were numbers and points to them, not people with unique personalities.

Fleming, having heard good things about a woman named Faye Wilson through the bank's grapevine, personally asked her in 1982 to get involved in our account. She first met him as her instructor in a credit analysis class, where they discovered they were real soul mates as advocates for customers. She admired his career, reputation, judgment, and analytical abilities and had quietly gone to him on several occasions to talk through some troubling issues. So when he asked her for help on our account, she did it for him.

Wilson is an amazing woman. She began her business career as a CPA in 1960 following her graduation from Duke University, then became a full-time mom when her daughter was born. Following her divorce, she went back to school during the same hours her daughter was in class, earned master's degrees in international relations in 1976 and business administration in 1977 from the University of Southern California, and then went into banking.

She joined Security Pacific in 1977 and enjoyed great success in her short time at the bank, fast-tracking through the organization. She handled the bank's house accounts, those with whom Security Pacific companies had the closest relationships. These included large multinational companies such as Carnation, Nestlé S.A. (following its acquisition of Carnation), Litton Industries, Lear Siegler, Avery International, Safeway, Von's, and many aerospace companies; they represented hundreds of millions of dollars in credit lines and syndicates.

As time went on, she certainly proved her brilliance in her dealings with both The Home Depot and the other companies she handled. She got to know our company and worked with us, whereas the other loan officer had only been interested in achieving more protection and guarantees for the bank.

Wilson is a reserved, unassuming woman who doesn't look like a powerhouse, but she speaks with great passion. She is an articulate woman who is not afraid to stand up and be heard. She is a lion in sheep's clothing. She is a killer who goes about her business as calmly as a librarian.

And she literally saved our company in 1985.

Just after we acquired Bowater, but before it turned nightmarish, it was clear we would continue to grow. As ever, the question was paying for that growth.

We began a new dialogue with Security Pacific National Bank and Wilson about putting together a new $200 to $225 million line of credit that would allow us to grow from fifty stores and annual sales of $700 million to a hundred stores and give us the funds to operate them. This also forced us to make wide-ranging decisions on whether we would lease or purchase property in the future; what our balance sheet would look like versus our obligations; and with regard to the stores themselves, the inventory it would take to open so many.

Wilson said that to do a loan this large, she would organize a consortium of banks who would share the risk. We were banking with a variety of institutions besides Security Pacific: a small bank in Louisiana; Citizens & Southern in Atlanta; First Atlanta; and Bankers Trust, through its local office in Atlanta.

Wilson said we needed to bring in another large New York bank such as J. P. Morgan. She also suggested a southeast bank with a strong Atlanta presence, Wachovia. They came to a meeting but ultimately declined to participate. We then looked at where The Home Depot might grow in the future and also sought to include banks in Texas and Chicago.

J. P. Morgan passed. First Atlanta, an Atlanta-headquartered bank that handled our import-related letters of credit (and was later acquired by Wachovia), stayed in, as did Bankers Trust and C & S.

C & S was a party to our previous credit line and handled trust business for us at the time. It was also our stock transfer agent.

The problem came when Wilson received a call from the C & S loan officer who had been in the syndication meetings with us. We later learned that he thought our expansion into California was too risky, so at the last minute, he unilaterally made the decision that the bank would not participate in the deal.

This set off alarms because here was a local bank, one that knew the company, knew the management, presumably had an ability to physically be involved day-to-day, looking at operations if they wished, and we had other business with them. Their withdrawal—for unexplained reasons—was less an issue of their share of the cash but the appearance of a problem at home. What would another bank, one we didn't already have a relationship with, say? "C & S must know something we don't know." It created a potential blackball effect.

Wilson called Ron Brill that afternoon and gave him the bad news. He relayed the development to us, and we felt sick. We expected C & S's decision would surely scuttle the syndicate.

But Wilson told us not to worry. "Don't you do anything," she said. "I will take care of this." She said that very calmly, as she said everything. She immediately started working the phones and worked through the night to keep the deal from collapsing.

None of the other syndicate members blinked. Wilson had been with the company and walked the analysts through the Bowater acquisition. Much as we had with Rip Fleming, her predecessor, we talked regularly with Wilson. We had a good understanding. She knew how detail-oriented the company was, and we knew that she didn't want bad news, but liked to know what was coming. So we— particularly Ron Brill—were very good about sending information to Security Pacific and were very regular about calling her with updates.

Security Pacific demonstrated its absolute confidence in us by picking up C & S's share, rather than reducing the total. In the great tradition of Rip Fleming, Wilson convinced her bank to actually increase its exposure.

Security Pacific had a new chief credit officer at the time, one who came in after Fleming's many Home Depot–related loan scuffles. He said to Wilson, "Are you willing to put your job on the line for this?"

"Yes," she said, "I am."

Had Security Pacific not taken on more risk, its partners in the syndicate would certainly have reconsidered their own situations. Wilson saved us from enduring that ignominy. It was the second time a banker from Security Pacific had saved our bacon.

The next morning, she called and told us the deal was done, and we closed on time. But we didn't know until later what she went through on our behalf.

The C & S withdrawal was a real learning experience for us. Not so much that anyone could have predicted the bank's decision, but that we can often find depth of character and brilliance in unexpected places. From that point on, we looked at Faye Wilson differently than we ever did before. She became our new tower of strength.

When the bank sent her to work with international clients at its Security Pacific Hoare Govett office in London in 1987, she was named that division's managing director of mergers and acquisitions. Our relationship with the bank changed dramatically then, because we no longer had anyone there to personally represent our interests. But because we frequently travel overseas, we stayed in close contact with Wilson. "Faye," we told her, "when you come back to the U.S., we want you on our board."

She understood who we were, how we ran our business, the culture—she understood everything about The Home Depot. She also loved to be in our stores. This was a woman who loved The Home Depot as much as we did.

If Wilson thought we were just being nice, the day she did return from Europe in mid-1991 she learned just how serious we were. Bernie called her that very day. Her new assignment was running the nonbank subsidiaries of Bank of America as chairman and president of a holding company called Security Pacific Financial Services.

"Welcome back," he said. "You helped us finance the first hundred stores. Now we would like you to help us with a 500-store buildout."

Wilson was speechless.

"But this time," he said, "we want you to do it as a member of our board of directors."

She became the first woman on the board and a wonderful role model for many of our female associates. In 1998, she retired from the bank and joined us in the newly created post of senior vice president of value initiatives. The position includes two areas of emphasis. First, she'll be evaluating the ways in which we enculturate new associates in our values. Second, she will help the company become a more inclusive organization overall, making sure we get the best employees, ensuring we welcome everyone with the same opportunities and the same training to become leaders.

I asked Faye to do this because, being on our board, she doesn't have to worry about the politics of the job. She can just do what's right. Besides, she's already retired from one brilliant career and isn't looking at this as a stepping-stone to her next job. Her only career goal is working herself out of a job.

■　■　■

We weren't done with C & S, incidentally. Naturally, we—as a corporation and as individuals—canceled all of our business with C & S. We sent a letter to all of our employees, encouraging them to pull their personal accounts from C & S.

We blamed the bank, even though the chairman of the board personally insisted that the fault lay with one mistaken loan officer. We said, "If you have procedures that allow one person to unilaterally almost kill a company, we don't want to do business with you."

In retrospect, it's interesting that C & S dropped out of the syndicate before anybody—including us—knew about the mess Bowater was becoming. When that news broke, someone at C & S probably enjoyed a moment of superiority to the banks in our syndicate. But that was short-lived. Not only did we survive Bowater, but we have long since outlived C & S, which disappeared in a merger with NationsBank in 1991.

But we wouldn't do business with NationsBank, either, until several years later, when we put together a new line of credit, $800 million, and finally invited the then preeminent southeastern bank to participate, which they gladly did.

The 1985 credit line closed in early November, the beginning of the fourth quarter, and it was in the fourth quarter that Bowater began punishing our bottom line. The loan agreement was amended to allow for that unexpected fourth-quarter dip in earnings.

A month later, our stock plummeted, thanks to Bowater.

■   ■   ■

Taking our concept into the notorious Northeast was one of the most controversial decisions this company ever made. For every person urging us to do it, there was another person equally opposed.

Those in favor believed that consumers accustomed to being mistreated and taken for granted by old-line retailers in the New York and Boston metropolitan areas would fall in love with our "whatever it takes to make the customer happy" commitment.

Those against such an expansion warned us about union strife, the vast difference in selling in the Sunbelt vs. the Northeast, and the challenge of finding decent labor.

In 1988, shortly before this debate came to a head, Ken Langone's mother died, and he had the unpleasant task of cleaning out her Long Island home prior to its sale. He asked the man helping him to pick up some shop-vac vacuum bags at Rickel, the home improvement chain with a store nearest the house.

The man returned empty-handed. "They don't have any bags," he said.

"Oh, they must," Ken insisted, and drove over to the store in disbelief.

Sure enough, they didn't have the bags, so he bought a broom instead.

Near the checkouts, Ken saw a sign that read: "Rickel's policy: Whenever there are more than four people in a line, Rickel will open a second checkout counter." Ken looked around and saw one line with four people waiting and two more lines each with two people waiting. Curious to test the policy, he lined up behind the fourth person in the longest line, figuring that as soon as they opened up that new checkout, he would probably be first in the next line. But nothing happened.

After waiting for the four people ahead of him to be rung up, Ken asked the young man at the cash register about the posted policy.

"Oh, forget it," he said. "Nobody here pays any attention to that."

Finishing the transaction, Ken stopped at a glass-enclosed cubicle near the exit where he saw the store manager. Ken knocked on the door.

"What do you want?" he said in a curt tone.

"I am a customer," Ken said.

"Well, what do you want?"

"I'm interested in that sign up there," Ken said, pointing to the checkout policy. "I was the fifth in line, and I had to wait."

"In 70 percent of the cases, we do it."

"Then why don't you put up a sign that says, '70 percent of the time when there are more than four people in line, we will open up another counter'?"

"What are you, a wise guy?"

"No," Ken said, "I am not a wise guy. But I'll tell you what I am. I am with a company, and we are coming up this way, and when we get here, we are going to kick your ass."

"Oh, yeah?" the manager said. "Who are you with?"

"The Home Depot."

"Well, let me tell *you* something," the manager said. "Wait till you get up here and you gotta deal with these animals. And then you will see how good it is up here."

"Why are you calling your customers animals?"

"Oh, I'm not talking about the customers," the manager said. "I'm talking about those bastards out there that work for me."

(Rickel is no longer in business, by the way.)

■   ■   ■

Opening a store in East Hanover, New Jersey, was unlike any other Home Depot grand opening. As northeastern customers were met for the first time by a crush of orange aprons and smiling faces, they didn't know what to think. "Is this some type of a religious organization?" we were asked, as if we were the Trekkies of hardware.

Analysts, vendors, and even the people we hired to work in these stores told us, "Business is going to be a lot different in the Northeast. You just don't understand the people here. They are rougher, short-tempered, intense, aggressive," etc. All of which is more or less true.

We said, "But we *do* understand them. We have been serving their parents in Miami for years!"

Treat people with respect and give them what they want, and you know what? They were no different in New Jersey and New York than they were in Atlanta, Texas, Florida, California, or anywhere else. They are as softhearted in the Northeast as anywhere in the country, they just put up a hard-bitten shell for survival. But it is pretty easy to get through to them, and they make great customers. They like being helped, shown how to do things, pointed toward the right product, given the right price.

The odds should have been against us entering the Northeast. Chains such as Grossman's, Channel, Rickel, Hechinger, and Pergament were household names. Grossman's in the Northeast was a dynamite company, financially strong, and it was eating up the world. Hechinger was the Bloomingdale's of our business. Both were dynamic chains, the envy of the industry—until we came knocking at their doors. These companies—as well as such Northeast mainstays as Channel, Rickel, and Pergament—didn't sell merchandise. They sold pieces. Buy some lumber here, toilets there. But we sell projects—here's everything you need to renovate your bathroom, including step-by-step instructions for installing a new toilet and grouting the floor tile.

But despite the incredible population density, those companies didn't think big. They looked at the limitations. They looked at numbers. They operated without imagination, creativity, and vision.

If we quickly sell 12 of something, we'll bring in 60 more. If we sell all 60, we don't order 72, we'll order 300. That takes courage and great confidence. Our regional presidents take the position of seeing how high up high really is. That is one reason we are successful in our volume sales.

And their prices were high. We brought them down. The big companies in the Northeast were Channel and Rickel. Rickel occasionally challenged us on price; Channel never bothered. (To be fair, both were also heavily laden with debt from leveraged buyouts.) But as good as we are on price, that is never the most important decision. More important is product and project knowledge. We wanted a "Wow!" experience in our stores. The customer should come in and say, "Look at that product display! Wow!"

If you wanted hardware or lumber twenty years ago, home center stores such as Channel or Rickel were set up like oversize Woolworth's. Low shelves, low ceilings, and inadequate inventory. They might not even have had what you wanted when you wanted it; chances were 50-50 that they would have to order what you need and you'd wait two weeks. By contrast, walk into a Home Depot for the first time, and it's packed from floor to high ceiling. Whatever you need, our stores usually have it in stock. We also put a larger percentage of our overall sales back into store payroll, putting more people on the sales floor than anyone else.

Our competition in the Northeast failed to respond aggressively when we came to town, guns blasting. They didn't examine their levels of service, even though they had to know ours would be extremely high. They didn't do a better job of staying in stock, even though they knew we would carry twice the volume and variety that they had. The lesson is that you can never stand pat; you must be in constant motion. There is always somebody brighter than you are. There is always somebody who has a new idea. And you can't ever, ever take it for granted that you own the business. Because everybody who does eventually disappears off the face of the Earth.

We learned that by studying people who failed and understanding why they failed. Failures—especially our own—are great teaching tools. If someone fell on his face prior, why would you do the same thing again?

■   ■   ■

While we now have a strong business in the Northeast, it is not one place. It took us longer to establish ourselves in Connecticut, for example, than it did in New Jersey. And Baltimore was not the same as Washington, D.C. Capitalizing in each market took a lot of hard work.

It took us a lot longer in the Northeast to establish a major presence. In the Southeast, in the Midwest and West, getting sites was easier.

By contrast, many of our competitors believe that if they open a store in a marketplace, the market is theirs and they can move on to the next one. We've never followed that dictum.

In fact, because we have grown the do-it-yourself market in every one of the markets where we have gone, in order to serve the existing customers we've had to open a number of additional stores to bleed off the high-volume stores. We call it cannibalization.

Sites were originally acquired in the Northeast on the basis of their ability to generate sales of $30 million each; once open, many of those sites actually brought us $60 to $80 million a year. Tomorrow, God knows where they will end up, depending on how many more we open near enough to cannibalize them. We severely underestimated the sales that dense populations such as those found in Paramus, New Jersey, and Long Island could generate, and compounded our error by overestimating the competition. We may even have underestimated how good our own product was.

We had to do so many things differently so quickly. It was sort of like basic training in the military; you learned how to do a lot of things, then you went to war, and then you threw it all away and improvised.

The only thing you really learned in basic training was how to improvise, really. When all was said and done, the goal was survival. For us, the Northeast was the retail equivalent of a war zone, but not in the way the skeptics predicted. Our volume was so unbelievably high, any concept of customer service above and beyond keeping product on the shelves went right out the window. We sold job lot quantities—the amount of goods that pro customers would order for one of their projects, such as 15 interior doors or 75 electrical junction boxes—and brought in massive amounts of products just to stay in stock over the weekend. We thought we were mass merchandising before, but when we got into a store that was doing a million dollars or two million dollars a week, that's when we really learned how to mass merchandise just to stay in stock.

It showed our flexibility and our enhanced ability to adapt, not only to positive developments but to negative ones, too. That was a very, very important issue that goes back to finding out what you are doing right and what you are doing wrong.

For one thing, we needed more people. Before then having 150 associates on a store's payroll was a lot. But in the Northeast, a single store might employ as many as 600 people. And we needed them quicker. We had to speed up the hiring, training, and enculturation process. Everything had to be accelerated.

That demand applied to our vendors as well. Our Northeast stores were hungrier for product than any other units in the company, so the vendors had to respond more quickly than they had before. The tempo picked up dramatically. Much to their own pleasant surprise, most manufacturers discovered they could keep up. Those that couldn't fell by the wayside.

If we had not adapted, we would have had so many ticked off customers we would have died.

As a company we didn't change our general business philosophy, training, or operational practices to enter the Northeast, but we were forced to radically reexamine our approach to merchandising in volume, and *that* changed the company a lot. The stores we opened there did many, many times higher volume than even we were accustomed to.

We grew within our abilities in the Northeast. There was always a desire to open more than we could handle, but we always opened *less* than we could handle. Instead of opening three or four stores in some markets, we opened just one or two. We made sure that we were staffed with the right kind of people; we spent a phenomenal amount of time and energy on training. If that worked, we could always add more stores later. The key was to do it right the first time.

There was always the issue of whether employees in the Northeast would treat customers as well as they do in the South, where people are generally more genteel. But we found wonderful people. We filtered a lot of people out, finding people in the orientation process. Selection of people became very critical. And they became as good or better than anybody else in this company.

The successful changes we made operationally in the Northeast were instantly applied in the South and the West as well. The paradigm that changed most was that we found that virtually every item that we carried, every line of goods, needed to be packaged in greater quantities. In the South, we would sell 60 electrical receptacles and then order 72 more. In the Northeast, we needed a thousand of the same item. So then we went back to the vendors and said, "We will no longer buy these in 48-packs. Don't even think about packing them 48 to a box. We want a 'coffin'! We want you to bundle up a thousand of them at a time." Once they recovered from the shock at the dramatic size of our orders, vendors quickly acceded to our demand.

■　■　■

During the first three years of our Northeast invasion, 1988–91, our stock just went crazy. Getting a presence to that part of the country exposed us to Wall Street in living color. For the first time, analysts and brokers saw how busy the stores really were. Seeing is believing; our stock once again was climbing upward.

Rating our stock a "Buy/Moderate Risk," analyst Wayne Hood of Prudential-Bache Securities wrote on March 21, 1990: "Home Depot remains our Single Best Idea." He credited three reasons: (1) vendor rebates were greater than expected; (2) sales of higher-margin merchandise were being emphasized; and (3) control over shrinkage had tightened. As a result, Hood noted, "operating income rose a whopping 48 percent."

Many fund managers are based in the Northeast. They may have visited a Home Depot store on an out-of-town retail trip organized by Merrill Lynch or Salomon Brothers, but they never experienced us the way a customer did until we entered their market. Then they walked in not as investors, but as customers.

That's when they began to realize that what we talked about was not only words but deeds. We were the real thing.

Still, analysts are funny people. Some of them will never leave New York, and thus resisted traveling across the river to New Jersey to see our first store. When we opened on Long Island, it was a little easier.

Why was it so important to us that these people actually visit our stores? Here's an example: For some reason, Moody's always rated us higher than Standard & Poor's. Ron Brill launched a campaign to influence Standard & Poor's to reconsider our rating by getting their analyst to experience The Home Depot in the flesh. Once we opened a store in Paramus, he called the appropriate analyst. "You have never seen one of our stores, right? I will fly to New York, pick you up in a limousine, and take you to Paramus," Ron offered. The guy said, "No, I don't have time." Time wasn't the problem; he just wouldn't leave New York. Ron went over the man's head and convinced his boss to make the trip, which did, in fact, have a positive influence on our bond rating.

■   ■   ■

A lot of people criticized us for taking too long to get into markets such as Seattle, Detroit, and Chicago. But our philosophy is to commit stores to markets where we already are established and have become the strongest player in the marketplace. Number one in number of stores, number one in assortment, pricing, service, and so on. We always felt that if we did our thing the best, we would be the leader in the marketplace and we could take that same package of "bests" and replicate it in the next market.

In California, our marketing campaigns were more specialized than they had been in Atlanta, Florida, or Texas. We entered the market in San Diego. The stores were laid out better than ever before. They were larger and had the capacity to hold more product. They were cleaner, brighter. Pricing was extremely aggressive. But what ultimately blew the Californians away was the high service level in our stores. The public took to The Home Depot like movie producers to cellular telephones. They went absolutely nuts "taking meetings" with us.

In San Diego, there is a company called Dixieline, which is a traditional outside lumber store with a small interior hardware store. Builders Emporium had 40,000-square-foot stores. We came in with a 100,000-square-foot store and blew them both away. We had the right mousetrap at the right time.

The volume of people through our doors grew all the time, and sales quickly reached $500,000 a week, a record for the time. Bryant Scott, who opened the San Diego store and was its first manager, told his merchants to start buying in anticipation of $600,000 weeks.

"You aren't buying enough stuff," he insisted. Garden products in particular were very well received. Department heads would order 50 plants and Scott would put a "1" in front of it. He also ordered more carts for carrying more stuff. He was aggressive, determined to take those store sales as high as they could go.

Once the stores reached $700,000 in weekly sales, Scott became convinced $1 million was within range.

I visited San Diego to see the fun for myself. The place was packed with incoming merchandise, flooding the aisles, making some of them virtually unpassable.

"Man, what are you doing?" I said, aghast.

"We have to have it to sell it," Scott explained confidently. "We are going to find out how high is high."

He did just that, making an incredible amount of money. And as we continued opening stores in the San Diego area—Oceanside, Chula Vista, Escondido, Balboa, and University—we promoted Scott to district manager. We had to—he owned the market.

I used to oversee quarterly staff meetings in which district managers would bring their financials and show them on a screen. Scott's stores were making more money than anybody else's, so he would stand up, post his financials, and his presentation would last, oh, about thirty-two seconds. I would look at the numbers, exhale, and say, "Keep sending the checks, Bryant. Keep sending those checks."

■   ■   ■

We had a merchant, Stephen Bebis, who was eventually promoted to vice president of merchandising. He held the position for only a couple of months, however, before being recruited away by the Molson Companies, which is best known for its Canadian brewery. Molson assigned him to start a Canadian-based home improvement chain. The Home Depot was not yet in Canada, so it wasn't directly competitive, but we—and our ex-merchant—knew we were going there eventually.

Aikenhead's Home Improvement Warehouse, as the nine Molson stores (six were open, three were under construction) were called, built a good reputation with customers, but Molson, seeing us looming on the horizon, decided that rather than do battle with us, it made more sense to join forces. We bought a 75 percent interest in Aikenhead's in 1994 and changed its name to The Home Depot Canada. (We bought out the rest of Molson's interest in 1998.) It was a much better operation than Bowater, which had made us wary of acquisitions. Aikenhead's had good people and some critical real estate that we wanted. They also had partners that would be important to have in a new and, for us, foreign marketplace.

In Aikenhead's, Molson had a business that was very successful— at least from a customer-service point of view. Customers loved the store. And based on that, Aikenhead's employees participated in a bonus plan that gave the impression the company was succeeding.

But in reality, the stores were losing fistfuls of money. That became a problem in merging the companies because we had to break the news to Aikenhead's employees that their stores were not financially viable—which is why Molson sold out to us.

It took a long time to get Aikenhead's payroll and operating expenses in line; it didn't happen overnight. We invested a year in converting their operational systems. And it took us almost two years to bring our values into this company. But it was still a better transition than Bowater, because by the time we bought Aikenhead, it could not, as a percentage, affect the bulk of our business the way Bowater had.

We also did something new. Rather than just tell the Aikenhead's employees what The Home Depot was, Larry Mercer, our executive vice president of operations, suggested we *show* them. He developed an exchange program that put many of them to work in our U.S. stores for months at a time. And we sent people from the United States to Canada so that we all learned each other's culture. (It later became the model for developing our first stores in Chile.)

The irony of Aikenhead's was that even though it had copied many Depot traits, what The Home Depot needed in Canada was a Canadian. Now that we have one, division president Annette M. Verschuren, the growth of our Canadian division has gone from good to spectacular.

■ ■ ■

The 24-hour home improvement center may be one of our boldest, most customer-friendly moves yet.

The decision to expand a store's hours to an around-the-clock schedule is something Larry Mercer and I pushed through after several years of trying. It is based on a very scientific method: We count headlights. How much traffic is driving by the store at midnight or three in the morning?

Our Flushing store in the New York City borough of Queens was the first to go 24 hours in June 1994. A huge portion of the population there works the midnight shift. Your off hours may be after six P.M. and on the weekends. Theirs might be one in the morning, and they wanted a place to shop—especially those planning to start their home improvement projects by two A.M. We wanted a Home Depot that served their needs.

There are already twenty of these stores, and there will be a significant increase in their number in the near future, usually in urban areas that tend to be congested during the day.

The 24-hour/seven-day-a-week stores created some communications and teaching problems for the company. We were already doing video training Sunday mornings at 6:30 or 7:00 A.M. and we had to push that back in some stores to 5:00 A.M. And instead of one store manager, each 24/7 unit has two.

■   ■   ■

We double the size of The Home Depot Inc. every 3.5 years. The base number of stores keeps growing, but we believe we have the infrastructure in place to double the company again in the next four years. When we went from four to eight stores in 1981—expanding from Atlanta into South Florida—it almost killed us, because the next four stores were higher volume than the first four stores, and we weren't ready for it. But we learn from our mistakes.

For the last decade, The Home Depot's growth has been very consistent, between 21 percent and 22 percent each year in terms of store count. This is not growth for growth's sake. It's a strategy for *profitable* growth in response to favorable trends that we see in the marketplace. They include an increase in households, growth in the overall industry, continued cultivation of existing customers, as well as consolidation in the industry and opportunities in the international marketplace.

As we have grown, the industry has grown, and we still don't have a huge market share. The do-it-yourself industry, based on 1996 numbers, is about $135 billion in annual sales. We still only do 15 percent of that total market—$20 billion in 1996. To put that in context, 85 percent of the products in our industry are sold outside of our stores, so when people ask if suppliers have the capacity to grow with us, sure they do. They are shipping more than 85 percent of what they make now to retailers other than us. That leaves a lot of business worth competing over.

And the fact is, $135 billion is an inaccurate depiction of the market. An important part of our mindset about growth was redefining *our* view of the home improvement industry. In 1996 we redefined the traditional measurement to include products already sold by us or our competitors, and sales to customers in businesses related to home improvement that were not included in the traditional measure. We looked at how all building materials are sold in the United States and Canada. With a limited number of exceptions, all of these areas are in some way related to our core business. The redefined industry as a whole is even more fragmented than the traditionally defined home improvement industry. It is everything from providing light bulbs for a Howard Johnson's Motor Lodge to supplying renovation materials for a single-family home. Instead of the $135-billion-a-year industry the consultants describe, we see close to a $365-billion-a-year market. The Home Depot's market share in the $365-billion industry is only about 5 percent, providing lots of opportunity for growth.

Of the $365 billion, $265 billion is spending by professional customers: electricians and plumbers, general contractors, repair and remodelers, and heavy construction. We then excluded areas outside our core business, such as steel beams, concrete, and other heavy construction, and wound up with a pro market of $215 billion. Our piece of this pie is very small—about 2.5 percent—and this is where we are looking at opportunities to gain market share. By rethinking "the pond in which we fish," we have expanded our market and given The Home Depot an almost limitless opportunity.

This pro market can be split in two: the smaller pro customer, who does repair and remodeling, and the large pro. The small pro typically spends less than $200,000 in total annual material purchases and makes most of those purchases at home centers or wholesale supply houses. The large pro spends more than $200,000 annually and rarely shops in home centers, instead making most purchases at wholesalers or other outlets. This latter group requires extensive price tiers, rebates, and large-scale deliveries.

Admittedly, the traditional Home Depot stores are not equipped to adequately serve all of the large pro customer's needs. The small pro, however, is already a Home Depot customer but only buys 10 percent of his or her materials from us. That's our real opportunity.

Service and relationships are most important to the smaller pros, less so pricing because we are already perceived as being price-competitive. They shop our stores for convenience sake, so we need to provide faster in-and-out service and go further in developing relationships with them.

To address these two primary issues, we are putting a separate pro service desk into our stores to quickly meet the pro's product and service needs. We are also reaching out to them with the *ProBook*, a specialty catalog of 15,000 products chosen especially for pros and business trades. Finally, we're adding new credit programs and a menu of delivery options at competitive prices to get products to the pro faster.

We realize we cannot serve all pro customers efficiently and profitably inside our existing stores. That's why we're initially focusing on one segment of the pro business. And we will *not* rob resources from the DIY customer to attract pro customers.

One of the significant advantages we do have with regard to the pro customers is that time is money. Our stores are open long hours, seven days a week. The average supply house where most pros do their business is open 7:00 A.M. to 4:30 P.M. and a couple of hours on Saturday.

We originally only carried home improvement products and home improvement brand names such as Black & Decker. Today we have grown beyond that, however, and we stock contractor brands such as Halo Lighting, DeWalt Power Tools, and Milwaukee Tool. Often whatever is good for the pro turns out to be doubly good for the do-it-yourselfer. It is not just a question of getting the job done better, either. They like tools, they like good products, and they get a kick out of having high-quality products that they can work with and show off to their neighbors.

The Home Depot has deliberately and continually expanded the hardware and home improvement market. We introduced new products, broadened selection, found or inspired merchandise that made projects easier to do yourself. Eventually we reached the point where we were stimulating manufacturers to make products that were more friendly in terms of appeal, application, construction, and preassembled parts.

When we first signed up Milwaukee Tool as a vendor, we talked their products up as a high-quality, high-end addition to our overall merchandise selection. A store manager in North Plainfield, New Jersey, got so excited about it he called Pat Farrah up on a Thursday and said, "Come see what I have done with these."

Well, instead of tucking the Milwaukee Tools in a nice place where only our pro customers would know to look for them, he built an end-cap display full of these professional tools that retailed for $130 each on average. The endcap was stacked floor to ceiling. Pat didn't even know that Milwaukee made that many saws in a year, let alone that he would ever see them in one place. But there they were on display, signed and ready to go.

Pat, a man who can be brought to tears by a gleaming stack of pliers, nonetheless thought there were not enough contractors in all of New Jersey to buy all these tools.

He was wrong. The following Monday, the manager called again and invited him back to the store. "You have to see this," he said.

Four days later, half of the tools in the display had been sold.

It told us that it wasn't just the pro buying these products; do-it-yourselfers were buying them, too. Just like one person buys a Chevy and another takes a BMW, some customers want the option of choosing a Milwaukee or a DeWalt over a no-name saw.

We helped create this breed of people who want to buy high-end hardware products. They want—and can afford—to emulate the pros.

When we first got to Atlanta, do-it-yourselfers were people who mowed their own lawns and maybe painted once in a while. We encouraged and taught them to do room additions, electrical wiring, and plumbing through our clinics. We took the fear out of a lot of projects. Instead of saying, "I can't do that," we put our customers in front of pros who showed them how. Since opening our first store in Atlanta, we have given confidence to DIYers all across North America that if the project did not go well, we would take care of them.

One of the key strategies of this company has always been to do things before we needed to do them. That may sound obvious, but lots of companies get painted into a corner, then they have to react instead of pre-act.

One of the reasons we own as much real estate as we do today— 70 percent of existing sites and nearly 100 percent of new locations— is that we want to control the store through the development cycle.

With the simultaneous consolidation of chains and overall growth of sales taking place in our industry, we don't want to end up in a few years accepting C and D quality locations because all the better sites are gone.

The Merchant, Act II

"Who Is Staring Out the Window, Wondering Where We Will Be in Five Years?"*

Pat Farrah was always looking for opportunities to make the stores better. Some days he communicated those ideas better than other days. Early associates had to be smart enough to separate his message from the way in which he delivered it, which was sometimes direct and unsympathetic. Some people couldn't handle that, especially when he used language that would not be considered politically correct these days. "This area is an abortion!" Pat would holler. But that critical eye for detail represented an important stage of our development. It made us better. It made us noncomplacent.

Pat is a hands-on guy, and when the company got to the size where he couldn't touch everything every day, it frustrated him. When he couldn't be in every store every day, when he couldn't be involved in everything, he lost it.

Whatever "control" is, he is the opposite. He is a product guy, but not one who is terribly well organized. He doesn't like operations. Where we are disciplined and know our outer limits, Pat had no limits. He worked hours that were inhuman. And he drove the people that worked for us to be just like him. He is a merchant, and that is what is important in this company, the merchandise.

* Bernie Marcus

One day, a top merchant came to see Arthur. "I have to talk to you about Pat," he said, a tone of desperation in his voice. "I can't take the strain of keeping up with him anymore. I have to leave the company." His announcement came as a complete shock.

We didn't know how serious the problem with Pat was until this merchant spoke up. He was exhausted, emotionally and physically. Here's why: Workdays with Pat sometimes started by seven A.M. or earlier. He might or might not eat lunch. Dinner was not often eaten until three in the morning. The next morning, he would start at seven A.M. all over again. This would go on seven days and nights in a row, because he always worked weekends.

Pat was destroying even the heartiest people working for him. He drove them, and he drove himself.

The time came for Pat to leave. His frustration level was getting bigger and bigger every day and was affecting the way he conducted his life and the way he dealt with people. Nobody could work for him. They all loved him, they all respected him, they thought he was a brilliant merchant, but you can't push people that far, that long, and expect them to be able to function. They just couldn't do it.

As for Pat, he was frustrated. He was the type of guy who expected that if he walked into a Home Depot, everybody would know him. He once told us how aggravated he was because he walked into several stores, and he would say, "Hey, you have to do this, and you have to do that," and they would say, "Who *are* you? Why are you telling us what to do?"

And he would say, "What do you mean, who am I? I'm Pat Farrah!"

"Burnout" is a shopworn phrase that doesn't quite explain this situation. It was more an issue of Pat not being able to adapt to the breadth of what we had become.

Pat has the capacity for creating something from nothing, but he had this greater need to be all over, to be the Home Depot ambassador of everything, and it reached a point where he couldn't be managed.

We had some stretches where I didn't speak to Pat for days at a time because I thought he was being too crazy. The problem simmered for six months as this madness, this hyperkinetic, frantic behavior rose to a boil.

When he left, it was one of the saddest days we have ever known, because he was a guy who we loved dearly, loved like a brother. We cared about his well-being and health, and his health was not good. He was not taking care of himself, and we were concerned about what was going to happen to him.

More important, he left the thing he loved the most, which was The Home Depot. He loved it because he was one of the creators of it, and leaving was a terrible, terrible day for him and for all of us. Not only that, he is such a fun guy. He was such an upbeat guy and so great to be around. His passion was an inspiration for us all.

When Pat left in 1985, we all thought our 31-store company was big, but it was tiny.

In many ways, Pat Farrah's departure in 1985 marked The Home Depot's coming of age. Whenever Pat was around, there was controversy. Life was never quiet and peaceful. The air was always electric, and after he was gone, we had to generate more of our own electricity. We missed him, but we also proved to ourselves that we could still run the business, even if it wasn't as much fun without him. We came to understand that the culture we created was bigger than any one person and would survive and flourish when the day came for any of the founders to move on.

The next ten years saw unbridled and virtually unrestrained expansion. As the number of stores and associates multiplied, we developed mature operational systems and settled into life as an unqualified retail success, both in the aisles and on Wall Street. It was a heady time and yet, because we're not a couple of 25-year-olds, it didn't go to our heads. We enjoyed success but stayed grounded at the same time.

■　■　■

A decade later, in late 1995, one of the happiest days of our lives occurred: Pat Farrah returned to the company.

We never lost touch with Pat. Pat has always been in the family; he was never banished. We always talked on the phone, we always did things together, such as playing golf. Arthur organizes an outing every year that always brought the four Home Depot partners together; Pat never missed it.

In his years away from us, he helped his kids, Michael and Shannon, into adulthood. He and his second wife, Ann, spent their time at homes in California, Florida, and Hawaii. He bought two ocean racers and a 62-foot sport fishing boat.

In a disorganized manner, we—including Ken Langone—began planting a seed for Pat's ultimate return a good two years before he actually came back. Ken even helped Pat attract $9 million to finance his other business, MG Products.

He sold merchandise to us through MG Products, so he would be in our stores, and every so often he would call one of us about something that distressed him in a Home Depot.

"You are running a terrible business, you have to do this, you have to do that. . . ."

Actually, he wouldn't say, "*You* have to do this. . . ." Pat would say, "*We* have to do this. . . . *We* are doing this wrong." In his mind, he never left The Home Depot. And everything he told us was dead-on accurate, and we listened closely to him.

Arthur began informal discussions with Pat in late 1994 about returning him to the fold. I harbored doubts about the sagacity of such a move, so we took our time. Finally, after a day of playing golf at Arthur's annual tournament in '95, Pat and I were walking together when he started telling me all the things we needed to fix in the stores.

"Pat," I said, "I am tired of listening to you tell me what we have to do. I think it's time for you to come back."

We all felt the same way.

People outside this company never quite understood our eagerness to bring Pat back into the fold. "The company was going great guns!" they said. "Why did you need him back?"

Certainly not because things had deteriorated. Sales per square foot and sales per store were both up dramatically in the ten years he was away. We had also seen improvement on gross margins and in the lowering of our cost of buying product. In fact, from 1985 to 1995, *everything* got better. His departure actually marked our coming of age.

But in terms of creating a spark, building the training environment, having a vision—we wanted that from Pat. A home run hitter like Mark McGwire is not a balanced player. Every couple of at-bats, he hits one out of the park. In between, however, he may just as often strike out. A team could probably win without him, but a McGwire is a great addition to a team. He thrills the fans; he also excites his own teammates. Everybody wants to see him play. So if you're looking for a long-ball player, you want a Mark McGwire or a Pat Farrah in your organization. We simply had not been able to duplicate many of Pat's strengths. He was such an unusual guy.

Today, sure, we're a huge success, but what about five years from now? Who is staring out the window, wondering where we will be then? The company was doing well because of its size, but like anything else, if you aren't always renewing your youth, you get old. We noticed, in the early 1990s, that we didn't have the same verve that we'd once had. We needed not only to revive ourselves, but we also needed some new thinking.

Sometimes you get so close to the trees you don't see the forest, right? There is a difference between a great company and an also-ran company. A great company goes beyond making money. A great company has a mission, a vision, a dream. We needed a road map back to the forest.

We also became a little fat, a little arrogant. "We're the biggest. . . . We're the best. . . . We can do whatever we want!" But that attitude also makes you lazy and sloppy, as we ultimately discovered when we found we were paying too much for certain products. That would have never happened on Pat's watch.

We gave our merchants too much latitude, only to learn that in certain categories, our competitors—and even smaller companies— were getting better deals than we were. We needed a revival of aggressiveness in dealing with certain vendors. They needed to be reminded that we must always be the cheapest guys in town.

The Home Depot needed Pat Farrah to keep us thinking like youngsters. We needed some aggressive behavior. We needed some craziness.

I consider myself a damn good merchant, but Pat is better. He is the best any of us have ever seen. We wanted him on the team back in the Homeco days, and we never stopped longing for him during the decade he was away.

Pat well knew when he returned that he was coming into a situation that was potentially fraught with risks for him and for the company. Therefore, his return demanded a greater level of patience and diplomacy than had been his hallmark in the past. The years away from the company mellowed the man without costing him his edge. Pat recognized that he might be a threat to some people, and he bent over backward not to be one. He grew into a marvelous developer of talent, so people who have a desire will grow by virtue of their proximity to him, and people who are threatened by Pat will be threatened by anybody, and probably shouldn't be with us.

Some people who used to work with Pat and are still with us felt that he deserted them when he left. When he came back years later, there were some bad feelings: "You have been gone all this time. You expect to step right back in and tell us what to do?" And they didn't like it. There was some reticence on a lot of people's parts, people who are fairly high up in the organization today who might have been merchants when Pat was the head merchant.

But if you spoke to those same people today, they would say it was terrific that he came back.

Bill Hamlin, our executive vice president of merchandising and a group president, deserves tremendous credit for creating the environment that allowed Pat Farrah to return. Bill is Pat's boss, so it fell to him to create a situation in which Pat could come back and once more make a substantial contribution—and not only that, but to establish a complementary, positive relationship with him. Few people I know could do that.

If Bill had said, "I don't want this guy back, I'm the senior merchant in this company," we would not have been able to bring Pat back. We value Bill's contribution too much to undermine him. It would have created a very divisive environment. But Bill worked hard to create a place where Pat could come back and be Pat, stardust, warts, and all.

As it turns out, Bill is a very good counterbalance for Pat. He knows how to get people to buy into and support Pat's ideas. He also knows how to diplomatically step on Pat's brakes, too. Because with 55,000 SKUs on average in every store—and 775 stores—we need good systems to focus us on what department needs attention. Bill's very good at that. The beauty is that they balance and respect each other, much the way Arthur and I do.

Pat brought a lot of the old culture back, the hands-on feeling. He is a wonderful motivator. He has trained our merchants and gotten them back to the basics, which, the bigger we become, the more they need to do.

In rejoining us, Pat realized he had nothing left to prove. The Home Depot is an enormous, over-the-top success, and he is one of the reasons. Pat doesn't have to worry about titles or status or anything else this time around. Everybody knows that he has immediate and direct access to us. Pat knows who he is, likes who he is.

But he is still a dangerous person. He could still bury us with inventory. In fact, it almost happened. When he first came back, we said, "Pat, you cannot order anything. You coordinate, you facilitate, you are not ordering. We are not giving you a pen."

So he pumped the merchants up, and they went out, and *they* would order all the inventory in response to whatever Pat said. When we confronted him, he was like the cute little "Not Me" ghost-child in the "Family Circus" comic strip. He would say, "I didn't do it; it wasn't me." But it was him; he goaded them on, saying things like, "Who in this room won't step up and order some of this?" So they *all* stepped up, and that quickly we were overinventoried.

Merchants get in a room, away from regular people, and they get a little crazy. Or instead of testing a product in one market, they order the product for every market, and we can't do that anymore. We have too many stores.

That ten years of seasoning away from us was good for all of us. The impact that Pat has had in this company in the last few years can't be measured. There is an indefatigable spirit he brought with him that we sorely missed.

Pat will look at something and say, "If you make it just that way, I can sell 300,000 of them, but if you make that blue instead of yellow,

I can sell 600,000 of them." Don't ask Pat to explain how he came up with those numbers, but it is scary how many times he is right. That is Pat's genius. He brings a special verve to our business that no one else can match. It's a style of looking at a product and knowing how we can make it better, or how we can get the vendor to do something differently and thereby drive more volume through the stores. Pat can instinctively tell us how to create a better value perception of us with consumers. How we can clean up SKU creep. It's all second nature to him.

Not everybody can be entrepreneurial from a creative standpoint, and we created that environment for Pat. We gave him a hothouse to flourish in twenty years ago, and we're doing it again now.

It is like we created a seed bed in which Pat could be planted, and then we kept the storms and the crap and the creditors and the banks and the this and the that and everybody away from him until he could grow.

We needed him; he needed us. We are incomplete without him; he stretches our parameters, and we protect his blind sides. When he came back, the first day we worked together in almost a decade was astounding. The magic hadn't left us. We all laughed, recognizing the fact that we were the same and the combination of us was still a beautiful thing.

Pat is a great part of this culture—the interrelationship with the associates and the interrelationship of the company with the communities in which we have our stores. You can learn something from him just by being around him for more than ten minutes. He walks into a store and immediately increases the level of morale. He is that dynamic. And at any moment, he might get up on a desk, start clapping his hands, and get a cheer going.

When we set up The Home Depot, we deliberately engineered a fine balance between the merchandising, operations, and financial groups. But merchandising was always key. It didn't mean the financials weren't important or that operations weren't important, but we knew that creating sales was the *most* important. The role of operations was supporting sales. The role of the financial group was capturing the dollars and reinvesting them.

When Pat returned, he brought back all of the passion that he had before—and much more. But at the same time, Pat recognized his own limitations. He still works terrible hours, and there is nothing we can do about it, but he does use people better, and he is training people now. He has learned that he must train people in order to get things accomplished. He understands what a real executive does, and we are strengthened because of it.

Strategic Partners

"We Had to Be Psychologists, Lovers, Romancers, and Con Artists"*

Our number one job in 1979 and the early 1980s was to get the vendors and manufacturers who sold us goods to see a vision: The Home Depot as the number one home improvement center in the world.

The relationship between us and the companies that sell product to us is a vital link in our success. Today we leverage our stores' enormous sales volume to get the best possible prices. But over time, these relationships grew from leaps of faith on the manufacturers' part to great nurturing and respect on both sides as The Home Depot became a brand name unto itself.

We had a singular vision that we sold over and over again. The first group we sold it to was the bankers. The second was the vendors. We used to tell these people that we would lead our industry before long—and be convincing when we said it, too. We dared them to look into our eyes when we said: "Do you think anything is going to stop us?" You must stick to a vision and turn people into believers.

We had to be psychologists, lovers, romancers, and con artists to get them aboard. Our ability to paint a picture of how that would take place—lowest prices, widest selection, and great customer service—was what convinced skeptical manufacturers to sell merchandise to us during the early years.

* Bernie Marcus

We would take the vendors out and use all of our guile to convince people to do business with us. We spent at least three nights a week schmoozing and pitching to vendors at Pano's and Paul's restaurant in Atlanta. We were pretty good dream weavers, especially with something in which we fervently believed, especially where our lives were on the line. We talked about what they normally would sell to a retail store. Then we would give them round numbers of what we thought we could move. The numbers that we threw out were ones they had never heard from people in our industry before. Most didn't believe us until we laid down immense orders.

We didn't have the buying power of our established competitors; on paper, we couldn't compete with Handy City or Handy Dan. But we were very good at selling futures. "You need to do this for us now," we'd tell vendors, "because, down the road, we will have fifty stores. Eventually we will be the biggest in the industry, so now is the time for you to get on board."

As in any long-term relationship, the key was getting to know the vendors and, at the same time, understanding what motivated them. Then *we* motivated them. We appealed to their greed, we appealed to their enthusiasm for new concepts, we appealed to their need to get their products exposed.

Manufacturers gave us target projections for sales lines, and then we would ask whether we could get incremental discounts as sales volumes increased. So if the cost of the product was $20, we would ask, "When sales hit $100,000, can we get a 2 percent discount?" And when we sold another $150,000, we asked for a 3 percent discount. At $400,000, we then asked for a 5 percent discount.

All the vendors looked at us like we were crazy anyway, not because of the discounts per se, but because there was no way in the world we would get that kind of business. Of course, we regularly exceeded projections, so when we received the 5 percent quantity discount we negotiated in the beginning on top of what was already considered a good price, the vendors were shocked. They never expected us to sell in such volumes.

In lieu of direct price breaks, there was always a fresh idea to get a manufacturer to provide co-op advertising instead.

■   ■   ■

By the time we expanded from two to four stores, we were buying product equivalent to the volume that Handy Dan ordered for all 66 of its stores. It was mind-boggling for the vendors and their salespeople.

The sales people, especially, wanted to believe in our numbers and potential. They had to be optimistic, otherwise they couldn't survive in the selling business. So we were selling to sellers, selling something that couldn't help but capture their commission-hardened hearts.

Pat Farrah and I had a grab bag of different routines that we used to win over stubborn vendors. The most basic approach was a Mutt and Jeff thing where Pat would start talking and talking. When he lost steam, I would jump in with fresh enthusiasm before the vendor could change the direction of the conversation. Then Pat would talk some more, then me. It was a mortar barrage that wore down the opposition.

Since then, we have learned they all feared that we would be bankrupt inside of two years. They felt this way because people like Frank Denny—who took over Handy Dan when Arthur and I were fired— told them that The Home Depot concept would never work. The numbers did not work, so how could these giant stores turn merchandise fast enough to pay the bills?

In a sense, Denny and the others were right. The numbers didn't work on the face of it, which is why I persuaded Arthur to be as aggressive as humanly possible with the numbers in the original business plan. There was no reason to expect a two- or even four-store southern hardware chain would not only be able to dictate who it bought product from—manufacturers over wholesale distributors— but price and terms as well.

■   ■   ■

Pat Farrah was always the emotional and spiritual leader of The Home Depot's merchants, those men and women who negotiated with vendors and manufacturers to acquire goods for sale in our stores.

Pat taught these merchants how to negotiate, how to handle themselves, how to walk away. "Don't be afraid to ask for more," he'd say. "That is really the biggest thing, don't be afraid to ask."

The senior buyers in this company working under Pat and Bill Hamlin, have always been put up on a pedestal. They are our cowboys, always on the road, flying, driving, going wherever the deals are made, from Atlanta to Beijing, from Sacramento to Sydney. They operate under tight schedules, sometimes wondering where they've been, where they are, or where they're going.

If you want merchants who chase deals like Dobermans, they are going to bite people once in a while. Pat's role with the merchants was to take this energy, both positive and negative, and tame the men and women who were too aggressive, juice those who were not aggressive enough, build the confidence in the neurotic ones, and control the ones who were overconfident.

■   ■   ■

Bruce Berg came to us from Wickes Companies, and if our merchants already had a cowboy reputation when Berg joined them, he was the first to look the part.

We were exactly the kind of place Berg was looking for, because we didn't care if he had a beard or not—he did—and we didn't care if he wore a suit or not—he did not. We were only interested in results.

Berg came here partly because he was drawn by the legend of Pat Farrah; unfortunately, Pat left the company less than six months later. The two didn't really get to know one another until Pat returned a decade later.

Many things have changed about this company over the years, but one thing has not: We accept people for what they are and who they are, as long as they are going in the same direction as we are. Some of them may travel at 105 mph, some at 75, but everybody is pretty much moving in the same direction. Those that don't usually leave the company of their own volition. Rarely do we have to tap somebody on the shoulder and say, "You don't understand the culture of the company." Those people tend to move on by themselves.

As for Berg, he fit in. One of his earliest assignments—and the one in which he had the greatest long-term impact—was straightening out our ceiling fan operation.

Pat bought ceiling fans like there was no tomorrow from every factory that made them and put a variety of brand names on them; the whole operation was out of control.

Berg put all those diverse products under a single brand-name umbrella, Hampton Bay. Today Hampton Bay is the largest-selling brand of ceiling fans in the world by quite a margin, and it is a brand name that is very well respected.

■   ■   ■

We fell in love a lot in the early days. But sometimes our love went unrequited.

Some large national manufacturers, companies such as 3M and Wagner Paint Sprayers, initially treated us as if we could be bankrupt in a week.

That was their opinion. Ours was that we didn't need their merchandise in our stores.

Eight years and several hundred stores later, 3M came back to the bargaining table admitting they had made a serious blunder with us. They did get back in, and they paid a very steep price for the opportunity. They were always important to us, but not at the price of putting up with their condescending behavior.

But even that relationship still needs to be tweaked now and again. We have ten stores in Minneapolis, where 3M is based, but one of their key guys on our account had never been in our store until we made an issue of it. Is that pathetic? It is amazing—even today—how many people will try to sell to us and they don't even know us. Step one for any vendor: Get to know us! Spend time in our stores, talk to our associates, talk to our customers. We often invite vendors to conduct their meetings with our merchants on the store sales floor, to get them to understand what this is about.

Porter Cable took eight years to convince that they should sell to us. Klein Tools took eleven years.

People in the industry call us the 800-pound gorilla. And we, in turn, say to vendors that when you start to dance with an 800-pound gorilla, you don't stop dancing until the gorilla wants to stop. That is why some manufacturers were reluctant to sell to The Home Depot once we became big. They missed the opportunity when the company was small, and now they look at it and wonder, "Do I really want to stick my hands in its mouth? Do I trust it that much?"

For many years, these manufacturers thought a stiff wind would blow us away. Then we began affecting their core businesses. Halo and Klein both sell into the electrical distribution channel. We eventually affected that channel using other suppliers. One day, the electrical trade magazines weren't talking about other electrical distributors, they were talking about the effect that The Home Depot had on their business.

The instinct of survival took over, and someone decided, "Get me that guy from Home Depot, the one who is always after me at the trade shows."

The traditional lines of distribution prior to The Home Depot were very strong. Typically, most manufacturers sold through distributors. There were very strong relationships built up over the years. It took a tremendous amount of energy for us to convince manufacturers that the world had changed.

We were not going to buy from any wholesaler or distributor. We had customers coming into our stores who were consumers of many of these products. When they couldn't buy these products in our stores, they bought something else. So we had to convince the manufacturers that they had to be in our stores because that's where their customers were. That was our selling point.

"Go outside one of our stores and interview our customers," we'd tell the manufacturers. "Find out how many of them were your customers and are no longer your customers."

Every business is there to please the customer. They had to understand that the way they did things was not working anymore. It took time to convince them that that type of distribution was going away and they needed to jump on the bandwagon.

There are few product lines today that we can't buy direct from the manufacturer. It didn't matter how many times they said no, because we would never stop asking. The job of Home Depot merchants is getting their own way. They are professional get-your-own-way people.

For many years, Weiser Lock was one of those manufacturers that didn't return our flirtatious advances. It already had a satisfactory form of distribution, utilizing a wholesaler in south Georgia, Addison Corp. (now Rugby Building Products, Inc.), that sold its product across the South. But we didn't want to buy anything from distributors, we wanted everything direct from manufacturers, drop-shipped direct from their plants to our stores, which was a radical way to do business in those days. That's because it was cheaper. We eliminated a layer of price markup with direct shipping. And it was faster. By not going through distributors, we got the goods much faster to our customers.

But Weiser didn't want to disrupt its distribution. The company figured if they cut a new deal with us it might make Addison angry with them, or it would eat into Addison's sales. We kept telling them that we had customers that Addison would never see. We personally guaranteed that Weiser would see incremental sales increases. In fact, we promised to increase Weiser's exposure.

We made that pitch to Phil Pryne, the president of Weiser, for four years. Finally, in the early 1980s, we wore him down and he gave in, tired of hearing our relentless song and dance. We picked up the full line of Weiser Locks, and they sold like crazy.

The very same year, Weiser's wholesaler, Addison, saw an 18 percent increase in sales because we had done the hard work of increasing the brand's name recognition in our advertising. We had burnished our point in green—and orange.

In fact, Weiser sales were so good at The Home Depot that when Pat retired in 1985, he had an unexpected visitor in fellow retiree Phil Pryne. Pryne had sold the business and moved to Alamitos Bay, California, where, by sheer coincidence, he lived seven houses away from Pat. On Christmas Eve, Pryne showed up at Pat's house with a big magnum of champagne.

"I just wanted to thank you for selling me on selling to you," he said. "That was the day my business went through the roof. That was the day I became a multimillionaire. Today I am living in a beautiful house on the water here because you made me sell to you. I wanted to thank you and let you know that I truly recognize you as the moving force that made my life."

Pat was stunned and delighted.

"There is only one thing I am angry about," Pryne added. "Couldn't you have convinced me to sell to you faster?"

■   ■   ■

There is a real art to negotiating and getting people to do what you want them to do and work to the death and be happy about it; it's largely because when we say we will do something, we will.

Now every once in a while, one of our merchants will make a commitment and we won't be able to fulfill it. Or there are cases in which a vendor thinks he got a raw deal from us. If that happens, we will make it right, period. We back our words 100 percent, and people know that. So even though they have to work really tight on their margins to sell to us, they aren't afraid to because they know that they will get back their risk with us.

Our criteria for which product lines we carry were defined right from the beginning as that merchandise in which our sales dominated the category. Second, we had to have top-of-mind awareness for the category. For example, when people think of kiddy swimming pools, they don't think first of The Home Depot, they think of Toys "R" Us, Target, or Wal-Mart. They will never think of us for kiddy swimming pools, so there is no reason for us to carry them.

But when people need a filter for their furnace, who do they think of? Us. So even if we don't make money on furnace filters, we must stock them.

And the third question is: Is it a product essential for the repair, refurbishing, remodeling, or fix-up of a home or business? If the answer is no to any of those questions, then we don't have any business carrying that product.

The sheer number of transactions we do in every store makes us attractive to vendors. The bigger we get, the more vendors will show up with phenomenally profitable opportunities to get their products visibility in our stores. But because we can't confuse our customers about what business we are in, we must often say no to some great deals.

■   ■   ■

The Home Depot concept took hard-selling in the early days because even if salespeople wanted to sell to us, when they pitched it to their company, the comptroller, CFO, or credit manager would turn the deal down. For our merchants, a sale meant not only convincing the salesperson, but also the CFO and eventually the CEO. We often had to deal with all three to get deals done.

Pat Farrah would say, "I need to have this," and then we would have to go after a manufacturer to sell it to us. It was difficult, especially when the merchandise in question came from someone who lost money on Pat at Homeco.

I knew Peter Gold of Price Pfister, a manufacturer of high-quality plumbing fixtures for the bath and kitchen, from my Handy Dan days. He declined our first advances to carry his lines, but I wouldn't take no for an answer.

"Peter," I said, "not only are you going to sell to us, but we are going to buy it cheaper than we did at Handy Dan. And I need extra advertising dollars, because we have no money, and we need invoice postdating on top of that." Normally their dating was end of the month (EOM) or 30-day dating. But we would get 60, 90, or even 150 days to pay our invoices. That was as important to us as buying the product cheaper. It eased our cash flow immeasurably. We didn't know when the cash was going to start flowing, so paying for anything was a crapshoot.

Gold appreciated our long friendship, but there were bigger issues confronting him. "If I sell to you," Gold said, "I have already been told that I will probably lose 20 percent of my business, maybe 25 percent. There are people who will immediately stop buying from me if I sell to you."

There were subtle threats like this from competitive retailers to almost every manufacturer. Gold did sell to us, and he did lose that other business. But his act, because he was very influential in the vendor community, convinced a lot of other vendors to sell us product.

After he sold his business, Gold joined our board and served with distinction.

■ ■ ■

Today, our stores represent a very important part of many vendors' overall business, both in terms of sales and bottom line. Doing business with us requires a great commitment of manufacturers' resources, because for us to stock their product across all of our stores, they must invest heavily in manufacturing and distribution, as well as money for displays, collateral, and advertising.

And while we are loyal to a fault, shelf space in The Home Depot is brutally competitive. We have an insatiable appetite for merchandise, to the point of frequently suggesting new national or regional products or line extensions to our vendors.

Occasionally, manufacturers run into trouble with us when they can't keep up with demand, but that's not for lack of warning from us. We keep our vendors thoroughly apprised of our expansion plans, for example, and we expect them to take steps to keep us fully stocked.

In the early days we did this because it was important to get their support, have them believe in the concept, and have an understanding of what we were trying to accomplish.

Today we tell the vendors where we are going and when we will be there. These manufacturers are not like Chicken Little where the sky will fall down on them one day. Home Depot stores are planned well in advance. At any time, we know how many and where our new sites will be for the next four to five years. We actively share with them the level of detail they need so that they have the distribution and manufacturing in place to keep up. There are some individual vendor situations where we are an awfully big piece of their pie, and that is not good for us or them. We don't want to get too dependent, and neither should they.

Despite our best efforts to work with and help them grow with us, some manufacturers still make the mistake of saying yes to us when they should say no, or at the very least, maybe. If they stretch themselves too far, everybody gets in trouble, and no one is served.

We do ask for a vendor's best price. And because of the velocity of our sales—not just the volume of products sold but the speed with which they come in the back door and go out the front—there are other ways we expect to be recognized by suppliers. That might mean making appropriate allowances for returns and higher levels of service in our high-volume stores. But most important, we insist they ship full orders—we can't sell product from empty shelves.

■ ■ ■

Over the years, as we experienced monumental growth spurts, business came full circle and we found out that we had to help the manufacturers help us.

Part of our vendor presentation each year is a preview of the year ahead in terms of new stores, demand for product, and expectations. We also use this opportunity to highlight or introduce new technology we are using to increase operational efficiency.

"If you are doing $30 million with us today," we'd say, "then most certainly, you will have to expand capacity and manufacturing capacity, because every four years we will double in size, and you must be much farther ahead of the curve to just keep pace."

We learned to do that the hard way, because until then we were growing at such a clip that we just sucked some manufacturers dry.

Today, manufacturers understand much better how much product we will sell and how fast. Their salespeople salivate to get in the door, and we must really temper their lust. "Let me tell you what is going to happen if we carry your product," we'll warn. "We will blow you away. We will suck everything out of your inventory." Meanwhile, they're not listening, doing their selling routine, saying, "That's fine, we have it covered." And sure enough, we will drain their inventories, and it takes them months to catch up.

We were forced to cease doing business with some vendors because they did not want to make the investment necessary to keep up with the demand. That happens even to the big kids on the block, because some of these manufacturing plants must invest hundreds of millions of dollars in equipment to satisfy our needs. Few boards of directors will vote to fund that just to satisfy one customer.

We are very loyal to these people—within reasonable limits—

especially those who bought the dream early on. However, it's not blind loyalty. If somebody else comes in and is able to sell to us a better quality product at a significant discount and the existing vendor can't match it, or deal within a tolerance level, we will, unfortunately, switch. We need to be price competitive.

That situation developed with a lighting manufacturer that had been with us forever, a wonderful company. A competitor of theirs came in and undercut them by 20 percent. They had to go back and sharpen their pencils, and they got within three points. That was good enough because they had brand name recognition, a track record with us, and they were very credible people, too, so we stayed with them. But we also gave their competitor an opportunity to sell to us, because they really forced the other company's hand.

We have taken a more proactive approach to our ongoing vendor relationships, initiating periodic product line reviews that have radically reduced our assortments in certain areas.

Incidentally, our policy is that no vendor can be cut off without the line being reviewed by a senior company officer. And when our merchants have a problem with a vendor, they ask a senior merchandising officer to come in. If they can't solve it—which is rare—Arthur or I will personally work with them to find a resolution.

■　■　■

If Johnson & Johnson brings out something new for babies, parents almost instinctively believe the product will be pure and safe, something they could use on their baby.

When people think about a home improvement item, the first place I would likewise hope they think of is The Home Depot. You know that the quality's going to be good because, since we guarantee to take any product back with no questions asked, why would we carry anything but the best quality?

We have now reached a place in life where we are becoming a brand in and of ourselves. Because of that, we are in a position to ask manufacturers to share their brand with us and let us be its caretaker.

Sometimes a brand name we want is exclusively tied to a competitor. In certain circumstances, we will create our own product name; in others, we will license an existing brand name and extend it into a new, related category.

For decades, Honda had only one channel of distribution for its lawn mowers—independent dealers. But that changed when some of their people went into a Home Depot store and met a department head who convinced them that we are just like their terrific independent dealers.

They approached us, believe it or not. We hadn't even thought of bringing in Honda because of their well-known commitment to independent dealers. They said that by the way we run our stores and the way our people respond to the customer, our goals are the same as theirs. They suggested we become the only mass merchant retailer for their products.

We take care of their customer just the way they would. We have the same commitment to total satisfaction, to the ongoing relationship and all the other things that Honda holds dear. So they have entrusted their jewel to us. The partnership clicked immediately, growing from lawn mowers and riders to string trimmers, generators, compressors, and pressure washers.

Then, using the same technique we'd used in the early days, we went to Pergo—manufacturer of the world's best-selling laminate flooring—and told them the Honda story.

"You have a distribution pattern very similar to Honda's," we said. "And you also need a large U.S. retailer to create interest and help grow your market and your market share, and we are it. We should be the only one. We will protect it just like it was our own name."

That made sense to them, and they developed an exclusive line of flooring products for us.

■   ■   ■

General Electric used to be our exclusive lightbulb supplier. In fact, GE was given 80 linear feet of shelf space—80 feet across and 10 feet high of selling space—in virtually all of our stores. Any vendor would kill for that kind of shelf commitment; GE had more exposure than any other vendor in our stores. That's the ongoing business GE lost by not shipping complete and on-time orders to us.

This was such a problem that in 1993 we were forced to cancel tens of millions of dollars worth of GE bulb business and switch to Philips. Every fourth quarter, GE ran its inventories down, creating out-of-stocks in our stores, which we couldn't stand for. Lightbulbs to us are like bread, milk or eggs to a grocer; customers expect to see them on the shelves when they come into the store. So GE lost our bulb business. *All* of our bulb business.

In fact, I was so concerned I personally flew to see GE's chairman of the board, Jack Welch, and delivered the news myself. "You can help put a man on the moon," I told him, "but you can't get a 60-watt bulb in our stores." Then I traveled to the Netherlands and cut a deal with Philips.

GE's lesson here was the same one we have to apply to ourselves: Never, ever, take the customer for granted.

When we dropped GE as a supplier, Welch personally wanted to know why. Once we told him, he understood our reasons and dealt with them. At the same time he never stopped looking for a way to get his products back in our stores. He worked hard to get back in our good graces and stay there.

When Pat Farrah returned from retirement in 1995, we challenged him to try to put something back together between the two companies. We began by introducing GE electrical panels and breakers into our stores, which quickly became a $30 million category for us. We also reintroduced GE light bulbs, but only in certain areas and certain categories.

Once the two sides made up and started doing business again, GE once more became one of our biggest suppliers. But nothing is ever easy. They wanted to sell us water softeners, but were reluctant to sell us appliances because they didn't want to disrupt their existing channels. Ultimately, we began selling their GE and Hotpoint brands.

We then saw a consumer survey showing that GE water heaters had name recognition. One problem with the survey results: GE didn't make water heaters. But the brand was so strong, consumers thought they did.

It encouraged us to suggest a new deal with GE: "Why don't you give us your name for water heaters?"

They ultimately agreed. We went out to six water heater manufacturers, gave them GE's manufacturing specs, and let them shoot it out. No matter who wins, The Home Depot will still be the only one selling GE water heaters.

All of these deals led Welch to assign one person, Jim Painter, to oversee all of GE's existing and potential business with The Home Depot. Welch gave Painter—whom we've dealt with for many years—a lot of clout. Now Painter can go directly to various GE divisions and say, "Hey, this is what we need to do with Home Depot." In 1998, Painter saved at least six deals. "Whatever inkling of an opportunity there is, we'll be there," Painter told us.

Jack Welch is widely regarded as one of the all-time best CEOs, and one of the reasons for this is that when he sees something that isn't working right, he reacts quickly and does something about it. And it doesn't stop with him; when he gets something rolling his whole organization follows suit. That's why he's great. And that's why we've begun to actively benchmark with GE in the last few years, borrowing some management development concepts. One of these is the workout. This involves getting all the people closely tied to any given business problem to lock themselves in a room together—for as long as two days—and work out potential solutions. Even if it's something we're doing well, how can we do it better?

■　　■　　■

Most recently, I brought Ridgid Tool into this company. I opened the door, and Pat Farrah ran with it.

The only home improvement company that has ever rivaled us in having its own franchise is Sears. They were the originator with proprietary brands such as Craftsman tools, Kenmore appliances, and Weatherbeater paint. We are starting to bite into their following a little and making them nervous.

Here's a little industry secret: For the last 40 years, Craftsman tools were actually manufactured by an American company named Emerson Tool Co. But the consultants said it didn't matter where Sears tools were made. Their advice: Drop the local suppliers and go offshore for less expensive stationary bench tools manufacturing.

If Sears sells 100 stationary bench tools, we sell 25. That is their niche. Sears has been growing the business for decades, and they had a tremendous partner in Emerson. Emerson manufactured Robo Grip for Sears; its own brand names include Western Forge and Ridgid Tool.

After forty years of building tools for Sears, Emerson lost the contract.

For ten years, I had been playing golf every year with people from Emerson. And almost every year, I brought something back for The Home Depot to sell. One year it was Skil Tools. The next it was Ridgid Plumbing.

Emerson never really wanted to sell to us because of their deal with Sears. But I never stopped pleading with Chuck Knight to open the door to us. Emerson made Sears's Craftsman tools, and I had been begging them to sell us those products. I said, "Just make them for us the way you make them for Sears. We will just put a different name on it."

"I would never do that to them, never, ever," Knight would say. "We have been doing their stuff for forty years, and I would never turn my back on them. That would be dishonest, unethical, immoral."

And I always came away from him wishing there were more people as loyal and moral as Chuck Knight.

In September 1997, I went to St. Louis for my annual golf game with the Emerson people. Ernie Lovelady picked me up at the airport and told me a story. "You are not going to believe this," he said.

After forty years, he said that Sears had hired a consultant who decided the company could no longer afford to buy American-made power tools; they had to go overseas. "They went through a process of review," he said, "and just like that, we were out. They informed us by phone.

"We are closing the plant in Paris, Tennessee, and getting out of the business," he continued. "Is there a possibility that you would take up the slack, that we could make the tools for you?"

Incidentally, my foursome that day included Chuck Knight and Arthur Martinez, the chairman of Sears.

My heart started beating faster.

"Well, I don't know," I said. "Maybe we could do it. But first, let me tell you how to sell to us. Take every one of those tools you made for Craftsman and make it better than it ever was. Increase the strength, add features. In other words, you can do whatever you want, but show us a better tool than you ever had for Craftsman.

"Next, you need a marketing program," I said. "And then you have to price it right, and you have to have the right promotion."

I spent hours telling him how to sell to The Home Depot. Then I called Pat Farrah, who was hysterically delighted.

This was an emotional rather than a financial issue for Chuck Knight. When he and I talked about doing this, he was visibly upset that this town was going to be wiped out. I don't think that the profit and loss entered into it as much as the fact that he was going to destroy people's lives. That also became a very critical factor for us, that we were going to save a town. It fit in perfectly with our values.

When the day came for Emerson's presentation, Pat got all our merchants together. Emerson came through, putting on a show that blew our minds. It was without a doubt one of the single most exciting presentations we had ever seen. They came up with a whole new tool line—item for item—to compete with Craftsman. The new stuff made Craftsman look like a 1950s design.

The Emerson people were angry because they had been abandoned, so they made us an offer we couldn't refuse.

But what to call the new line?

Emerson owns several brand names, but the best known in plumbing circles is Ridgid Tool, which was famous for years for its cheesecake calendars showing attractive women demonstrating their products. Giving us the Ridgid name for an entire product line—woodworking stationary tools, wet-dry vacs, stationary bench tools, a line of plumbing tools, and more—was just the cherry on top.

There isn't a tradesman who doesn't know the name Ridgid and its lifetime warranty. And the name Ridgid Tools is ours. Ridgid Tools: *Made in America . . . 75-year heritage . . . available only at The Home Depot.* Ridgid became one of the most successful new product launches in our history.

Emerson also committed—at my suggestion—a marketing person

who works only with us, almost like being our associate except that they are paying the salary. This person will live and die Ridgid Tools in our stores.

Developing the new Ridgid lines for The Home Depot was a partnership between our two companies that energized everybody. The normal corporate bureaucracy was set aside. Our two management teams wanted to do something and do it quickly, like two brand new entrepreneurial companies just starting out rather than two major corporations who had been around the block a few times.

We took busloads of Home Depot associates to Paris, Tennessee, on August 28, 1998, for a celebratory barbecue at the 600,000-square-foot Emerson plant there. That plant was significant because without our business to pick up the slack from Sears going overseas, 650 employees—6 percent of the town's population—would have been out of work.

When we arrived, Charles Knight, chairman of Emerson, took us on a tour of the manufacturing facilities. We oohed and aahed over the sight of a huge Home Depot logo painted on their factory floor. As we walked, the Ridgid employees autographed our special Home Depot–Ridgid aprons. Then it was on to the warehouse, where thousands of boxes of Ridgid bench saws were piled high.

"Pat," somebody shouted to Pat Farrah, "you better make sure those boxes are full!"

So he and I—remembering Pat's tricks from our early days—leaned on several stacks of boxes to be sure they were full. They were.

During the barbecue, I told the good people of Paris what they could expect from our relationship in the months and years to come. "I made a promise to Chuck. I said, I don't think that this factory is gonna be big enough to handle the amount of merchandise that we're going to be shipping out. So you better make plans to build on another building and hire more people, because we're going to have this place running three shifts, 24 hours a day, seven days a week."

And while Pat was being covered from head to toe with Ridgid Tool decals by Emerson factory workers, Ken Langone related another piece of Home Depot lore to Knight. Losing Sears's business, Ken said, "was like being kicked in the ass by a golden horseshoe."

■   ■   ■

Vendors are always welcome to come to our stores, tie on an orange Home Depot apron, and work in their appropriate department for a day.

Ron Cooper of Price Pfister went one step further. He put aprons on six of his people and put them to work in our faucet aisle. Then he borrowed two of our people and sent them over to a factory, where they took a tour and offered input on some new designs. We encourage these kinds of relationships. It makes us grow closer together; we lean toward Price Pfister because of those things.

Then there is Jay Blau, the owner of a plastic pot manufacturing company called Dynamic Design Inc.

Fifteen minutes before closing at one of our stores, one of our associates spotted a man in a suit on top of a ladder, pulling pots down off the top of a rack. By coincidence, the associate was our pot merchant.

"Sir, I'm sorry; we are closing," he said. "On top of that, I can't really have you climbing the ladder."

"Oh, it's okay," the man said. "I am only a customer part of the time. I am the president of Dynamic Design, and this stuff needs to be out, okay? I want to pack it down."

The two of them worked for the next hour, unpacking merchandise. Those are the kinds of vendors we want. Six months later, Dynamic Design won our vendor of the year award for its category.

■   ■   ■

A store walk is one of our most valuable tools for dealing with our vendors. For example, after contracting with GE Credit in the early 1990s to provide our professional customers with a revolving line of credit, a store walk revealed how the explosive growth of this program had hurt one aspect of our customer service.

In the nineties our credit program's growth was so rapid—worth $4 billion in 1998 alone—that the GE division servicing these needs couldn't keep up, in spite of growing by 40 percent themselves. GE Credit couldn't hire and train people fast enough to answer the phones and provide adequate customer service once they did. Since the credit service was being offered under Home Depot's name, this hurt us as well. Our passion for customer service was not something that GE's people on the phones understood at first, and caused a lot of frustration with our store associates.

On a store walk with more than a dozen store and regional managers, Pat Farrah encountered the credit problem first-hand. He spotted a professional contractor pushing a large cart loaded down with kitchen cabinets and, without telling the man much more than his name, engaged him in conversation.

"What kind of project are you working on?" Pat asked.

"I specialize in multifamily fire rehabs," the man said.

"That's great. Where do you shop when you are not shopping here?"

"Do you really want to know?"

"Yeah," Pat said, "I do."

The man gave Pat the name of another local retailer.

"Where do you get lumber and stuff like that?" Pat asked.

"Over there."

"Over there, too? They have it?"

"My average month's bill over there is about $12,000," the man said, widening Pat's eyes. "I spend about $4,000 here; my credit line here only goes up to $4,000. I have a $20,000 line of credit at (the other store)."

The contractor went on to say that his payments to GE Credit were not getting credited to his account very quickly, forcing him to pay by check on some purchases.

"Do you guys hear this?" Pat howled. "He has a $4,000 limit on his credit here, and $20,000 at the other place. And he needs three kitchens this afternoon. But because we can't process his payments in a timely manner, he has to pay us with a check. Unbelievable.

"I believe we can do something about that. Sir, meet Mike McCabe. He's a vice president of operations in this company. Mike, this is a guy who we need to handle differently. GE has gotta bump his credit limit up. That's number one. Number two, what would you like to see here that you haven't been able to find yet?"

"It is easier to load over there," the man said, referring to the other store. "They make it really fast to get in and out."

Pat turned and addressed the Home Depot managers who were focused on every word spoken between himself and the contractor. Pat directed McCabe to either fix the man's credit on the spot or take his phone number and get it done within the hour.

Then Pat made it worth the man's while to speak so frankly. "Let's walk over to the tool corral, and you pick out a tool on us. How about that?"

"Great!" the man said.

Only then did Pat let the man know who he was talking with. "I am one of the founders of this company. We started in 1979, and we are particularly concerned about seeing that guys like you get taken care of."

"That would be really good," the man said, "because this store is only four minutes from my shop."

An hour after letting the contractor pick out a free power tool, Pat received an update on the man's credit situation. His limit was immediately increased to $10,000. Pat also noticed that everyone in the store knew the man as a regular customer, which confirmed his story in ways a credit check can't. We have to act fast in situations like that, because this was a guy who wanted to give us his business. All we needed to do was take it and go to bat for him.

As a result of incidents such as this one, a dozen senior-level managers from GE Credit came to Atlanta in 1998 and walked one of our stores in an effort to fix our joint growing pains. Bill Hamlin, our executive vice president of merchandising, led the charge for us, telling GE in no uncertain terms how frustrated he was with the situation.

"On the mixed-up billing process," Hamlin said, "it is almost like we should apologize to our professional customers. We need your help in rebuilding those relationships."

The GE executives agreed.

"We want to get back on the bandwagon and start pushing this program," one of the GE Credit executives said. And, from that point on, they got involved and took significant steps to fix the problem.

We are now receiving a tremendous amount of support and commitment from GE Credit's senior management, which is drawing on the parent company's vast resources to get ahead of the curve. Two cross-company teams are working closely together to improve payment processes as well as totally rewrite credit policy and procedures for both companies. As a result of all this—and most important—the actual GE employees on the phones dealing with our credit customers have a much better understanding of Home Depot's attitude about taking care of those customers.

And all of these improvements started by our being ground engaged and in our stores, walking with our vendors, touching the merchandise and listening to our customers. We never would have discovered the credit situation if we'd been parked in our offices on the twenty-second floor.

How We Manage

"You Are Wearing an Invisible Collar"*

Want to know the management secrets of The Home Depot?

Number one, we are not that smart.

Number two, we know we are not that smart.

And because we are not that smart, we have learned that we must listen. And in listening, we learned that the consumer dictates who we must be, what we must be, what our content is, and what services we must give them. We have now successfully listened and responded for twenty years.

People who talk a lot don't ever hear anything. The art of communication doesn't mean speaking. The art of communication means speaking and listening. It's like in an argument. When a married couple has an argument and he says, "Don't ever do that again," and she yells back at him, well, he's probably not listening to what she yells back. He's thinking of his next answer. We want our people to understand that when you're busy in an argument and you don't listen to people, there's at least half a chance that you are not right. You've got to listen.

In this chapter, we have collected the fourteen essential management concepts that govern The Home Depot. These, like our values,

* Arthur Blank

237

are what set us apart from the rest of our industry. If you really want to know what's different about our company, keep reading.

1. THE INVISIBLE FENCE

One of the big advantages that we have over most of our competitors is being decentralized. It allows us to be close to the customers and access the best knowledge in the field. That way we can do not only what is right for the stores, but also respond to the marketplace and support the associates in the stores.

We began decentralizing operations away from Atlanta when our West Coast expansion was in full bloom and we created an autonomous California-based division to handle business in that part of the country. That eventually became the model for the whole company: We now have additional regional divisional headquarters in the Northeast, Midwest, Southeast, Southwest, and Canada. In addition, EXPO Design Center has its own individual management structure.

We entered the Northeast market without regional offices in place, something we wouldn't do today. I tried running the Northeast myself for the first year, but quickly realized we needed someone on the ground there full-time, every day, learning, listening, and responding to the market as a native. I turned over that responsibility to Larry Mercer and went looking for a counterpart to him in the Southeast.

That's when Bruce Berg was asked to fly up to New York for a meeting. He was surprised to find a limousine waiting for him with me inside.

"How would you like to be president of the Southeast division?" I asked.

"Yeah," Berg said nonchalantly, "that would be okay."

"Okay," I said. "You're the president of the Southeast division."

The limo was quiet for a few moments as Berg soaked up what had just transpired.

"Hey, Art," he said, breaking the silence, "what does the president of the Southeast division *do*?"

"We'll talk about that later."

Later was two weeks later.

"Bruce, let me put your new responsibilities this way," I explained. "Think of your new job as being enclosed by an invisible fence and you are wearing a collar. Out there, somewhere, is a fence, and you are going to keep running around in the yard doing your thing. At some point, you will inevitably go beyond the boundaries of what your job responsibilities should be and you will hit that fence. And when you do, you will get buzzed."

"Art," Berg asked, "have you ever hit an invisible fence?"

"No."

"Well, I have, and it really hurts."

And sure enough, he was zapped by the fence quite a few times. That's because the role of a Home Depot regional president is a somewhat amorphous position. If things go right in the division, everyone is rewarded. But if anything goes wrong in the division, there is only one call I will make.

We learned together where that fence is; it is in different places for different people, and it moves all the time. The division presidents have a tremendous amount of autonomy. They should—with multi-billion-dollar individual businesses under their management, they are effectively running the largest home improvement businesses around. For each of them, that fence will have a different effect, a different amount of juice. It's not a fixed fence for all of them. What works in Maine might not necessarily click in Atlanta or Seattle. Take Vern Joslyn, for example, the president of our largest division, the Northeast. Vern is always the first one to try anything new and, subsequently, everyone in the division follows his lead as entrepreneurial risk-taker.

For new division presidents, I might draw the circle around them a little tighter for a time until they become more comfortable and can run freer; they're not going to run into the street and get hit by a car.

When Hurricane Andrew hit South Florida, the invisible fence moved and Berg got buzzed. Since we didn't have a clue in Atlanta what to do, we pretty much left dealing with the storm and its aftermath up to Berg. The system worked, too, until Berg got a bright idea one day about building a huge blacktop addition on the land where our four-day-old Cutler Ridge store had been flattened by the hurricane; Berg needed a place to store all his incoming lumber and building materials.

It was the right decision, but he forgot to tell me about it. On a rare day when Berg was playing hooky on his boat, I called him. Berg got tangled up in the fence pretty good that day.

"Look at the sign on our stores," I said. "Does it say 'Bruce's Depot'?"

"No, it says The Home Depot."

"Well then, don't you think that you should tell *me* when you decide to pave four or five acres and pour $100,000 into a store?"

"Yeah," Berg said sheepishly, "I should have."

I didn't have a problem with the decision—especially at a store hitting $3 million a week in sales, but Berg should have shared the plan with me *before* it happened. "If we are going to work together," I said, "if you are going to be an officer of mine, I will give you great latitude. But other things, I want you to tell me about."

"I don't know the difference."

"Remember the invisible fence?"

"This sucks, man," Berg said. "I don't know where the boundaries are."

"You will get it; don't worry."

Not long after that, Bernie gave Berg some advice.

"First, build trust with Arthur," he said. "Then the fence will be much more elastic."

The invisible fence is not just for our seven division presidents. It is used and applied throughout the company, up to and especially in the stores. Our store managers and their assistant managers have more operating and decision-making leeway than in any other retail chain in America. We want them to roam and test parameters to see how far they can move out on the fringe of the property.

Those who can deal with the fence experiment more. They bring more unconventional thinking to the table rather than always toeing the line.

We don't build a straitjacket around our division presidents, and that is by design. We want them to be flexible; we want them to be entrepreneurial. We would rather have them push harder in that direction than not, and if we impose our own limits on them, they will stay well within those boundaries all the time. But sometimes they need to go beyond that, and that is another element of our company's culture.

We insist, we *demand* that our people take risks, and then take responsibility for those risks. "It is *your* business, *your* division, *your* market, *your* store, *your* aisle, and *your* customer. It is not a Home Depot customer, it is *your* customer."

We have a policy procedure manual, and in it there is a chapter called "Merchandising." When you open up to that chapter, there are no pages.

That's our way of teaching people to think and to think on their feet. Don't wait for some Home Depot bureaucrat to give you an answer or fix your problem. And don't blame somebody else. If you have something that needs to be fixed, fix it! If there are resources to tap into, tap into them! Like we tell our customers . . . *do it yourself.*

This is a very basic business. We are not trying to put people on the moon. There are still things that require a scalpel; others call for a chain saw.

Bruce Berg still bumps up against the invisible fence because he would rather ask for forgiveness than permission. The difference between then and now, as Bernie intimated, is trust. I tend to be more forgiving when our people are entrepreneurial, particularly if it is in the customer's interest.

Operations may change dramatically from one region to another, but the company's principles stay the same. Nobody tinkers with the principles.

Our managers should never feel our presence over their shoulders. We don't feel compelled to check everything they do. We expect them to make decisions and to make mistakes. We are relentless in our desire for our people to have confidence in themselves. We respect confrontation. And we expect it, too.

2. THE THREE BUNDLES

Empowerment is a primary, almost magical management issue for us. We believe the answers to most challenges are in all of us, and we rally people to think and believe in themselves and make good decisions.

Transferring the decision-making responsibility through the ranks is done on the basis of three "bundles," a concept suggested to us by GE Chairman Jack Welch:

Bundle 1: This is the nonnegotiable bundle. There are very few Bundle 1s in The Home Depot; those are the things we do the same across the company. Many of these are operational in nature, areas where investment in systems dictates a more uniform compliance. They are usually transparent to the customer, things that have to be done to maintain key consistencies between the stores.

Bundle 2: This is the entrepreneurial bundle. Entrepreneurship comes into play here because this involves challenges in which the company provides only a minimum standard. If a store can extend that standard, great! We say, "Your store will carry such-and-such product lines. How you sell or display them is up to you." As a result, we get the benefit of some extraordinary creativity in this bundle; many of these ideas get distributed companywide as part of the "Best Practices" program.

For example, when we introduced the Ridgid Tool line, one of our stores' teams had the bizarre but inspired idea of setting up a miniature golf course in their parking lot. To show how powerful new Ridgid blower-vacs were, they invited customers to sink putts using blowers instead of clubs. That was a great idea.

When we introduced a new saw blade, another enterprising store team brought a junk car into its parking lot and demonstrated the new blade by sawing the car in half! Then they moved half of the car inside and set up an endcap display around it. That sold a lot of saw blades. We also discovered a market for these saws in firefighters who previously used lesser saw blades and reciprocating saws to literally cut car-accident victims out of their cars.

On another level, when our store managers teach department head management classes, there may be four or five main things we want them to teach. But by the time the class is done, they usually teach at least ten things.

The entrepreneurship bundle works at every level of the company. We even use it to further our community programs by giving the stores a budget for spending in their own communities. We don't tell them exactly how to spend the money. Instead, they find causes and become attached to those causes, emotionally and financially. The empowerment is great.

Bundle 3: This is when we give associates complete autonomy to make their own decisions in the way they operate their store. They don't make the decision about the assortment in the store, although they do talk to the merchants about what their customers are looking for, so in a sense they're responsible for the fine-tuning of the assortment. But they're totally responsible for the amount of merchandise that we have in stock. They're responsible for being sure our pricing is right in the stores, for building the displays, for signing, hiring, and training. And they're responsible for paying people what they're worth, which is the backbone of our entire organization. The people in our stores are responsible for moving people along in the company—and for deciding who doesn't move along. All of those things come from the individuals making those decisions in their stores.

Our managers and associates have great freedom to experiment at the store level. You can go into one Dallas store and see things you won't see across town at another Dallas store. As big as we are, we've largely resisted a cookie-cutter type of approach. That has been helpful, because people generate good ideas in every store.

That's the area in which you find the difference between us and other home improvement chains. We expect the associates to run their store like it is their own business, tailoring a great deal of the product selection to local needs and buying local products. Our garden departments are a classic example, where no two are the same.

But there's a great responsibility that goes with that; you're running your business more as an owner than a staff member.

There are virtually no plan-o-grams involved in assembling and operating a Home Depot. If you're not familiar with plan-o-grams, Kmart is famous for them. They send out a blueprint or photo showing where each item goes on a peg or on a shelf. It has a model number or picture of the item. Even if you had never worked a day in retailing, you could set that Kmart shelf exactly right. A child could do that. We don't work that way.

Take the front endcaps at a Home Depot store, the product displays built up in front of each cash register. Almost without exception, the choice of products and the manner in which they are presented is almost entirely up to the staff of the store. We will certainly criticize it if we don't like what they put there, but it's entirely up to them. We give them complete autonomy. The endcaps are a signature of that store.

Our message is simple: We want excitement. *You* figure out what excitement will be in *your* market. That's the fun of running a Home Depot store.

3. HIRE PEOPLE WHO ARE OVERQUALIFIED WITH A VIEW TOWARD GROWTH IN THE FUTURE

From the beginning, The Home Depot has hired overqualified people with a view toward our growth in the future. The first merchants and store managers came to us as vice presidents of merchandising at larger companies with responsibilities for managing many stores. We didn't want to start low and outgrow our ability to cope.

A personal meeting I had with Charles Lazarus, founder of Toys "R" Us, in the early 1990s had a big effect on the manner in which we expanded. Both of us were participating in a conference at a time when The Home Depot was a public company but still rather small.

Over lunch, I asked Lazarus, "Is there anything you could share with me that you think would be helpful to our company?"

"The most difficult thing which I have had to do," he said, "and I think I have done well, but it was very hard, was look at the people who have helped me build this company, get to half a billion, then a billion and so on, and recognize that at some point along the way, they ran out of steam. They were terrific people, but they did not have the capacity to take me from a billion to $5 billion, from $5 billion to $10 billion. Recognizing that and dealing with it will be your greatest challenge."

He was telling us that we have a responsibility to shareholders and to the other folks inside the company to have people in critical positions who have the horsepower to do the job.

It was a valuable lesson and warning: Don't outgrow the ability of people to take you to the next level.

4. HAVE A FINANCIAL CONSCIENCE

For our formative years and beyond, Executive Vice President and Chief Administrative Officer Ron Brill was responsible for all of The Home Depot's nonretail product purchasing. That is, everything we bought for our own use, not for resale. He was our financial conscience, the man who watched the dollars and gave us a regular sense of fiscal reality.

Brill outlawed office photocopiers and fax machines for our stores until the mid-1990s. He feared the generation of incremental additional expense. When we started, there was no money spent that didn't need to be spent. Copy machines get abused, because it is hard to put controls on them. Besides, our stores never really had an office where you could put a copy machine.

If someone absolutely needed a photocopy, he or she went out to Kinko's or Sir Speedy. Today, the average store does about $43 million in sales, so we can afford a copier in each one.

When Ron came up with a sales formula for approving copiers— as well as much-in-demand forklifts and trucks—one of our regional vice presidents still wouldn't approve the expense. "We did without it for all these years," he said. "We are still not going to do it."

One year, I wanted to round the store P & Ls to an even $1,000. Ron refused. "On a consolidated basis," he said, "we will do that, so the numbers you see are in thousands. But I don't want store managers to think that $800 isn't important; I want them to think *$100* is important." So even today, a store that is doing $120 million will know its sales down to the dollar, because the store managers have to focus in on every dollar.

If you don't watch the dollars, they add up very quickly. Today, we are approaching 1,000 stores. A piece of equipment we want to put in each store that costs $609 means an expense of $609,000, so we really better know that we are going to get a payback on it.

In April 1996, Ron launched a strategic review that led to greater financial efficiencies in the way we open new stores. A year later, the average preopening cost per store had dropped $10,000. Multiply that by 100 or 200 new stores per year and you can see the savings build.

Our greatest secret weapon in the battle against costs was Ron. He just always said no. He listened to reason, but his first approach was always to say no. You had to have a compelling reason to spend The Home Depot's money. If you made a good case for something, he might open up the purse strings.

Unless your name was Pat Farrah.

Brill was always giving Pat a hard time over expenses. That's why he became the victim of an infamous Pat Farrah prank.

One of Ron's big issues with Pat was his travel expenses—what they were and how he reported them. The rules were different for Pat—or so Pat liked to believe.

In the early 1980s, Pat would take his merchants to exotic places for catalog meetings. Occasionally he would charter a plane, which might cost $2,500. Well, Ron thought that was an outrageous expense and wouldn't reimburse him. If he wanted to do that, "You pay for it," Ron would say. Ron would investigate the comparable cost of commercial coach tickets on the same routes and that is how much he would reimburse Pat for his merchants.

Pat also had a problem filing his travel expenses on a timely basis, so we ended up passing the rule that anything older than 90 days, you eat. At a time when we weren't making much money, Pat once turned in a year's worth of expenses in one report. That was such a big hit it actually distorted our earnings.

We were overinventoried on ceiling fans at one point. Gross margins might have been low one month, so Ron and Pat would get into it: "Your inventories are too high, your margins too low." Their confrontations—both verbally and in terms of their physical size difference—had the makings of a good Abbott and Costello routine.

Both men wear gold Rolex watches. Pat's was the "President" model; Ron's was the "Submariner," a diver's watch. It was one of the first nice things he bought himself when the company went public and started making money.

One day, Pat asked to see how Ron's watch fit him. He slipped off his own watch, put Ron's on, and stepped into the hallway.

"Hey, Ron," Pat called, "come out here a minute."

Ron went into the hallway and saw Pat taking off his watch.

"You know," Pat said, clearly agitated, "I am so tired of you giving me a hard time!"

He took Ron's watch off his wrist, raised it over his head, and threw it down on the slate floor with all his might, breaking the treasured watch into pieces.

Ron was shattered. That watch was the most expensive thing he had ever spent money on other than a car or a house, and he was aghast. Then he looked more carefully at the watch pieces on the floor and noticed a price tag on the back.

As a gag, Pat had bought a counterfeit Rolex and set up the whole scene, complete with a dozen or so witnesses who were in on the joke.

5. ONE-MAN SHOWS DON'T CUT IT WITH US

Monday mornings were always interesting with Pat. Bernie kept a slot in his schedule between 8:30 and 10:00 A.M., because he knew that Pat was going to walk in, slam the door shut, and pace back and forth, telling him what occurred in a store that weekend.

You have to understand something here. In the retail business, there is always something going wrong. Nobody runs a perfect business, Home Depot included. But you can't let your frustrations get to you.

Every time Pat would see something going wrong, he didn't deal with it very well. He couldn't delegate responsibility for correcting something; he had to do it himself. Immediately, if not sooner.

He walked in one day and told Bernie about his weekend visit to the Fort Lauderdale store. It was on a Saturday, and the endcaps were all wrong, merchandise was displayed improperly, and it was the wrong kind of merchandise at that. So he took a forklift and literally destroyed the endcaps.

Merchandising is a magical game. Consumers walk into a place, and if they don't see something that is exciting, something that says, "Buy me!" then you won't be in business long. The point of the endcaps in any store is to present ideas, things people might not have thought of buying, things that will suggest a project that they hadn't before considered.

If Pat, the consummate merchant, went into a store and didn't see the kinds of provocative, suggestive endcaps he expected, it aggravated him.

"Do you know how many hours I put in in that store?" he said. He literally worked around the clock from Saturday afternoon until Sunday afternoon, redoing the endcaps.

"Did the district manager work with you?" Bernie asked.

"No."

"Did the store manager work with you?"

"No."

"In other words," Bernie said, "you did this yourself?"

"Yep."

"Well Pat, then you accomplished *nothing* because you trained nobody, you taught nobody. You did it yourself and you want me to have sympathy for you? I would have felt a whole lot better if you had the district manager there, if you showed him what you were doing, if you explained to him why you were doing it. *That* is teaching and training. That is really what you have to do.

"You are a one-man show," Bernie continued. "A one-man show doesn't make it in this company."

And then Bernie threw Pat out of his office.

Pat did not understand that as the company got bigger, that we all had to become more teacher than doer, that teaching was more important than anything else. He would rather do something himself and get the personal satisfaction of it being done than wait and get the satisfaction of training other people to do it.

The lesson for Pat was a simple one. For him to know how to do something and not share that knowledge with somebody else was to waste his knowledge. Bernie's role has always been to challenge people, to make them better, to create people who would be self-sufficient, who would be able to operate.

6. "HOW WOULD YOU LIKE YOUR EGGS?"

One of the quickest things that can sink a company is a communication problem.

We must communicate to our stores why we do the things that we do and let them understand the logic behind our actions. The day that they think we are stupid is the day we are dead in the water. A business is only as good as the legs it stands on. And the legs this company stands on are the people who work with us.

So we periodically need to get in front of our associates and talk to them. We have several formal and informal vehicles for doing this. On the formal side, Bernie and I often go on location to our stores to shoot "Breakfast with Bernie and Arthur," a lively give-and-take Home Depot pep rally with our associates that is broadcast live via satellite to all of our store locations. The "Breakfast" shows usually originate from the stores to give them a natural feel to which all of our associates can relate.

During "Breakfast," Bernie and I banter with each other and then turn the microphone over to our associates for questions about whatever is on their minds. The "Breakfast" show is a mass communication effort aimed at touching issues of interest to every associate in the company. For example:

"There's nothing worse than when a customer comes up to me and says, 'I can't find anybody to help me,' or 'Why are the lines so long?' " began Lisa Carnabuci, an associate at one of our New York area stores. "With the growth we're predicting on Long Island, is there any program to train and find more quality people so they'll be prepared to give the kind of quality service that our customers demand?"

It was a good question; the growth of our Northeast stores continues increasing as fast as we can hire associates.

"We are finding exactly how high is up in terms of staffing," I told her. "We have doubled the staffing in certain paint departments. We have doubled in many lumber departments during the week. In some stores, we are adding 30 percent to 40 percent more associates on the weekends.

"We are very much concerned about the same issues that you are," I continued. "The standards have to be raised because the competitors who are left today are better and getting more aggressive."

The "Breakfast" shows also include slickly produced company news segments with reports on everything from international developments (including lighthearted moments such as our Waterloo, Iowa, store's development of a horse-and-buggy parking area for Mennonite customers who shun cars) to announcements on the latest in product-knowledge classes.

Since 1990, we have also participated in 150 "Welcome Aboard" satellite telecasts. These live programs are aimed at new associates as part of a comprehensive enculturation process.

Bernie and I also have individual programs that put us in front of our managers on a regular basis.

For the last few years, I have been conducting quarterly "World Tours" in which—over the course of three nonstop weeks—I visited every division, met with all the district managers, discussed the company's future strategic plans, and sought out the latest candidates for our best-practices program.

All the words of wisdom didn't come from me. Hopefully a few did, but these tours also included virtually all senior managers of the company—typically Bill Hamlin, Larry Mercer, Senior Vice President of Human Resources Steve Messana, Ron Brill, Senior Vice President of Finance and Accounting Marshall Day, and others. They all participate because it's the responsibility of every officer of our company to constantly be taking our people to the next level.

And the reason we do it on the road rather than Atlanta is, number one, to save money because there are a lot more district managers and store managers than there are senior managers. And we want to be in the environment where they feel most comfortable.

At the start of each "World Tour" meeting, each division presented to us the five or six best practices that they wanted to share with the other divisions. Then the division presidents packaged the three very best ideas. We don't do the same things in the Southwest that we do in the Northeast. Or we may not do them as well in one division as in the other. They each have different strengths and weaknesses, but the one thing that they all have in common is being entrepreneurs. Sometimes those of us back at the Store Support Center in Atlanta won't know what they are experimenting with in some of these divisions. But by the end of the three-week tour, we returned to each division president a book with all the best practices and accompanying documentation that showed what the division did and what the sales results were.

"Best practices" was something that we didn't do as well before the "World Tours" began, to be frank. It's not that people didn't share, but in a culture such as ours that so strongly values new ideas, it was harder for some managers to receive ideas from other people than to create their own.

Today, thanks to our best-practices program, the best store manager we have could have zero creativity. But if that person is a sponge and is willing to think about taking all the best ideas from the whole 775-store system, it would be a pretty effective approach. You would have to be smart to do that.

I mention the "World Tours" in the past tense because in 1999, we intend them to be led not by me but by our new group presidents, Bill Hamlin and Larry Mercer.

As for Bernie, he conducts at least eight "Bernie Road Shows" a year in which he personally shapes and develops the talents of our division presidents, district managers, and, most important, store managers and associates in the company. Working alongside him on these appearances are our merchandising gurus, Bill Hamlin, Pat Farrah, and Denny Ryan.

The first day in a division, Bernie conducts a store walk with senior executives; all the merchants and district managers and officers of that division walk the store. They go through all the merchandising philosophy and concepts—why we do what we do—so everybody understands why we're merchandising a product, why we bought it, how we priced it, and what we expect from the manufacturer. They go shelf by shelf, line by line. It's an immensely effective training tool.

That night, Bernie solicits questions from the district managers and officers. Everybody in attendance has what Bernie calls "immunity" during these meetings. That means managers can ask any kind of question no matter how blunt, invasive, or even offensive it might be. These meetings are intended to be naked, honest exchanges of information and opinions. Bernie insists on it—no pussyfooting around. If he doesn't get a frank discussion, he won't hesitate to berate the managers to stop being milquetoasts. If he has to, he'll challenge them.

The next day, he'll study all their issues, what is and isn't working. If there is something he can't answer directly, he'll reach the appropriate company officer who can. When they walk out of a meeting with Bernie, they have an answer to everything that they wanted to know. They feel more secure.

Over the years, these road shows have basically changed the way we merchandise products in the stores because Bernie and I relearn our business firsthand from people on the floor of the stores. The associates know more about the products and what the customers are looking for than we do. It is a changing, teaching experience.

This is a merchandise-driven company, and that is why we are successful. You can only do so much with computers and numbers. What it comes down to is what customers see in the stores with their own eyes, what says to them, "Buy me!" "Try me!"

Uncertainty is one of the driving factors in failure for a company. When our associates' focus starts moving off the customer onto their own personal thing and they start spending their days more concerned about what management is doing, as in "What are they doing?

Why are they doing this? Why would they institute this program or that policy?" that suggests a breakdown in internal communications. I have made improving internal communication a big priority.

Here's an example. One day, Bernie and Bill Hamlin were visiting a Home Depot, and a customer complained that the store was always running out of certain merchandise.

"Like what?" Bernie asked.

"Electrical boxes," he said.

Curious, Bernie invited the man to accompany them back to the electrical department, where he sought out an associate. He didn't identify himself.

"I need some electric boxes," Bernie said.

"We're out of them," the young man said.

"How come?" Bill asked.

"Well, I never order enough because I have no place to put them."

"Do you get much call for these?" Bill asked.

"Lots," the associate said. He explained that he ordered six at a time, because that was all he had room for at a time.

"What would happen," Bill asked, "if you ordered 12?"

"I'd sell them."

"What would happen if you ordered 24?"

"I'd probably sell them out."

"What would happen if you ordered 60?" Bill asked.

"Oh," the associate said, "that would probably be just about enough."

"Then why don't you do it?"

Again, he answered that there was no room for them. So Bill suggested piling them up on the floor in front of the rack where the fittings are normally set.

"I can't put boxes on the floor," the associate said, terrified. "Bernie doesn't want anything on the floor."

"Bernie who?" Bernie asked, still enjoying his anonymity.

"Bernie Marcus, the chairman of The Home Depot."

"Oh," Bernie said, "*Bernie Marcus* doesn't want you to do that?"

So what is bureaucracy? Bureaucracy was this young man—who

happens to be a district manager for us today. They finally explained to the associate that Bernie Marcus was standing right in front of him and that Bernie Marcus never said anything of the kind.

We believe our associates know we're not stupid.

So if they see something that doesn't make sense, they should question it. If their suggestion makes sense, we'll change to accommodate it. We know how to move and change with the times.

Bureaucracy is giving in to stupidity and ignoring common sense. When you know something is wrong and you don't challenge it, you have become bureaucratic.

Entrepreneurs don't act that way.

The reason this is so important is that the root cause of creating a bureaucratic environment is when people are afraid to make mistakes. And when they are afraid to make mistakes, they write more memos, call additional meetings, or ask for meetings to be extended. All of those things are manifestations of people who are afraid to make decisions because they're afraid to make mistakes.

We encourage people to make decisions. Planning is great; analysis is great. But most of the time when you get 80 percent of the facts, that's really all you need to make a decision. To get to the last 20 percent could take forever. Make a decision and get on with it! We want our people to be unafraid of making mistakes. The only time people don't make mistakes is when they're asleep. And if you are wrong, all we ask is that you be willing to step back, admit "That's not working," and try path B or C.

What we try to do with my "World Tours" and Bernie's "Road Shows" is to answer questions, encourage risk and decision-making, and take the mystique out of senior management. The questions they ask us are the questions that affect their lives. When we leave that room we want our people to feel secure about the management of this company, that we are not gambling their lives at the craps table.

In addition to those issues, there are basic company philosophies and values that we want to impart to them at every opportunity. We want to reemphasize customer service, ethics, morality, and culture.

The importance of getting our values across to our associates is why we went to the expense of building a closed-circuit satellite television network that we call HDTV.

Rob Hallam, who is now our director of internal communication, was the passion behind developing HDTV in 1989 as a vehicle for us to communicate to the thousands of new employees joining us each month. That strategy has grown to include other methods, such as print and electronic communication.

■　　■　　■

One of the best management tools we have for overseeing the vast number of Home Depots is the store walk. It's nothing more than a visit—preferably unannounced—by anyone from the two of us to a board member to an officer of the company to a district manager. We walk the aisles, examine the displays, the signage, eavesdrop on associates' conversations with customers, and talk to the customers ourselves. On announced store walks, we become part of the action, donning orange aprons and working while we inspect the facilities.

The number one value of our store walks is that they keep our district managers close to the action. It keeps them from getting disconnected. So many things happen on a store walk, the most important of which are role-modeling and teaching. It's looking at something and noting what's right and what's wrong.

We will walk around and talk to the associates if there are no customers around, but when somebody needs help, the chairman of the board and president will provide that help. We have to set the example for the store people. There is nothing more important. We are not more important than the customer. Neither is anything we are trying to communicate on the floor of the store, because if we don't have that customer, it doesn't mean anything anyway.

Walking a store with Bernie is not unlike being there with your neighbor or your spouse. He spots the real commonsense, basic stuff they would, such as the lawn mower gas tank without a cap on it. "How do you expect to sell it without putting the cap on it?" Or he'll notice that the handles are not working on the gas grills. Or the broken bags of charcoal. Or a sign that doesn't have a price on it.

I, on the other hand, will have done my homework on that store. I know its payroll, turns, and shrinkage. But what I will also tell you and show you is how this store has performed on a particular level and what it needs to improve. I learned the merchandise end of the store walks from Pat Farrah, however, and will focus on these opportunities from a sales perspective.

A Pat Farrah walk is more of an offensive maneuver. He has the ball, and he is going for the score. His unyielding love of merchandise and his relationship to the merchandise causes him to relate to it differently than we do. Pat can field strip it, tell you how much it weighs, what kind of motor it has, and put it back together again. He knows the three sizes we should or should not carry and how many colors it comes in.

Store walks are such an important and valuable tool to this company that they're required not just of our executives, but of our board of directors, too. Ken Langone started the tradition and institutionalized it after other directors pestered him about how he knew so much inside dope on the stores. It flattens the management pyramid by creating communication from the very top to the very bottom of the company. And because our board travels so much, they cover a tremendous amount of ground, especially when they visit the stores unannounced and unidentified.

The best store walks are unannounced and unexpected by the store's management and associates. But sometimes they call us and beg to be walked. When they are that proud, we just have to go.

The bigger the stores get and the more well known Bernie and I personally become within the company, the more problematic an announced store walk becomes. So the challenge today is to keep these walks unannounced so the stores don't spend a week getting ready for them at the expense of the customer.

Often store managers will take us from area to area, but they don't take credit for what goes on; they want us to meet the people who really make it happen. "Show Bernie and Arthur what you did here!" It shows that they really have a team operating, managing, and controlling their stores. If you don't have a team, you can't operate a store like ours.

During a typical store walk, we will either ask for or randomly invite 15 to 20 associates to meet us in the break room—with no managers present—and we will sit with them and talk about the business. You would be stunned by what we find out.

In Canada, we had just introduced an ESOP program (called the Group Registered Retirement Savings Plan in Canada) when Bernie walked a store there. But the associates didn't have a clue about how to participate in the plan. Nobody really explained it to them. That opened up a Pandora's box; we discovered we were doing a very bad job of marketing these things to our own people!

In fact, our ESOP program came out of a conversation with a kitchen designer who was leaving the company. During a store walk, Bruce Berg introduced the man and Bernie said, "Why are you leaving?" And the man said, "Because I don't have a retirement plan here."

Bernie stopped dead in his tracks and spent the next 45 minutes talking to the man one-on-one. When they were done, Bernie turned to Berg. "You know, Bruce, we have to do something to hang on to people like that."

Six months later, Ron Brill rolled out our ESOP.

Incidentally, another reason for the ESOP program was to protect our young, suddenly rich associates from themselves. Many sold stock as fast as they earned it in those heady early days, whether to buy a new couch or a sports car. This company is rife with tales of $1 million couches—luxury items bought with stock in the early days of the program before the share value soared—because that's how valuable the first stock options became. Stock in the ESOP program became something you couldn't get right away; we instituted a seven-year vesting period so it had a chance to build value over time.

The culture of this company intentionally beats down our associates' fear of bureaucracy, opening up very honest face-to-face interaction. Smart associates are not afraid of us.

We discover great things by walking the stores. Then it is a matter of taking it and seeing how far we can spread it. If it is a great presentation of snow shovels, that probably won't work in Miami, but the same presentation might work for dirt shovels. When we get a concept that works, something that is successful, we spread it around.

Our "Best Practices" program came out of what we learned on store walks. If something is really great in Phoenix, why are we not doing it in New Orleans?

Here are two examples:

- Signs are very important to The Home Depot. Great big stores require great big signs, and many years ago, Jeff Anderson, then a department head in our Jonesboro store with a strong entrepreneurial streak, went a little overboard on signage. He took signs that were 17″ by 22″ and put them on all the storm doors, screen doors, and windows. Previously, those big signs were used just on endcaps.

  Suddenly, when you walked into his building materials and millwork department, these big signs exploded in your face. The only thing written on the signs was the price. It demonstrated how proud we were of our prices, and it put some excitement in the department.

  Denny Ryan was the first executive to see the signs. He was so excited, he raced back and told Bernie about it.

  Bernie went straight over and took a look, but he was not nearly as excited as Ryan was. He came back and said, "Are you totally blind? I walked in that store, but I hardly made it back to the building materials department because there were so many other things wrong with the store."

  At the time Ryan was responsible for the merchandising of building materials, and he walked in that store with blinders on. He saw his building materials department, and it was magnificent. The signage concept was subsequently rolled out everywhere in the country. But what he didn't see was the whole rest of the store! He was looking myopically at things.

  But those signs really were something special, something you'll still see in every Home Depot store today. We started calling them BFSs—big fat signs—although the middle initial originally stood for something more profane. We have cleaned up our "business" language since then. Pretty soon we were putting BFSs on everything. And we created even bigger signs that we call RBFSs, which are really big fat signs.

- "Depot Dons" originated at our store in Chula Vista, California, which is right on the Mexican border, south of San Diego.

  When non-English-speaking Hispanics would come in, some of our employees had a hard time communicating how to do things such as patching a wall or installing windows screens. Don Sheresh, an associate in the store, was Anglo, but bilingual. He needed visual tools for his weekend clinics and came up with the idea of putting "how-to" project examples on endcaps. At the end of certain aisles, he created a step-by-step-by-step visual how-to guide.

  The "Depot Don" concept caught fire immediately and spread across the entire company. Today, you'll find this "best practice" in virtually every aisle of every Home Depot. It was such a good idea, most of our competitors copied it outright as well.

There's a natural tension between "best practices" and entrepreneurism. A best-practice approach of taking ideas from somewhere else is much harder to implant in an entrepreneurial system. In an entrepreneurial system, managers want to initiate their own ideas, making them defensive about ideas that come from somewhere else.

Our company is still learning how to balance the two. The corollary is that our competitors can often copy our ideas and spread them through their organizations faster than we can do our own.

Load 'n' Go, the Kids' Workshops, Tool Corrals, and Depot Dons are all best practices that have been knocked off by our competition. The good news is some of our bad ideas have been copied, too; sometimes they run with a red herring and get burned by it.

What we are trying to do on store walks is engage our associates. This is a people business, and our goal is anything from engaging them in strategic conversation to just getting to know each other so we can transfer culture and ideas. It's about building relationships so people are open to learning; it's about creating a teachable moment.

We expect them to make some notes, but generally, the goal is to communicate at a higher level about concepts and ideas and potential ways for us both to improve the business. We are looking for input from them as much as anything else.

We are the coaches. We don't run the stores for them. We don't make all their decisions. We have guidelines, but the rest of it is kind of free-form.

The tips or the hints we want to get across are things like, "Look at the customer's eyes. Do they understand what you are telling them? Read your signs, look at the pricing. Does it make sense? Look at the stock levels. Look at the cleanliness of the product. Look at the lighting. Look at what your customer is seeing. Be critical. Do something about it."

A lot of people think there is some sort of magic, a silver bullet that one of us will provide and it will change their lives. But there isn't. You know what we do offer? It is an environment that allows people to flourish, and the rest is coaching, mentoring, and support.

Stop and focus, don't just run up and down the aisles. Some managers manage by walking fast and looking worried. We would rather have them take their time, focus, see what the customer is seeing, talk to the customer, and interact, because that is where you get all your answers.

Our people are shopkeepers. As long as they run their business well or reasonably well, we don't bother them.

We hire people who couldn't work for anybody else, who might otherwise be well-suited to being self-employed or running their own shop, and many of them become store managers. They still don't work for anybody, really. If they are good, they work for themselves. We don't tell them what to do, and there isn't anybody that runs in from Atlanta and says, "Oh, no, no, don't do that, do this."

When you look at the return on sales of this company and it is 40 percent higher than the next best competitor, you need to keep the troops fired up all the time. With a 40 percent gap, it is easy to become soft.

■　　■　　■

During a store walk more than ten years ago, Ken Langone took more than a dozen associates into their break room and chatted with them.

One young man said he was unhappy with his last review.

"I am not qualified to talk to you about that," Ken said. "But we have an open-door policy here. Start with your department head and then talk to your assistant manager and then your store manager. In that process, you will find out exactly how they arrived at your evaluation."

That should have been the end of it, except Ken discovered the problem was bigger than this one associate's evaluation.

"Well, I can talk to the department head, and I can talk to the assistant manager," the young man said, "but I can't talk to the store manager."

"Why not?"

"There is a policy in this store that you can't talk to the store manager."

"That's too bad," Ken said, puzzled. "He must be a very busy guy, but I tell you what . . ." Ken stood up, walked to the blackboard, and wrote his New York office number on it. "This is *my* number. I want all of you here to spread it around the store. I can make shit happen. If you ever have a problem because your store manager is too busy, you call me and we will try to solve the problem together."

On his way out of the store, Ken ran into the store manager. "How did the associates meeting go?"

"Very well," Ken said. "But look, I know you are very busy, in fact, you are so busy you can't talk to your people, so I hope you don't mind, but for now, when they have a problem, they are going to call me."

He solved that one pretty quick, didn't he?

"Do me a favor," Ken tells associates during their meetings. "When a supervisor calls you up with a stupid request, do it. Then, when you get done doing it, say, 'Now that I've done that, tell me how it is going to help me help the customer.' Make them focus on what the connect is between what they are telling you to do and what your mission is. Because your mission is simple: Sell somebody who comes in off the street *something*."

Once we get our values instilled in associates, then we don't have to manage them. They manage themselves, and they are able to make independent, on-target decisions without having to get a tremendous amount of direction from above.

7. BERNIE'S TEST

Bernie has a little test to see how long it takes for an associate to recognize him. It is an interesting test. If he walks around a store for 45 minutes or an hour and no one recognizes him, he knows there is a serious problem in the store.

Can you guess why?

Eye contact.

They are not looking at his face. Nobody has looked at his face. That is why they haven't spotted him; they haven't acknowledged him. In fact, he has walked into stores where he has bumped into associates and ends up saying, "I'm sorry." They don't even say they are sorry. And he knows, as a result, that we must have a bad manager and an even worse store.

In South Florida, Bernie once spent an hour and a half in a store, putting his face right into the associates' faces, and nobody ever recognized him. Why not? Within this company, he is very recognizable, as am I. We appear on publications and videos seen by every associate. We are as visible within our company as any chief executive anywhere in the world.

The flip side of this test is the places where it takes an associate five seconds to say, "Hey, aren't you Bernie Marcus?"

Bernie was getting out of his car in the parking lot of a Home Depot store in Tucson, Arizona, and a lot engineer looked at him and said, "Oh, my God, it's you!" Typically, it takes no more than five or ten minutes. It has nothing to do with his ego. It has to do with the fact that they are not looking at his face or anybody else's. Many people are used to going into stores where the employees don't make eye contact. They don't acknowledge you; they couldn't care less about you. That should not happen in a Home Depot.

The only way to find out how our people are responding to customers is to go out there—alone, not with an entourage. When Bernie goes in a store and they pick him out in five minutes, he feels good about it. Then he walks around the store and sees what the store really looks like. It is not prepared for him, it is prepared for the customer, which is really the critical thing. They are not in stock because they know Bernie is coming, they are in stock because they know the customer is coming.

Walking those stores, Bernie becomes the dumbest person that you ever saw. He asks the dumbest questions. He has learned never to educate himself on anything, so he will pick something up and say, "How does this work?" And he wants someone who says, "Oh, let me show you." Then he wanders from one department to the next, learning pretty fast whether or not we have a training problem in that store. It becomes self-evident if the managers are not doing their jobs. We are so careful about who we hire that if we don't teach them and train them, we end up with people who are just like those in our competitors' stores.

The whole issue is what we call being "ground-engaged." Pat Farrah spends 70 percent of his time in the stores, Bill Hamlin and Larry Mercer a little less than that. Bernie and I probably spend 25 to 30 percent of our time in the stores. The balance is spent training managers in our culture and teaching merchandising.

8. GONNA GO 'ROUND IN CIRCLES

Our "360 Feedback" is a way of providing Home Depot officers and managers with insight into their leadership style. The primary purpose of 360 is for the development of Home Depot leaders. It is not the same as a performance appraisal because it focuses primarily on leadership skills and is not tied to salaries or bonuses. However, performance appraisal and 360 are used together to help determine what kind of management development and which job assignments make the most sense.

The name "360" comes from the fact that the managers receive feedback from everyone that works around them—their boss, their peers and the people that report to them. The process involves filling out a survey that rates the manager on leadership qualities that we value at The Home Depot. Not only do the people that work around the manager fill out the survey, but the managers also rate themselves on the same leadership skills.

Honest answers are needed if the 360 is going to help our leaders recognize their strengths and weaknesses. I believe it is one of the most powerful development processes we have ever gone through.

Even though this feedback is for the development of the manager, the 360 report can pack a punch. Imagine being the manager getting that report full of honest feedback from trusted associates and finding out you're viewed as unapproachable—or worse?

However, not all the information on the 360 report is negative. Studies on receiving feedback have shown that people tend to ignore the positives. All managers—myself and Bernie included—go through a 360 every eighteen months. And most of the Home Depot leaders who have received their results classified them as "eye opening."

9. ESTABLISH TIES THAT BIND—AND STRENGTHEN THEM

In recent years, two important dynamics have affected the ranks of our senior officers.

Number one, our company has grown so quickly that someone is always being promoted into senior officer ranks. And at the pace at which we are all moving, we need ways of communicating effectively on the fly. In a low-growth or no-growth kind of environment, people can be in meetings all the time and all be part of the same things, but in our situation, where everybody is physically going in different directions all at the same time, trust is really important, because we can't be every place at once. We must rely on each other implicitly.

Number two, my visibility within the company has been steadily expanding as Bernie turns over more and more of the day-to-day operations and decision making.

For these reasons, I have looked for opportunities to build on my relationships with our senior officers and smooth the transition between me and Bernie. Participating in Outward Bound's team-building experiences have encouraged within us the ability to communicate sometimes without even saying a word. These outings build trust, because trust is all you have on trips into the rugged middle of nowhere with nothing more than what you can carry on your back.

I am the more physically active of the company's cofounders—I'm the one who has run the New York City and Los Angeles marathons, who skis, who rides the rapids. Taking outdoor trips with the senior officers has given them a new personal intimacy and familiarity with me that until recently many only shared with Bernie.

Our Outward Bound–type trips, where we get out of the office and away from the phone, let people see each other in a different light. It recommits us to each other. We rediscover the dynamics that make it all work.

Several years ago, our Western division officers participated in an Outward Bound program on a working dude ranch in the southern part of Utah where *Butch Cassidy and the Sundance Kid* was filmed. In fact, it's the site of the cave where Butch and Sundance hid out in real life. The Western group had a great experience there and suggested I try it.

I found the notion irresistible and organized a retreat to the Hole in the Wall Ranch in southern Utah in October 1991. It was our first real officer bonding trip. Along with me were twenty-four Home Depot officers, including Bruce Berg, Dick Hammill, Marshall Day, and Lynn Martineau—virtually everyone but Bernie and Bill Harris.

Getting there was more than half the fun: They took us three at a time in single-engine Piper Cub airplanes that flew for two thrilling hours about 200 feet off the ground, over nothing but brush, just like you see in old movie westerns.

It was supposed to be 60 degrees when we arrived. The plan was to ride horses by day and camp out by night. But it was actually 26 degrees, and it was trying to snow. The next two days it *did* snow. As Berg put it, "It was colder than a well digger's ass out there."

That wouldn't be so bad at a four-star mountain resort, but this place was in the middle of nowhere. The "ranch" didn't have beds— no one ever slept there. Flying out wasn't an option in that weather. Besides, that is not The Home Depot way. Who was going to be the wimp to stand up and say, "I don't want to do this"? We had no choice but to see the trip out to its bitter end.

Most of us laid our sleeping bags out on the hardwood floors, but two guys had their own ideas of rustic comfort: Hammill and Andy McKenna, our senior vice president of strategic planning, slept on the floor of an old school bus; Berg, figuring the inevitable snoring in the bus would keep him awake, found a full granary and crawled inside to keep warm. What he didn't think of right away was that granaries attract rats. So he spent his nights warm, although his bunk mates still snored—and squealed—in their sleep.

The cold created some unexpected hardships. No one was prepared for anything near that kind of wet, bitter cold, so several people dressed around the clock in virtually all the clothing they brought with them.

If you ever had nightmares about using a drafty outhouse on a windy, 20-degree Utah morning, then you can imagine what our entire three-day visit was like.

It got dark early, so we would go inside, where we ate dinner standing up because there wasn't enough room to do anything else. There was no electricity, so at night all twenty-five of us—plus five ranch hands—went in the one room with a fireplace and huddled together. By seven P.M. we'd be in the room with the fireplace—no TV, no radio, no nothing—and we just kind of stared at each other for four hours before finding enough floor to call a bed.

Not that the trip was a disaster; it really wasn't.

The owner of the ranch, A. C., was a colorful, if somewhat cantankerous, former rodeo star. A. C. would get up in the morning, climb in his little Piper Cub, and fly around his property to find his horses. Then he and another cowhand would use a truck to bring the horses in.

That first—and only—clear day, A. C. wanted to ride fast, so he gave a command and all the horses started running like the wind. That was fine with Berg and Martineau, who had either lived or worked on ranches and were comfortable around horses. But Marshall Day, a city slicker who had never ridden before, threw his reins in the air, grabbed hold of the saddlehorn, and held on for dear life.

At least he stayed in the saddle. Berg's horse did a 90-degree turn when he wasn't looking, and his body kept going straight. Mr. Cowboy hit the ground and rolled a couple of times before getting up. That's when we all started laughing at him.

Berg got the last laugh, however, when we watched one of the cowhands rope a would-be steer that had not yet been castrated.

Most of us had never seen this done before. The guy had the animal on the end of the rope, then he used a pocket knife to removed its testicles. The steer was not a happy camper at all about it, as you might imagine.

I was wearing a bright yellow rain suit and I dismounted from my horse to get a closer look.

Sure enough, as soon as it was untied, the steer went right after me, and I ran away from it—the worst thing you can do under the circumstances. That 400-pound steer smacked me in the butt, and once everyone was sure I wasn't hurt, they cracked up.

Hammill was another first-time rider. Instead of guiding his horse around a tree, it led him right toward a large, low-hanging branch. He panicked, ending flat on the ground. The horse kept going without him. As he rebounded off the branch and landed with a thud on the hard ground, Hammill got up and said, "Wouldn't it be great to go sailing next year?"

So a year later, the same group went sailing—a first for me. Over five days, we cruised in and out of the British Virgin Islands, with five or six officers to a 50-foot yacht.

While many people wrestled with sea sickness, I demonstrated a very healthy *respect* for the ocean water, a mix of uncertainty and curiosity. I went snorkeling for the first time with Hammill, jumping off the back of the boat and swimming quite a distance to the nearest reef.

When we got back, Hammill and I were at the back of the boat, hanging on to the ladder, when I quietly said, "Thank you."

"For what?"

"For helping me overcome a fear," I said. "I don't think I would have ever gone sailing before we took this trip, especially in this deep water."

I have gone sailing every year since.

10. SHUT UP AND SHOW THEM WHAT YOU WANT

Another colorful Home Depot guy is our Southeast merchandising manager for hardware, Terry Kinskey. Many years ago, Kinskey—

then a district manager—was unhappy with the state of our old original store on Memorial Drive in Decatur, Georgia. He had been trying to work within the system to get the store cleaned up, but to no avail. When the store manager went on vacation for a week, Kinskey personally took charge, promoting seven trainees to the title of assistant manager. In the manager's absence, he and his crew blitzed the store in a stretch of twenty-hour work days, cleaning, repairing, and remerchandising.

There was product buried in corners of that store that never saw the light of day, bearing price tags that were five years old. There were 50 reconditioned lawn mowers that looked atrocious. Kinskey and Co. wiped down the lawn mowers with WD-40 and hawked them like carnival barkers for 50 to 75 percent off until they were all gone.

When the manager returned, the store looked brand-new. Kinskey's crusade sent a pretty powerful message.

You're probably wondering why Kinskey didn't just fire the manager, whose name was Ashok Patel. But that's not the way we do business. Patel was relatively new to our company, overseeing our oldest and perhaps most difficult store.

Leaders in this organization don't want to crush somebody trying to get something done—even if it's not yet working out. Kinskey looked at it as an opportunity to help the store and teach Patel and the people that he just promoted. Instead of talking, Kinskey showed him what he expected.

By the way, Patel not only grasped the lesson, but Kinskey eventually promoted him to regional merchandising manager, a liaison between the buyers and our Atlanta stores.

Kinskey also stands tall as an example of another Home Depot value: "Do the right thing, don't just do things right."

When he was a store manager, Kinskey had a person working for him who he believed deserved a raise of 30 percent. It was an outrageous amount. Kinskey went to his district manager, made his case, and was turned down. But instead of shrugging his shoulders and walking out, he stood up on the desk and started stamping his feet. "This guy deserves this raise!" he insisted. He felt so strongly that a 30 percent raise was the right thing for this associate that he would not take no for an answer. He got in everybody's face over this. He stood up for what was right.

One of the most important issues we face, especially at a time of enormous growth, is producing enough qualified people to run and work in all the new stores. We want these people to carry on the Home Depot values and use them as the basics for making the right decisions in their stores. We think it's important enough so that this message is personally delivered in every training class.

The week-long classes for assistant managers, managers, and district managers start with me and end with Bernie. Even our investors find it hard to believe that the founders of the company still participate in training managers, expounding The Home Depot's explicit values, as if that were beneath us.

"Bernie, you don't really still teach those classes, do you?" one man asked.

"Yeah, I do," Bernie said. "So does Arthur. So do most of our officers."

"How can you do that? This company is going on $30 billion in sales. You can't do that!"

"Sure we can. We have to," Bernie said. "And when the company does $45 billion and when the company does $70 billion, whether I am here or not, the officers of the company will still participate in the training, because we set the stage. When you start handing it off to people who do it professionally, you don't get the same emotion, the same direction, because we are the 'they' when people say, 'This is what they believe.' And they have to hear it from our mouths. We have to set the stage for what the philosophy of the company is."

Our role is to set programs, to visualize the future, to listen carefully, to train and teach, and then allow these people to do their own thing.

11. KILL BUREAUCRACY

If anything ever kills the personality of this company, it will be creeping bureaucracy. It is always there, unseen, and it's always trying to cover us like a fungus. Every bureaucrat who sends out a piece of paper to the stores that is not necessary is part of that.

We fight the bureaucratic urge by giving our store managers the freedom—some might call it a very long leash—and the confidence in themselves that they would never have someplace else.

At the same time, we are our own worst critic. You won't often hear us sitting around patting ourselves on the back. In fact, if you sat in on a board meeting or one of our staff meetings or literally any time we are together with the merchants or operating people, you would think we were going broke. You might even think, "Geez, I better sell my stock." We treat everything like a potential catastrophe, so we *don't* have a catastrophe on our hands.

When we acquired National Blind and Wallpaper Factory, its president, David Katzman, sat in on his first mini–staff meeting with all the Home Depot presidents and key officers. About halfway through the morning, I stopped what I was doing, looked at Katzman, and said, "Don't look so worried. Things are actually very good here."

"I was starting to get nervous," Katzman admitted. "I was wondering, 'What am I in for here? Wait till they get to me.' "

And that was a relatively routine meeting. Bernie, Pat, Ken, and I have raging debates over the way things are being done. An outsider would most certainly have thought that the whole company was going down the toilet. There are no calluses on our backs from patting each other. But if you took a consensus as to what we felt described our true effectiveness as a retailer, we are probably at about 65 percent satisfaction today.

12. HIRE THE BEST

There is an aversion in most organizations and among most managers to hiring people who are smarter than they are. What has made us successful? From the time we started in retail, we have always believed in hiring the best people.

Don't just hire good people and let their potential go to waste. Give up responsibility and authority to them. Challenge them to surpass you. And every time they show sparks of genius, your own career will take off because you are responsible for them.

Some people are afraid to hire smarter people. They're insecure;

"That person is going to take my job!" Baloney. They're going to help you up.

13. INVERTED PYRAMID

If we broke down the management structure at The Home Depot on a blackboard, Bernie Marcus and Arthur Blank would be at the bottom; the stores would be at the top.

The people at the stores are the most important—after customers—because they interface with the customer, and since Bernie and I really couldn't begin to tell you how to wire a house, we are the least important when it comes to satisfying a customer.

The sign at the front entrance of our main offices in Atlanta says "Store Support Center." Not "World Headquarters." It is not a corporate ivory tower. It is truly the store support center. We want everybody in this building to know that we are here to support the stores.

If a store calls anyone in the Store Support Center—from the chairman of the board and president to the janitor—our instruction to them is to stop what you are doing and take the store call. Sometimes it is hard for people to be efficient internally because of that, but that doesn't matter. Internally, our number one customer is the Home Depot stores. When they have a problem and they run to the phone, because of the chaotic atmosphere of a Home Depot store, it is not like they have been thinking about making this call for a couple of hours. They have a need *right now*, so we have to be there for them.

Don Keough, a member of our board of directors and a retired president and CEO of The Coca-Cola Company, told us a great story that we repeat in every management training session.

The day he was made president of Coca-Cola, Keough walked out of the board meeting, got on an elevator, and punched the number of a floor he had never been on before. Then he wandered the floor, looking around, and randomly walked into the office of a business manager he had never met before.

"Hi," he said. "I'm Don Keough, the new president of Coca-Cola. I would like to know what *you* do to sell Coca-Cola."

The guy looked at him and said, "I don't sell Coca-Cola, I'm in the accounting department. I have nothing to do with sales."

Keough shook his head, disappointed.

"*Everybody* that works in this building has to be involved in selling a can of Coca-Cola," he said.

And that is exactly what we say to our people at the Store Support Center. In our inverted management structure, everyone's career depends on how the associates in the stores function. If the people in the Store Support Center or divisional offices don't feel like they are selling a product to customers in the stores, then they are part of a bureaucracy, and they will stymie the stores, not help them.

We don't care what your job is. What have you done to help a customer in our stores today? What have you done to sell a product to our customers? What have you done to bring a customer into our stores? What have you done to make a manufacturer want to sell to our company? You have a role, and if you don't think you do, you don't belong here. If you don't know what that role is, *you need to find out.*

14. RESPECT FOR THE INDIVIDUAL

What's the secret of the partnership between Bernie and me?

There has never been anything significant undertaken by our company that the two of us didn't work together closely on. And there has not been a major decision made since 1979 that we were not in agreement with each other about.

That doesn't mean we never differ, but we have the kind of respect for each other where, if one of us feels strongly about something, the other won't fight him on it even if we don't agree.

We believe that's a real strength of The Home Depot. In other companies, founders have differences and people internally take advantage of that. But when people come to us individually, 98 percent of the time they will hear the same answer from either one of us.

That's significant because we are the oddest couple that has ever come down the pike. Forget Mutt and Jeff or Oscar and Felix—our physical and emotional differences are so obvious to everybody who knows us that it is a miracle that we survived 20 years together because we are such polar opposites.

Personalities created The Home Depot. If it had been conceived of by any of a thousand other people, they could not have created what we did.

Personality was our "X" factor, especially in the early days. Each one of us was a strong-willed personality: Bernie, Pat, and Ken were the extroverted giant-slayers; I was the reserved, less bombastic businessman who counterbalanced the excesses of the other three. In The Home Depot, our personalities became magnified. You know how manufacturers combine one drug with another to make a stronger new drug? That's why our partnership works. We each possess a different combustible element that won't ignite without the others.

Think about all the obstacles that we overcame: being fired, bankruptcy, opening stores on a used wing and a short prayer. So we worked together, and we had experiences together that were just unbelievable.

At this point, we should probably be over what created The Home Depot.

We are not.

When we sit in our meetings, we are no different than we were the first year of our business. We talk about how we have done things wrong, how badly we run our business, how we are not treating our customers properly. The topics and tone are no different than they were two decades ago.

We have customers on a lease, a short lease. Its terms state they will be with us just as long as we take care of them. The longer we take care of them, the longer that lease goes. They will even forgive us a misstep once or twice. They will say, "You know, I have shopped here all of these years and this store is usually terrific, so I'll give them another try." But we can't mess with the lease more than twice. We will lose them. Just like that. They will be gone. And we won't know it until they take their family and friends with them.

Nobody belongs to anybody, and we have seen that with companies who have gone down the drain. The landscape has changed radically in twenty years. Consider a partial list of chains that couldn't keep pace: Handy Dan, Handy City, Handyman, House Works, Homecrafters Warehouse, Rickel, Channel Home Centers, National Lumber and Supply Co., Builders Emporium, Forest City, Pay 'N Pak, Lindsley Lumber, Mr. Goodbuys, and Mr. HOW.

After twenty years, we are not jaded. We think we run an imperfect business. We have a long way to go. On a scale of zero to 100, we would internally rate ourselves about a 67. Compared to our competitors, we are like 110, but based on our expectations, we think there are too many opportunities out there that we are not exploiting for us to rate any higher.

The Communities We Serve

"Our Culture Is About Making Sure People Understand That They Are Empowered to Do What Is Right"*

When The Home Depot went public, we realized that we had the financial capacity and the wherewithal to give back to the communities where we did business.

There is a concept in Judaism called *tzedaka,* which means "to give back." It is considered a mitzvah, a good deed, to give to somebody who doesn't have, and we believe strongly in giving back to the community.

The beauty of that philosophy is that we don't tell our people that that is something they have to do. We don't keep track of how many homes they build for Habitat for Humanity or how many days they work for Christmas in April*USA or how many other community things they do.

In the early days, when we couldn't give money, we gave ourselves, we gave time, we gave product. We did what we could. Now we give money, too. But we never do it because we are trying to increase business in the community. We do it because we feel that we take an awful lot out of these communities. Meanwhile there are people in these very same communities who are disadvantaged, who need a helping hand.

* Arthur Blank

■   ■   ■

No one knew that Hurricane Andrew would be as devastating as it was to the area south of Miami known as South Dade, becoming the single largest disaster to ever strike the United States—25 deaths, 108,000 homes destroyed, and $20 billion in damage.

Our three-day-old Cutler Ridge store closed down at 11 P.M. on Saturday night. By then, everybody knew a hurricane was coming. All night and on into the wee hours of Sunday morning, assistant store manager David Bloom listened to news reports about the storm's expected path. Unable to sleep and knowing the rush of shoppers that morning light would bring, he decided the best place for him was back at his store. At four A.M., he found his store manager already there, waiting for him.

Within two hours, there were so many people waiting at the locked front door that the line extended a quarter of a mile, down the side of the building and over to U.S. 1. People were so desperate that they offered $100 for lumber carts to load their purchases. The thick, humid air was dank with panic. Bloom kept the mob under control by letting thirty people in at a time every four minutes. That gave them enough time to get what they needed and get to the registers.

Every associate showed up for work Sunday, even those who weren't scheduled. Management's intention was to close early so associates could make preparations for their own homes. Of course, by late afternoon, there wasn't anything left to sell, so closing wasn't a problem. When we inevitably ran out of lumber for covering windows, people started ripping pegboards out of the display racks. Some bought particle board or even flimsy paneling to cover windows. Anything that was flat and big, they took.

■   ■   ■

Home Depot tracks every hurricane from the time it leaves Africa to wherever it ends up.

In Tampa, where our Southeast regional division office is based, Bryant Scott was nowhere to be found. Unfortunately, the newly promoted vice president of merchandising chose that weekend to take his family out on their boat, oblivious to the very existence of Andrew, let alone the hurricane's threat to South Dade.

When Scott finally returned Sunday afternoon, just hours before Andrew began battering Florida, his answering machine was completely filled up.

Within an hour, Scott and his merchants—who had started without him the night before—were mobilized and following our hurricane preparedness plans, moving generators, batteries, tape, plastic, and lumber toward South Dade. We had been in that market since 1981 and had already been through several hurricanes and near misses, so we had a contingency plan in place.

■   ■   ■

Eight people showed up for work at the Cutler Ridge store after the storm cleared. What they found was astonishing: 75 percent of the store was virtually flattened. It had ceased to exist. Whatever you saw on TV didn't do the situation justice. You just can't appreciate the devastation of seeing acres and acres, mile after mile of flattened homes and businesses through a 19-inch, two-dimensional screen.

David Bloom couldn't easily find his way to the store after the hurricane. All the usual landmarks, from street signs to an entire shopping mall, were missing.

Maria Perez worked in our Kendall store. Her home was destroyed by the hurricane. When Bryant Scott arrived to inspect the damage for the first time, he found Perez and several of her fellow associates actually inside what was left of the store, cleaning it up. She didn't have a house left to live in, but she and the others were trying to get the store ready for customers. You can't teach that to people. It sounds hokey, but that is how close a lot of associates are to this company.

That same morning, Bruce Berg flew to South Florida from our Southeast division headquarters in Tampa via helicopter. The first Home Depot store he saw was at West Bird Road. It was still under construction and wasn't affected too much. At the Kendall store, all of the merchandise was destroyed, the roof peeled off with a heavenly can opener.

But by the time he got to Cutler Ridge, Berg had seen the true path of Andrew's indiscriminate destruction. There were telephone poles across the roads, live wires arcing everywhere. Cars were smashed and in odd, impossible positions. The doors were ripped off of some. As he landed in the parking lot, conversation stopped abruptly. Just four days old, the store was destroyed.

Berg got out of the helicopter, and he didn't have a clue what to do. Nobody prepares you for something like that.

What he had were questions: Did anybody spend the night in the store? Were they all right? How many associates have we heard from? Does anybody know where the rest are? What do they need?

He went into the store, because he didn't know any better. It was structurally unsound, but there was nobody there to tell him that, so he and the others crept around in ankle-deep water looking at blown-over racks and merchandise.

In Jacksonville, Tim Bolton (now vice president of human resources for our Southeast division) and one of our area store managers rented two 40-foot motor homes, drained the petty cash from their local Home Depot stores, and brought all the supplies they could carry to our people in South Dade.

The motor homes were intended as command points for management working in the disaster zone. The supplies were to help get our associates on their feet as quickly as possible.

In all, four stores were completely shut down by the storm. Others were in disarray. Within days, we erected a 6,000-square-foot tent next to what had been the Cutler Ridge store. There were six registers; the power supply was a box nailed to an oak tree in the parking lot. We opened a temporary store in northern Dade County to service builders, and we rushed the opening of the new store on West Bird Road. We also repaired the roof and reopened the Kendall store, which was immediately mobbed. There were 1,100 cars trying to park in a small lot built for 425 cars. Berg put on an orange apron and became "General Homer Patton." Associates in the store couldn't believe their eyes, watching their division president telling people where they could and couldn't park and ordering tow trucks by the dozens to tow violators.

It takes some serious logistical thinking to get back in business after a natural disaster such as that one. Can you sell from the parking lot? Can you get security? And every other retailer in the market was thinking the same things, especially in our industry. We found ourselves competing for things like motor homes, which were snapped up as far north as the Carolinas.

Sending people down to South Dade from the Southeast regional office in Tampa or from Home Depot stores wasn't simple. Hotel rooms were at a premium up and down the coast because of all the displaced persons. Our people found lodgings in Deerfield Beach, 60 miles north, which equated—with traffic at a crawl—to a three-hour commute in each direction. Their days started at five A.M. and ended around midnight. They worked on three or four hours sleep for weeks.

■ ■ ■

During the crisis, our stores in South Dade didn't raise a single price, much to the chagrin of certain vendors and competitors. To them, life is a commodity business, and they jacked up their prices to take advantage of one of life's misfortunes.

A few days after the hurricane hit, Bruce Berg called me. I was on board the company jet, preparing for takeoff. "I just want you to know that we are holding our prices to what they were the day before the hurricane," Berg said.

"That is exactly what I would expect," I said.

Notice that Berg didn't call for permission, he called me to say, "This is what we are doing, and it will cost us millions of dollars" in potential profits. Our culture is about making sure people understand that they are empowered to do what is right. We worry about the other stuff later, just do what is right now.

Berg—without advance, explicit support—did what he felt was right. We were not going to make money on somebody else's misfortune. We have given back since the first day we have been in business. That was a no-brainer. "Miami is in trouble, so we will help." It was the right thing to do.

Bernie supported that decision by appearing on the network news shows threatening to publicly name any vendors who raised prices, thereby taking advantage of the tragedy. He publicly called them on the carpet and said, "You will not do this." Some vendors held the line; others didn't. Caught in the middle, we held our prices steady and took a big loss on many products. There were five items we sold at cost, including plywood, wafer board, and plastic to cover up windows.

■ ■ ■

An emergency response team met twice a day at eleven A.M. and three P.M. in Atlanta to support the Southeast division any way it could. It showed us what we could do together, demonstrating to us the impact we could have, and it was extraordinary.

We had been in Florida longer than anywhere but Atlanta. We lost four stores. Our employees were impacted. It hit us on a lot of different fronts.

It was another defining moment for us because it was the first time since we had been in business that something of that magnitude had happened in a market we served. We were vested in South Florida not only with customers but with our own associates. We had a big people investment there. That's why everybody dropped everything they were doing and pitched in.

We literally sent truckloads of cash because there were no banks open to cash paychecks. We coordinated a program that insured our employees continued to be paid even if the damaged stores were closed or even if we couldn't immediately locate the employees. We had seventy employees and their families who lost their homes, and we helped find them temporary apartments and hotels, food, water, and even gas grills for cooking their meals. We also provided crisis counseling and no-interest loans.

Home Depot associates from coast to coast sent sixty truckloads of relief supplies to their counterparts in South Florida. We rented an 80,000-square-foot warehouse to store all of the donated goods from our stores. We gave as much as we could to our associates and distributed the rest to the local community.

■ ■ ■

Meanwhile, people were calling in to talk radio shows, where they enjoy the veil of anonymity, saying things like, "My brother-in-law told me that The Home Depot is gouging. He paid $30 a sheet for plywood there. I only paid $7 at XYZ Lumber." Well, his brother-in-law probably did pay $30 a sheet if he bought cabinet grade plywood instead of CDX. And his brother-in-law was probably the same naive person who, before the hurricane hit, didn't know the difference between cabinet grade birch and CDX. It was very frustrating.

A local TV station took these radio talk shows as gospel and made an across-the-board report that our industry was price-gouging. They didn't talk to us, they just put it on the air. That infuriated Bruce Berg, because we were selling so many vital building goods at our cost, and he responded by calling up several radio and TV stations and screaming at them. It wasn't the best approach, because everyone's nerves were raw and frayed. Besides, nobody believed Berg was who he said he was because of the language he used. He was absolutely livid.

Then the state attorney, responding to the TV report, came after us.

"Are you people gouging customers?" he asked. "Let us see your costs."

That was all Berg could stand.

"Why don't you get out of Tallahassee and come on down here and look at our costs and see what we are selling this stuff for?" he responded.

In the end, of course, the governor cited us as corporate citizens of the year. But that was after the fireworks.

We did get a lot of positive press because we pumped more generators and chain saws into the market and offered more product knowledge than anyone else, and we gave away water, foodstuffs, and anything else we could.

Certain product lines, such as drapery hardware, were dropped from stock at these stores. Priority items were generators, chain saws, polyethylene, plywood, nails, and whatever you need to clean up after a storm, such as wet-vacs, mops, and brooms.

Within a few days we also recognized the extreme need for propane-powered gas grills. How else were people with no electricity going to cook? South Florida is an all-electric market that hardly uses any natural gas. Barbecues were the only way they could cook. Our first order was for five truckloads of barbecue grills and five truck-loads of gas.

We started buying six-mil polyethylene, which was being used to cover partially destroyed roofs. Then the army came in and bought all the polyethylene we had, so we ordered more. "How much do you want?" the manufacturer's rep asked. "You start sending truckloads," Berg told him, "and we'll tell you when to stop."

At times, product knowledge was our most valuable commodity. There were people buying 5,000-watt generators, which they ex-pected would run a whole house just as if it were still wired to Florida Power and Light. It won't. Our people must have explained a thou-sand times that it will run a refrigerator, two light bulbs, a toaster and a fan, but you can't hook it up to your air conditioner. Most people had no idea. They thought they had just bought a nuclear power plant for their backyard.

And all of this was happening in three languages: English, Span-ish, and retiree.

■ ■ ■

The underground market was another problem, because demand for product was outrageous. People would come in and buy a prod-uct from our fenced-in stores, then would turn around and sell it at a premium price in our very own parking lot. One guy drove a truck with eight generators in the flatbed right into our parking lot, trying to sell them for twice our price. And if we had a truckload of genera-tors coming on a Home Depot truck, we had to cover it because our drivers could be in jeopardy from people clamoring for the product that was inside. Lumber was tarped over for the same reason.

Most stores in the affected areas received a truckload of Johns-Manville insulation daily; at Cutler Ridge, it was two truckloads daily.

We had 38 people at any time unloading trucks at any given store. We did mass hires not only to get the merchandise into the store but to sell it to the customers. We brought on more than 200 permanent associates in two weeks at the Hialeah store alone. These people were in addition to our normal associate base of 200 people. In all, we hired 2,000 people for a dozen affected South Dade stores within a six-week time period. Getting them all processed, oriented, trained, and out on the sales floor took a titanic effort.

We did not lower our standards from the point of what we required in terms of background checks, drug tests, and those types of things. But did we conduct detailed interviews? No.

After the storm, finding qualified people was a challenge because anybody with a chain saw could make $15 or more an hour.

Cutler Ridge opened with 117 associates, 16 cashiers and 18 cash registers. Post-Andrew, that store employed 657 associates, including 131 cashiers at 68 cash registers. We were always running out of orange aprons, needless to say.

David Bloom went to a Kmart and bought four king-sized sheets, stapled them together, and sprayed "Now Hiring" on them. Then he hung the sign two stories high on the back of the building facing the Florida Turnpike.

■　　■　　■

Even with our buying power and pull, there were certain supplies that were virtually impossible to keep in stock. We couldn't get tin tabs, for instance, which you use for attaching black felt paper to roofs before installing tile. Desperate, we found a local tin-can maker who had the necessary stamping machines and we put him in the business of making tin tabs.

There was literally a roofing shortage in the United States because so many of these materials were diverted to South Dade. Some manufacturers did have bona fide, unplanned shipping costs associated with supplying the market. They passed these along, but we just took it in the shorts and margin.

Lenny Kapiloff was a building materials merchant in the Southeast division. He bought all the doors and windows, shingles, roofing, and Sheetrock for the stores. That made him very important, because with so many blown-off roofs and every window in South Dade broken, we needed tons of glass and felt paper. Kapiloff bought felt paper from Canada, California, and Mexico; wherever it was available, he bought it. We quickly exhausted whatever the Southeast division's regular suppliers could produce. A truckload of felt paper was 1,100 rolls; it would arrive at a store and be sold within twenty minutes. He called his counterparts in our Western division and asked for the names of their suppliers. Then he would order as much felt paper as they would sell him. It was never enough.

We never bought felt paper from Celotex before the hurricane because it was too expensive. But after the storm we bought all they could make—even at a dollar more a roll than anyone else charged. They turned on the factory for us. And the Celotex people showed up every morning with fresh bagels and donuts to thank us.

Cost was irrelevant. Availability was the only issue. Kapiloff bought so much product that instead of trucks, it was eventually delivered by rail cars. That increased shipping costs, but at least we had the merchandise.

In November, just when we had a steady supply of felt paper, the Dade County Commission changed the kind of felt paper that was necessary for rebuilding. It required paper of a heavier weight, and it also had to have a yellow stripe on it. The yellow stripe was so that overworked building inspectors could see from the street that it met code without examining it. So we had to switch to a different grade of paper and put a yellow stripe on it. That was a killer.

Even Celotex couldn't produce enough material to meet demand, so Kapiloff went to some extraordinary lengths. He called a friend at a roofing company in Wilmington, Delaware, and asked about the availability of roofing materials there. He was directed to a local company that had its entire inventory in 105 trucks. Kapiloff bought 105 truckloads.

By November, the Cutler Ridge store was receiving eight truckloads of felt paper and ten truckloads of shingles a day.

Toward the middle of November, one of the companies that sold us interior doors told Kapiloff that it was raising door prices by two dollars apiece. They were maxed out in terms of production and felt it was a fair increase and a reasonable time to do it.

We were buying 6,000 doors a week for these stores, so we were maxing out everybody's production limits. It was either take the two-dollar price increase, or we wouldn't get doors. Since they could certainly sell our order elsewhere in the market, we accepted the price increase.

At the time, Kapiloff was also the buyer for our Houston stores, so he called Southern Millwork, which supplied doors to the Houston stores, and asked if they would ship into South Dade. The company agreed to send us six trucks, three times a week, all of which went directly to our Cutler Ridge store. That relationship blossomed, so eventually Southern Millwork set up in business right in Miami. To show our appreciation for helping us in a pinch—and to reduce our reliance on the manufacturer that increased prices in the midst of a crisis—we put Southern Millwork's products in all of our South Florida stores, from Cutler Ridge north to Boca Raton.

Three months later, we pushed the other supplier completely out of our South Florida stores, although we still do business with them elsewhere in the state.

■   ■   ■

Our window manufacturer, Keller, was based in Miami and worked twenty-four hours a day making us windows.

We had another vendor, Home Advantage, from whom we bought window glass. That company went to the extraordinary length of putting someone on its payroll in each of our South Dade stores to cut glass on the spot.

The president of Leslie Locke, Ralph Pepper, called Kapiloff to see what he could do to help.

"Do you have any people who can answer phones?" Kapiloff said, half-joking.

But on Monday, Pepper actually sent someone down for a week just to answer phones. It was bizarre, but it just goes to show you the lengths people went to to get through a crisis.

Poly America hadn't been selling us polyethylene up to that point, but they bellied up to the bar, too. We started a lot of new manufacturer relationships down there and expanded the dimensions of many existing relationships.

Bernie personally got involved with Georgia-Pacific, a substantial lumber supplier of ours, and told them that we would not tolerate price increases. For a certain amount of time, they froze prices on the plywood they sold to us in South Dade.

■ ■ ■

One day, Kapiloff and Berg found themselves working as lot guys, meaning they were shagging carts from a store's parking lot because there were so many customers and not enough available bodies to return carts to the store.

The company bought lunch and dinner for associates at the affected stores for at least the first month following the storm because everyone was working twelve- and fourteen-hour days. And late in November, Berg came through again for his Cutler Ridge crew, many of whom were still months away from returning to their homes, by throwing them a Thanksgiving dinner at the store.

What was a grand opening compared to this? What was setting up three stores at once? It was a cakewalk. Anybody that went through Hurricane Andrew knows that you can live through anything, because a lot of them lost their homes.

Every night, our team took a half hour for a debriefing. What issues did you face today? What could we do better tomorrow? Notes from those sessions later were used to update our companywide disaster-recovery plan.

Preparation was critical. You must have a flexible plan. The main lesson of our post–Hurricane Andrew experience is that whatever you give to the community, you will get it back tenfold. And when our stores were fully functional, people in Miami wouldn't think of shopping anywhere else. We created an enduring bond with the community.

The decentralized nature of our company was another factor in our quick and vital response to the tragedy. If we were a centralized company, micromanaging every move from Atlanta, we would not have reacted as swiftly as we did. Instead, we had people on-scene in Florida who understood their responsibility to the market, their customers, and our culture. We had a plan, mobilized quickly, and had employees who willingly gave up several months of their home lives to help the people of South Florida get their lives back.

When the Cutler Ridge store reopened, it grossed $3 million a week. Before Andrew it was not a high-volume store, budgeted for no more than $500,000 a week, but after the hurricane, it was the highest volume store in the company.

As a result of Hurricane Andrew, do we have a strong market position in South Dade? Yes. Do we own the market? No. We lease our customers. They are free to go whenever they want to. Sometimes the lease charges are quite expensive, but that is part of the culture of the company. We can't ever take them for granted because as soon as we do, they will find somebody else who will take better care of them. We can disappoint our customers once and they will put up with it. Twice? Not likely. Many have forgotten all about what we did for them after Hurricane Andrew, so we don't sit back and feel secure in South Dade because of what we did six years ago.

Hurricane Andrew was a moment of maturation for us as a participant in our communities. But it was just a springboard. In all our orientations and culture and values talks, store managers and district managers are reminded they will be held accountable for what they are doing in their communities.

■   ■   ■

Forty-five minutes after terrorists exploded a bomb outside the Alfred P. Murrah Federal Building in Oklahoma City, Rich Loyd, The Home Depot district manager for that area, was on his cell phone with our director of community affairs, Suzanne Apple.

"Something awful has happened here," he said. "I am sending my managers with truckloads of supplies. Rescue workers need masks, shovels, garbage bags, and garbage cans, and I am sending them everything we have."

Loyd wasn't calling to ask permission. And Apple knew better than to ask, "How are we going to pay for this?"

So when the first firefighters arrived, our people were already there because one of our two stores in the city was close by. Nobody called Atlanta first and asked, "Should we make donations to this?" They instinctively provided $70,000 worth of supplies and told us about it later. It was the right thing to do.

One of our associates, Don Shaw, realized that because of the bio-hazard, all the rescue workers had to take showers after they finished combing through the building. But the showers were cold, rigged through a city fire hydrant. Our associate went back to the store, got a portable generator and hot water heaters, which he rigged so the rescue workers could have warm showers. Again, nobody delayed action by calling Atlanta and asking, "Is this okay?"

In the first hours following the bombing, Bernie heard about the explosion and was desperately trying to get hold of Loyd or any key people at the Oklahoma City store. He was quite agitated until he learned they were already on the scene, behaving exactly as he would have expected. That was classic Home Depot as far as we're concerned.

As for Loyd, he is now the director of training in our Southwest division office.

■　■　■

Another recent example of this extreme community involvement came in December 1997 as ice storms ravaged New England and Southeastern Canada. Because the Ottawa Home Depot stores were out of commission, our people mobilized six truckloads of supplies and volunteers from Toronto to drive to Ottawa.

They rode through neighborhoods, randomly helping people secure their homes, patch roofs, fix broken pipes, and cut dangerous tree limbs. They were like a roving Peace Corps. In this case, they didn't just help their immediate community, they went to a neighboring Home Depot community that needed help.

■　■　■

One of the favorite company-supported programs is KaBOOM!, through which we build playgrounds for children all over the United

States. Our associates work long hours, five, six, even seven days a week. Yet, during a day off, they eagerly work many hours under all kinds of weather conditions to build something special for children. And they can't wait until they do another one.

Kids in these neighborhoods actually draw their own playground, showing us what they would like to see in swings and jungle gyms. We work in conjunction with Boys and Girls Clubs and our employees come out and convert urban blight into urban might—teeter-totters, slides, monkey bars, and swings.

For example, we built a playground in Chicago's Bridgeport neighborhood on a site where a playground burned down 40 years before and was never rebuilt. Six hundred Home Depot people worked side by side with gang members for three days and brought the playground back to life.

One of the gang members later had tears in his eyes, thanking us. "I didn't have a place to play when I grew up in this neighborhood, and I got in trouble," he said. "Now I have a two-year-old and a two-month-old, and they finally will have a place to play."

A woman who lived in one of the adjacent housing projects was likewise touched. "I have lived here for thirty years," she said, "and we have never had a place to just sit outside and talk to each other while our children played."

Coincidentally, that playground was under construction during the same weekend that the Chicago Bulls won one of their many NBA championships. The city was like Times Square on New Year's Eve. People honked their horns all night. Fireworks exploded. Police blocked off certain streets. But instead of joining in the hoopla, the gang members who worked with our people organized themselves on the site to protect the materials that we had delivered for building the next day. They took turns guarding them so nothing would happen and the playground would become a reality in their community.

■   ■   ■

Christmas in April★USA is a volunteer home repair program working with low-income and disabled inner-city home owners. Over the years, we have invested almost a quarter of a million dollars in

Christmas in April*USA projects. The group then cumulatively spends another $750,000 on additional supplies in our local stores.

An outgrowth of our Christmas in April*USA and Habitat for Humanity partnerships is the opportunity it gives our managers to see associates in a different light. Jeannine may have been tagged as a good plumbing salesperson, but not management material, until her store manager saw her captain a Christmas in April*USA project and realized her management potential.

We say we are in the relationship business, that we build a relationship with our customers. Well, that relationship doesn't stop at the door of our stores; it extends to the entire community that store serves, so we have very deliberately done more than just sign checks. We strive to make the local connection.

Habitat International came to us in 1991 and asked us to be a national corporate sponsor. "Write a check to us," they said, "and we will distribute it to our affiliates."

But we said no. Writing checks is just about money. If we really want to have an impact in these communities and if, in fact, we want it to be about more than money, then we have to build relationships.

We told Habitat we would be delighted to be a national partner of theirs, but we wanted to do more than write a check and get back to business. We offered training, volunteers, materials, and then some cash. That is a much more comprehensive approach with a bigger impact.

It also provides a team-building opportunity for our district managers and store managers. More recently, our vendors have expressed an interest in becoming more active in projects such as KaBOOM! and Habitat for Humanity, which will only strengthen their relationship with customers and The Home Depot people.

■   ■   ■

In New York City, the most skeptical city on the planet, The Home Depot culture works as well as it does anywhere.

The local ABC-TV affiliate, Channel 7, does a periodic consumer affairs feature on its evening news in which it identifies rip-off artists. One night, their reporter told the story about a man with eight kids whose house burned down. He unknowingly hired a fly-by-night contractor to rebuild the house with insurance money. But when the house was a third complete, the contractor allegedly had already run through all the money, leaving the family homeless.

It was a very sad story. But several weeks later, it had a very happy ending.

Associates in our Long Island store saw the report and asked their store manager if they organized the labor to finish the house, whether the store could donate the materials. Seeing it as a wonderful training and team-building opportunity, the manager agreed. Within days, an army of orange aprons descended upon the house. Our men and women worked through the night doing electrical, plumbing, drywalling, spackling, wallpapering, whatever it took. They built a new roof, new ceilings, installed carpeting, doors, windows, and lights.

The day they gave the house keys over to the father and he and his kids moved back into his house, everybody was crying. That is the kind of thing that happens in every single Home Depot store.

Most people only think about us for big events such as hurricanes, but it is little pieces of life like this that are just as important to our way of life.

■   ■   ■

The City of Hope is a great medical and research center in Duarte, California. It offers free care for patients suffering from catastrophic maladies such as cancer and leukemia; heart, blood, and respiratory afflictions; diabetes and other disorders of heredity and metabolism.

Bernie's first exposure to the City of Hope was back at Vornado, the parent company of Two Guys. Vornado had a corporate commitment to raise money for the City of Hope, and Bernie participated then through work.

Years later, at Handy Dan, a distraught young employee in his early thirties came to see Bernie.

"What is the matter?" Bernie asked.

"The doctor just told me I have five months to live," the young man said. "They told me all I can do is go home and die. I have an incurable form of cancer. There's nothing they can do about it."

Bernie called an old contact at the City of Hope and asked if they would consider the employee's case. The doctor at the City of Hope agreed, and the center treated him with an experimental drug that saved his life.

For Bernie, the City of Hope became much more than just another charity on a list from that point on. He and I were touched by the institution's compassion and led an effort to make the City of Hope an official charity of the hardware and home improvement industry. The first year, we raised $250,000; by 1998, the industry raised $10.1 million, most of it at an industry dinner during the annual National Hardware Managers Association convention.

Each year, the City of Hope and its Beckman Research Institute honor someone at this dinner with its "Spirit of Life" award. Bernie was feted while at Handy Dan and at The Home Depot; in August 1990, it was my turn.

One of the traditions of this dinner is that the honoree gets to request a guest speaker of his or her choice. Considering our history, some thought my choice was a curious one: Ross Perot.

Perot graciously accepted, flying in at his own expense, and he made a great controversial speech about our growing involvement in the Persian Gulf.

But before the dinner, Perot sat down with us for a personal chat about what could have been.

"I don't make many mistakes in my life," Perot said, "but I have to admit, that was one of the best mistakes I ever made, without question."

We all knew that The Home Depot would not be the company it is today if Perot had been the major stockholder. But he was very magnanimous about it, a true gentleman.

"I am proud of what you guys have done," he said. "Everything you said you were going to do, you did. And fellas, I shop these stores all the time. I buy everything in your stores."

■　■　■

In 1989, we budgeted almost $1.5 million for charitable contributions, but we had no idea how to spend it. Each year up until then, responsibility for community giving had been rotated among Bernie, me, and Ron Brill. But as the dollar amount grew we realized that deciding who to give back to was becoming a full-time job.

There was no other asset that we would budget a million dollars for and have no plan where to send it. That's when we hired Suzanne Apple to help. Her job was to take our general vision of *tzedaka* and make it work in the real world. The biggest challenge was making it something that wasn't just about us. We didn't want glory for ourselves or The Home Depot; we wanted proactive results.

Apple's first move was to decentralize the dollars and to train our district managers to be active in their communities. We developed three focus areas for the giving program: affordable housing, youth at risk, and the environment.

At the same time, we targeted eight communities nationwide in which we became proactively involved: Dallas, Miami, Tampa, Orlando, Atlanta, Los Angeles, San Diego, and Phoenix. Those were our major markets in 1989, and we targeted additional dollars for them. Apple then went door-to-door to charitable groups in these communities looking for opportunities, soliciting proposals from them for us to do a project.

A great example of how this worked was in Tampa. The local preservation organization, along with United Methodist Social Services, was trying to develop a plan for low-cost housing in 1989.

Apple walked into their meeting and said, "We want to be part of this." We helped them get a Habitat for Humanity affiliate started in the community, provided $50,000 in construction materials, and our district manager offered in-store volunteer training for Habitat volunteers from GTE, Tampa Electric, banks, churches, and synagogues. We weren't the only catalyst, of course, but we helped pull that group together a little bit.

By 1992, we budgeted $4 million for community projects. A year later we gave the program a name, Team Depot, and provided formal community-relations training for our managers. In 1998, we spent $12.5 million on community projects.

Through Team Depot, we stimulate associates to do things and support them financially, but they either do it or they don't; it is up to them, and we find that most stores are doing it. The kind of people who willingly do these things are the kind of people that we want to attract to The Home Depot.

Whenever there is a problem in a community served by The Home Depot, our associates will be a part of the solution. This is all part of the Christian-Judaic feeling that we think you should have in an ethical business.

It is more informal than formal in our company. Our people believe the way we believe, and at The Home Depot they found a place where they can act on these kinds of feelings. Whenever there is a Habitat for Humanity, whenever there is any community need, our people volunteer.

Associates are encouraged by making their schedules more flexible around their individual community involvement tasks, such as tutoring in the schools, and we launched an employee matching gift program. Since Team Depot's creation, company giving has grown in tandem with The Home Depot's own 25 percent annual growth.

The greatest pleasure we all take in Team Depot is hearing what our associates did *after* they have done it. Just as they do in making retail-oriented decisions, they don't call and ask for permission, they just do it, and they know we will support them in doing it.

PART III

The Future

"Responding to Change Is One of the Reasons for the Success of The Home Depot"*

Twenty years after we started this company on a truckload of fireplace screens and a warehouse of ceiling fans, you would think we would be satiated. We are wealthy beyond our dreams, successful, even somewhat famous. We get our pictures in the papers, and we appear on magazine covers. Even better, we've made millionaires out of more than 1,000 of our associates.

We probably have more self-made blue-collar millionaires on our payroll than anyone else in corporate America. Why do they still work here after striking it rich? Because they love their jobs as much today as they did when they started. The Home Depot is a fun place to work! There will always be pressures and days when they think—as we do—"Why am I here? This is aggravating—I have enough money to go anywhere." But the less need there is to stay on, the less pressure there is. And The Home Depot, as a company, has been great to these people, who know they make an important and ongoing contribution to our success and their own.

The Home Depot is one of the few companies where people who have been here a long time should have a significant amount of money socked away. And they still wear blue jeans to work and abhor ties, sport coats, and other standard business attire. You can always

* Arthur Blank

tell the people on our elevators who don't work here because that's the way *they* dress.

The competitiveness of the home improvement industry motivates my work at The Home Depot. I get to transfer that piece of my personality from when I was younger, as it related to sports and my studies, and apply it to the business arena today.

When you think about the retail business, every day you plan out certain things, but there are so many things you don't control in the marketplace, and every day you have to react, every day you have to plan, every day the circumstances change. It could be something as simple as the weather. How does it affect the business? How will you deal with competition? How do you deal with opportunity? How do you deal with customers who are changing all the time?

One of the things I love about retail is that it is not stable. It is always shifting. There are always dynamics taking place. To be successful in retail, you must be willing to stick to your values, understanding not just what your values are but that every day they will be painted against a different environment and you must be ready for that. Responding to change is one of the reasons for the success of The Home Depot.

■　　■　　■

What's next?

We spent a large part of 1997 contemplating where our growth will come from in future years. The answer included five categories:

- Continued expansion of our core business
- Increased sales to professional customers
- International expansion
- Specialty-store expansion
- Convenience stores

INTERNATIONAL

Being in Canada only whetted our appetite for expansion beyond U.S. borders. It provided an initial training ground for conducting business outside the U.S. and adapting to non-U.S. markets.

That's why Bill Peña, the president of our South American division, spent six months visiting fifteen countries in three key regions—Asia, Europe, and Latin America—focusing specifically on developed, as opposed to emerging, countries. In each country, the goal was to benchmark with other companies and spend time learning about the local home improvement market, housing patterns, and cultural differences.

One of the frustrations that caused was when Peña gave us his recommendations. "The truth," he said, "is that the whole world needs what we have." Peña found opportunities for us everywhere. Our estimates indicate the combined international do-it-yourself and pro market is larger than the entire U.S. market. Worldwide, we found that home improvement retailers provide relatively poor service, even though the customers to whom we spoke indicated good service was universally important to them. We were particularly encouraged by this, given The Home Depot's strength in this area.

The desire for good customer service is universal, but the housing and product needs are very different throughout the world, and sometimes within regions. Therefore, it is essential that we adapt to market differences in the areas of product selection and store services.

In addition, we realize that critical mass in international markets will take longer than has been our experience in the United States and even Canada. International home improvement market development and diversity are unique from country to country, so it's not possible to take a successful model and transplant it to another country. Each country requires its own model, which adapts to local customs, cultures, demographics, and geography.

Finally, in most countries we visited, we found that the DIY and pro customer markets were segmented—most markets had different stores or outlets for each customer.

It became a question of where to begin.

Helping guide us were two Home Depot board members with significant international experience: Don Keough, former president and CEO of Coca-Cola, and John Clendenin, former chairman of Bell-South. They have provided guidance, experience, and support throughout the international-development process. We also spent time with a number of global companies—Wal-Mart, Toys "R" Us, Carrefour, Office Depot, Sports Authority, and McDonald's. Finally, we learned from global partners of ours, such as Black & Decker, Bosch, Masco, 3M, Hitachi, and Honda. They all told us roughly the same thing: You must maintain your company values, whether you are operating in China or Russia, in the United States or South Africa. You must then mold them to that country's values.

Along the way, we also helped the Tianjin North Building Materials Trade Co. open Home Way, China's first warehouse home center, in 1995. As a result, Home Way bears some clear resemblance to The Home Depot—in its layout, signage, colors, and even their own version of a familiar company mascot. That led to some suggestion that China might be our first non-English-speaking market, but we have enough markets closer to home to try first.

We're not out to open in as many countries as possible just to say we're there. We're not in this to collect flags. So during the next five years, we will selectively plant seeds, the first in Chile. There has never been anything like The Home Depot in Chile before.

We determined Chile was the best place to start for a number of reasons. First of all, it has the most developed DIY/pro market in Latin America. In addition, housing is becoming more westernized, which means it doesn't require a 100 percent merchandise change for us. At this stage in its development, Chile represents a 1970s or early 1980s retail opportunity compared to the United States.

We picked probably the best non-English-speaking country in the world to export our concept. Because of the stable economy, stable government, and high education levels, Chile appears to have what it takes to support the concept. And the Chilean government supports foreign investment.

We wanted to go into a country in which we had a reasonable expectation of doing well and where we could form a partnership with the right people. Eventually, we believe, South America will be a big profit center for the company and provide the quickest return at the lowest risk of the countries we reviewed.

Our first store in Chile opened on August 28, 1998. Bill Hamlin and I were there that day, and we had tears in our eyes, watching our

400 Chilean associates giving customer service equal to the greatest level we ever saw in our stores in the United States or Canada. When we saw the Chilean customers respond the same way to our three-legged stool (widest product assortment, best products, and excellent customer service)—5,000 miles away—it really reinforced the potential the company has over the long haul. It was the single biggest opening in our history, drawing 25,000 people in a single day. Our second Chilean store also opened strong in December 1998.

Language was not a barrier to exporting our culture and values; once more, our culture proved itself exportable. We married our company culture to Chile's national culture and created a hybrid that is still recognizable to one and all as a Home Depot store. That really raised the bar for me as to where we can go with this company. It gave me a lot more confidence to move ahead, even more quickly than we originally expected. So in addition to three more stores in Chile scheduled to open in fiscal 1999, we will also enter the Buenos Aires, Argentina, market for the first time in the fourth quarter of fiscal 1999.

Whenever possible, we will use regional manufacturers in Chile, as we have in the United States and Canada, because we recognize everyone has civic pride and they will want to see products with which they are already familiar as well as select imports. That's also because of import duties and currency fluctuations. I think one of the main reasons for our instant success was the establishment of a full-blown buying office *in* Chile *for* Chile. We were determined to get the mix right the first time, despite the start-up expense. In fact, we now believe in putting all divisional operating infrastructure in place before opening new stores, not the other way around.

In fact, 70 percent of the goods we sell in Chile are manufactured in that country. When Chilean president Eduardo Frei Ruiz-Tagle and his wife entered the store to look around, he could not believe that 70 percent of that product was made in his own country. He had never seen it brought together in that way before. If we were trying to run this store from Atlanta, Georgia, I know we would not have been able to do that.

The success we've had is from regionally building the stores that are right for their communities.

Incidentally, as we did when we acquired the Aikenhead's stores in Canada, we spent a lot of effort bringing 35 to 40 Chilean associates to train in the United States for six months to a year before that store opened. So it was a blending of the culture of our company and the culture, building codes, and even the weather of the country and the products we found there.

Now the question becomes, will there be a short-circuit between the customer and our associates? Will our company culture transcend the language difference? Our Chilean partner, S.A.C.I. Falabella, supplies the logistics and distribution capabilities to provide a smoother and more cost-effective flow of goods to the stores. They also have the most widely carried credit card in Chile, with 4 million cardholders in-country—more than Visa or anyone else.

But Falabella will not have a Bernie or Arthur or Pat. Will they adequately judge the customer's input, and respond? That will be the most critical factor in gauging our success outside the United States in non-English-speaking areas.

Chile is not a big market, but if the first two stores continue to do well, we can eventually open a dozen stores there. Argentina is an even bigger market. Surprisingly, our first store in Puerto Rico had the strongest opening, sales-wise, in the history of the company. If things continue to go well, it will give us real comfort that there is an international side to this business. In 10 or 15 years, it would not surprise me if people look back and say the summer of 1998 was one of the significant milestones in our success.

SPECIALTY CONCEPTS

Why does The Home Depot even need to be in another business?

To continue meeting Wall Street's expectations and trading in the same multiple to which we have become accustomed, we must go beyond our traditional base.

That's why, in addition to The Home Depot, we own and operate the EXPO Design Centers.

Although the first EXPO Design Center opened in 1991, it took us six years and four prototypes before we settled on the model that satisfied our return-on-investment model.

EXPO is a kitchen and bath project-based business that complements The Home Depot. It came about because there was once a great location in San Diego that we wanted but it was only two miles away from an existing Home Depot store. We were concerned that one of our competitors would take it if we didn't. We came up with the idea of putting what became EXPO in that space, which turned out to be a real plus. Barry Silverman, now president of our Southwest division, developed many of EXPO's original merchandising concepts.

As a concept, EXPO was a good one in those days, but not a great one. It tried too hard to be something new, a showcase for upscale kitchen and bath designs sold to customers in an intimate, one-on-one relationship with our designers, while at the same time offering cash-and-carry products à la The Home Depot. The format was not conducive to the big consultative sales we saw as EXPO's future.

Steve Smith (who had been with EXPO from the beginning), Bryant Scott, and I took the concept back to the drawing board; we worked until midnight at my kitchen table reinventing EXPO. From then on, Bryant and Steve began building EXPO's that presented a strictly showroom atmosphere with virtually no cash-and-carry items. So while the original concept was less than perfect, Scott and Smith made it profitable and expandable.

Our insistence on getting a good shareholder return—one of this company's key values—sent them back to the drawing boards time and time again. We just couldn't get it right financially until then.

It has become apparent that there are other customer needs that must be met and so we have branched out into other arenas as well as other countries. Home Depot is and always will be evolving to find new and better or additional ways to serve our customers.

Of course, spinning off concepts from The Home Depot is not without its pitfalls. We launched a chain called The Home Depot CrossRoads in 1995 that was intended to service rural markets and we quickly regretted it. Stores opened in places such as Waterloo,

Iowa; Quincy, Illinois; and Columbia, Missouri. They were massive facilities with almost 100,000 square feet under roof and another 100,000 square feet outside. The merchandise mix included everything from tractor tires to carpet. We must have been out of our minds. Thankfully, we came to our senses before too much damage was done and we converted the CrossRoads stores into Home Depots, writing off the whole idea as one of our sillier moments. Nothing ventured, nothing gained. At least we're willing to take chances. And we did learn a great deal about the needs of farmers and ranchers, which we now accommodate in many Home Depot stores where appropriate.

■　■　■

We came to the realization a few years ago that not every customer shops at The Home Depot for all their needs, all the time. They may shop with someone else by phone, through a catalog, or via the Internet. And we want to capture that purchase in the future.

That's why we acquired two direct-based companies in the mid-1990s, Maintenance Warehouse, based in San Diego, and National Blind and Wallpaper, which is based in Detroit. Each ships product directly to the customer, whether it be the professional or the DIY customer. We see tremendous opportunities in that kind of relationship with customers who don't want to come into a store to shop or don't have the time.

The ongoing business of both companies was profitable; neither is a turnaround. On top of that, they brought some important capabilities that benefit our stores, some that we are using today, some we will apply in the near future.

Half of National Blind and Wallpaper's business is in wallpaper, half is in window coverings. We carry both of those categories inside The Home Depot, but they have certain product lines that we don't, and can offer the convenience of phone ordering. It's a cost-effective way of doing business.

We can also integrate their unique and efficient systems into our stores so all of our customers can enjoy enhanced custom-ordering capabilities.

For example, The Home Depot has a special order process for blinds that tends to be time-consuming; it's not something we specialize in as a core competency. But for National Blind and Wallpaper, it is. Their people are excellent at handling special order details and completing a sale. And the same process that might take up to twenty-five minutes in a Home Depot store could take only five to seven minutes on the telephone.

Our first pilot program to integrate National Blind and Wallpaper into The Home Depot came in ten Detroit stores; we put telephones in the decor departments and created the Special Order Center. When our store associates reach the point of placing an order, they hook the customer up with the Special Order Center. That frees the store associate to help the next customer and the blinds customer gets their order in quickly and accurately.

Our goal after validating the results is to expand this program throughout the company

This is what the mergers and acquisitions people call synergy. It's an overused word, but I think we have a great deal of synergy with National Blind and Wallpaper. There are many products that The Home Depot handles on a special order basis, things that a phone center could support, which is why we see this getting bigger in the future. So as much as we acquired a profitable company, we more importantly acquired a capability we very much needed.

Maintenance Warehouse, meanwhile, is a leading direct mail marketer of maintenance, repair, and operations products to the lodging and multi-family housing facilities maintenance market in the United States. We will increase its product offerings, expand catalog circulation, target direct marketing programs and enhance delivery services. It ties back to the $365 billion overall construction industry pie. One of its categories is maintenance—a $15 billion piece of the pie. Maintenance Warehouse was a $150 million bite when we acquired it, but still one of the largest operators in its industry. And they can ship to 90 percent of the U.S. in one day, suggesting unlimited growth potential.

Another fun fact: Maintenance Warehouse has the best service record in the industry. It has almost a 99 percent "fill" rate, meaning that 99 percent of the time, orders get shipped 100 percent complete.

It is an excellent company on the operations end, very good on logistics and delivery, picking one of this, two of these, and putting the order in a UPS box and shipping it.

We are putting Maintenance Warehouse catalogues in all the stores, so if there's something we don't have, our associates will be able to get those products delivered the next day directly to the customer's work site. And because Maintenance Warehouse focuses exclusively on one market—property maintenance—it carries a wider variety of selected products and more of them than The Home Depot does. So if an apartment maintenance manager needs 200 faucet aerators, a specialty item Home Depot doesn't normally stock in that quantity, we can still take care of their need within twenty-four hours through Maintenance Warehouse.

Another thing Maintenance Warehouse does well is catalog and database marketing. Its people are experts at segmentation and reaching people through direct mail.

We have not yet tapped all the potential synergies between The Home Depot and Maintenance Warehouse, but as we put together our e-commerce business, we're going to look to Maintenance Warehouse as a potential order-fulfillment operation. That distribution capability is going to be very important in the future.

Like many retail companies, we're generally excited about the Internet although we are proceeding carefully into e-commerce.

We've had a World Wide Web site since 1995, growing it from mostly financial information to include more customer service and product information. We want to build it further into a site that adds value and drives business into the stores, a place where we can further build the brand. For example, in 1998 we partnered with Mindersoft, Inc., to offer an Internet-based service called HomeMinder. Customers can sign up free for this reminder service, which will send them e-mail alerts on everything from planting bulbs to changing air filters to replacing the batteries in their smoke detectors. Customers can also elect to receive ongoing home-improvement tips tailored to their specific interests and skill levels.

1998 was also the year we began offering the public an opportunity to buy shares of our stock directly from Home Depot via our Internet site. We were the first company to make this option available to people who weren't already shareholders. And, for those existing or potential shareholders who would like to attend our annual meeting in Atlanta but can't make the trip, in 1999 we plan to broadcast that meeting on-line, following the lead of Dell, Intel, and others. Finally, we will be offering our annual report online and are already allowing shareholders to vote their proxies via our Internet site. This is more convenient to them and saves us money.

In 1999, we are testing a limited range of products for sale online. We must come up with a formula that's right for us: the right price ranges, and whether the range of products sold will be branded or not. The nice thing about e-commerce is that you can change on the fly. I'm sure we will. Overall, direct-sales capability should become one more way we can meet our customers' needs and provide total customer satisfaction.

In 1998, we also acquired an Atlanta-based truck rental company named Load 'n' Go. It was a concept dreamed up with us in mind in 1995, and we tested it at four Nashville stores. The idea is that customers can rent a truck from us to haul especially large purchases. This is more convenient, flexible, and inexpensive for the customer than having us make deliveries. By the end of 1999, Load 'n' Go will be in approximately 600 stores.

We now walk very carefully through the acquisitions we make because Wall Street has very high expectations of our return on investment (ROI). If we pick up a company that has a low ROI, Wall Street will punish us. Wall Street has to see synergies or bridge-building. There are very few companies that we could buy that would carry a 50-times profits-to-earnings (PE) ratio.

The majority of the acquisitions we will look at tend to be smaller, businesses that are much more specialized than we are, companies we can learn from and use the leverage of our hundreds of stores to grow.

Another important issue for us in considering an acquisition is culture. If ours is not akin to what we're acquiring, it represents a major problem. Is what they believe in similar to what we believe in? If not, we're going to have to work very hard to make it fit, and it may not be worth it. That's why we generally prefer to build from within.

VILLAGER'S HARDWARE

We believe that there will always be room for a good neighborhood hardware convenience store operator, in part because we have expanded the overall hardware market.

As do-it-yourselfers become more confident, they take on bigger projects. If they are going to spend $200 or more, they may feel it is worth pulling into a parking lot of 500 cars. But sometimes, for those bigger projects, they don't want to go back to a big-box store for a convenience purchase. There's a percentage of people who don't want to set foot in large superstores of any kind—Toys "R" Us, Wal-Mart, or ours. Our Villager's Hardware convenience stores will cater to those people. These people feel more comfortable driving up to a store where they can park their car right in front, go in, get a can of paint or a hammer, walk out, and be done in five minutes.

Some convenience store operators create a special reason why customers shop there other than just convenience. For instance, Sears recently bought Orchard Supply Hardware, a California company that we have competed with for years. Orchard has an unusual convenience store format with a lawn and garden focus, particularly in soil and fertilizers and things of that nature. Service levels are very high. It is a small store with a unique product niche, and there will always be room for that concept.

A convenience store that understands which of the shopping attributes it can compete with versus which ones it shouldn't will always be successful in the marketplace. That's why, in 1999, we launched a pilot program, Villager's Hardware, in New Jersey.

Our effort is to leverage our brand name, downscale, and create a more intimate store. At some times, in some places, for some people, less Home Depot will actually be more.

■　■　■

People often describe me as complex or complicated, and I am probably not an easy man to live with, at home or at work. Part of that comes from my fiercely competitive nature; part of it is my grinding need to climb, to achieve, to do.

On the other hand, there is another side to me, a somewhat contemplative, quiet side, where I draw back from all of this doing and competing to think and reassess.

That's my balance; my brain is competitive; my heart isn't. It is fed by love and caring and cooperation. It's a funny kind of mix inside of me, but this is my yin and yang. I need both of these sides of my personality. Fortunately, The Home Depot provides an outlet for both competition and caring.

I'm not a devoutly religious Jew, but I do see myself as a religious person. In my own way I have internalized a lot of the values and outlook and sensitivities of Jewish life without necessarily going through the formality of prayer, although I do enjoy attending services with my family. I like the quiet splendor of being in the synagogue, the kind of isolation it provides from the outside world.

I think I bring a sense of values and decency to business that represents the very best part of not only Judaism but of Christianity as well. I believe in the value of relationships, and I, like Bernie, have tried to carry that into the company.

■   ■   ■

On May 28, 1997, I assumed the title of chief executive officer of The Home Depot, Inc., although that represented a transition in day-to-day responsibilities that had already taken place.

Inside the company, it wasn't a big deal; externally, it gave the business press something new to write about.

At the same time, it was a wake-up call, challenging Bernie and me with regard to future succession at the top of the company. Do we have the best kinds of options for backing us up? Although we think there are some extraordinarily talented people within the company today, we told our senior staff that we think there probably needs to be another three or four players brought into the company at a senior level who can give us a deeper pool to consider for future succession.

The company should have more choices than we have today, and they should be in place and ready to go. Our philosophy has always been to answer the bell before it rings, and that is true when it comes to succession as well.

We are not in a rush. When it is appropriate for me to drop one title and give it to somebody, I will do that.

My job today includes focusing on strategic issues related to our core business—merchandising, operations, and systems support. Second is pursuing growth initiatives such as opening international stores, expanding EXPO and developing new specialty concepts and producing earnings. A great deal of my time is spent focusing our opportunities forward even if they won't be significant in terms of revenue for a number of years.

I am also leading us through organizational and structural changes, bringing in people from the outside who will get us ready for the next five- to seven-year growth spurt. This ties in with succession planning.

There may never be another tag-team partnership atop this company doing "Breakfast with Bernie and Arthur," but there will always be a similar balance of personalities and styles. I am sensitive to surrounding myself with people who are equally competent but also different from me. We believe that the best marriage is two people who share the same values but are different in many ways, because as long as you aren't fighting over values, difference helps you grow. The two of us developed personally and professionally over the last two decades because, while our values are the same, our styles are quite different.

This company is more than "The Bernie and Arthur Show." It is Bernie and me and all these other folks who, every day, run this business the way we always promised it would be run.

It is very hard to replace founders. Where do you find someone with Bernie's emotion or my problem-solving and financial insight? But this company is not going to self-destruct because Bernie retired. I could take some time off and The Home Depot wouldn't miss a beat. We have everyone backed up so that nobody is indispensable.

First-generation Home Depot people such as Larry Mercer, Bill Hamlin, Lynn Martineau, Vern Joslyn, and Bryant Scott lived through the same tough times that we lived through. We are confident of their ability to carry on in our stead.

If we do the job properly, if we continue enculturating our people with the values that built this company, we can alleviate the pain that normally occurs with a transition from the company's founders to professional managers.

The people who follow us will have to be better than we were; we expect to leave the company in better hands than those that created it. That's what I tell people who are running our stores. Your job is not to train people who are as good as you. Your job is to train people to be even better than you. We need to judge ourselves not on the quality of work we do today but on the quality of people we train to lead us tomorrow.

Despite the change in his title, Bernie still spends almost as much time on the business of The Home Depot as he did before his "retirement." The biggest difference is he spends more time working out of Florida, still actively involved with merchandising—the Ridgid deal is ample evidence of that—and working directly with our senior-level executives. It is very hard for somebody like Bernie to leave a company like this, and nobody would think of asking him to give it up.

He also feels a genuine sense of loyalty and obligation to the people who have helped make him what he is today. During management-training classes, Bernie says, "I am a product of what you are. If you weren't as good as you are, I wouldn't be where I am today. I am a famous individual. I have my picture in magazines, I have my name on buildings. But when we started this company, I was nothing. I was broke before The Home Depot."

Bernie keeps his hand in the company via telephone, fax, and face-to-face meetings. He plays golf or dines with our vendors, business partners, board members, and managers several times a week. He also gets a copy of every major piece of correspondence, memo, or policy that I make. The relationship continues to be one of complete partnership.

Years ago, we had conversations about succession with Sam Walton, and he felt very strongly that David Glass was the only guy who could follow him. You won't ever find another Sam Walton, but Glass is a great substitute for him. When Walton picked Glass, he did that knowing that one day he was not going to be there and Glass could run the business. In fact, he is probably running it even better than Walton did.

We are working toward that goal, of what happens when Bernie and I are not here anymore. We have a lot of strong people in the wings.

Right now, we have the luxury of time, but if something unexpected were to happen to any one of us, the company would survive.

Legacy
"We Took a Lot of Chances"*

When a company is small and it is in constant communication with the people in the organization, meeting them face to face every day or once a week, it is a very simple matter for everyone to understand what the company is all about.

When a company reaches our size, communicating our values and beliefs is more challenging. Arthur and I can no longer personally train all of our associates, but we can train our core people, from senior officers through district and store managers. They spend hours with us, they understand our philosophy, they understand the essence of who we are. We say, "You've heard it straight from our mouths. Now get out there and walk the walk, talk the talk."

Carrying that message to 160,000 associates today—or 500,000 in five years—is a job we entrust to them.

This goes back to all of my history in retailing. I have never had anybody work for me in retailing that didn't work for me out of love, as opposed to fear. We carried this approach into building The Home Depot. We care about each other, and we care about the customer. The things that we do for customers inside and outside of the stores demonstrate our commitment to them. And then when something

* Bernie Marcus

happens within the company, we circle the wagons. We help each other.

Now how do you get that message out? By every means of communication that you can, of course, but living it is the best way. For us it means walking the stores and hugging people, or the fact that our associates call us Bernie and Arthur and Pat, the fact that we will drop what we are doing to personally wait on customers in the store, the fact that we are willing to stop and teach and train somebody on the spot. We will go into a store and take five or ten or fifteen associates into a break room, buy them a cup of coffee, and say, "Tell us what we can do better, tell us how we are treating you."

We know we can't possibly touch 160,000 people this way, but all of our associates know we are out there doing it. They know we are accessible to them.

Let me go back to the essence of what the company is: Role-modeling. Every manager and every district manager in this company is a trainer and a teacher. Their role is to listen, react, and get things done. If they can't do that, they shouldn't be in the positions that they are in. Look at the influence they have on us. They hire the people. They train the people. They are in control of producing and nurturing our most vital crops—the associates in the stores.

■ ▓ ■

When I was a kid, the first opportunity I ever faced was on a merry-go-round. It had a brass ring on a mechanical arm, and if you reached out from your pony and grabbed the brass ring, you would get a free ride. I was the kid who always reached out. Sometimes I fell off the horse, but I always got right back up and tried again. Most of my friends, on the other hand, never even tried. They never reached for that brass ring. That was the original risk/reward.

I believe opportunities are still out there for anybody with the courage to reach out. But recognizing these opportunities is the difference between people who are successful and people who are not.

Many of the things that happened to us at The Home Depot go back to our willingness to take risks, over and over and over again.

And everything that ever happened to us, all the lucky breaks, were opportunities that presented themselves. Arthur, Pat, and I reached out for a lot of brass rings to start this company, and we didn't fall off the horse more than a few times.

Some people look at The Home Depot today, and they say, wow, you were in the right place at the right time. The truth is, it has often been a struggle. It looks easy now—and the stories are fun to retell given the distance of years—but people forget there was a lot of pain, a lot of times where we lived on the edge. We took a lot of chances.

We also had tremendous opportunities that turned into breaks. Knowing a banker such as Rip Fleming was also a big break. Enjoying a critical business and personal relationship with Ken Langone was paramount to our success. Even working for Sandy Sigoloff was a break. Without Sandy, where would we be today?

When I look back at my life today, I feel good about myself and the life I have led. I feel as though I've accomplished a great deal of good in my life for my family, my business associates, and my community. I think that I've given back to the world what I've taken out. I feel good about having helped create a company that's made its mark in the world.

But I get the most joy—outside of my family—from watching the people we helped up the ladder and seeing the success that they have also enjoyed. They joined us as kids, many just out of high school. Well, they're not kids anymore. They're men and women who, if it wasn't for The Home Depot, might never have realized their potential. They found their place in this company, a place where a square peg can fit into a round hole.

I get chills thinking about these people and what they've accomplished, many rising from lot attendants to positions of great authority, respected leaders in their fields, the managers and officers of this company. They're running multi-million- and multi-*billion*-dollar businesses, they're personally worth scads of money, and they're all giving back to their communities, just as Arthur and I do. Every one of them is charitable. Not because we said they have to do it. They do it because they're good people with good values. The Home Depot's values.

Index